QUALITATIVE SOCIAL RESEARCH

SAGE was founded in 1965 by Sara Miller McCune to support the dissemination of usable knowledge by publishing innovative and high-quality research and teaching content. Today, we publish more than 850 journals, including those of more than 300 learned societies, more than 800 new books per year, and a growing range of library products including archives, data, case studies, reports, and video. SAGE remains majority-owned by our founder, and after Sara's lifetime will become owned by a charitable trust that secures our continued independence.

Los Angeles | London | New Delhi | Singapore | Washington DC

QUALITATIVE SOCIAL RESEARCH

CONTEMPORARY METHODS FOR THE DIGITAL AGE

VIVIENNE WALLER
KAREN FARQUHARSON
DEBORAH DEMPSEY

Los Angeles | London | New Delhi
Singapore | Washington DC

Los Angeles | London | New Delhi
Singapore | Washington DC

SAGE Publications Ltd
1 Oliver's Yard
55 City Road
London EC1Y 1SP

SAGE Publications Inc.
2455 Teller Road
Thousand Oaks, California 91320

SAGE Publications India Pvt Ltd
B 1/I 1 Mohan Cooperative Industrial Area
Mathura Road
New Delhi 110 044

SAGE Publications Asia-Pacific Pte Ltd
3 Church Street
#10-04 Samsung Hub
Singapore 049483

Editor: Jai Seaman
Assistant Editor: James Piper
Production editor: Katie Forsythe
Copyeditor: Audrey Scriven
Proofreader: Sarah Bury
Indexer: Marian Anderson
Marketing manager: Sally Ransom
Cover design: Shaun Mercier
Typeset by: C&M Digitals (P) Ltd, Chennai, India
Printed and bound by CPI Group (UK) Ltd,
Croydon, CR0 4YY

© Vivienne Waller, Karen Farquharson and
Deborah Dempsey 2016

First published 2016

Apart from any fair dealing for the purposes of research or
private study, or criticism or review, as permitted under the
Copyright, Designs and Patents Act, 1988, this publication
may be reproduced, stored or transmitted in any form, or by
any means, only with the prior permission in writing of the
publishers, or in the case of reprographic reproduction,
in accordance with the terms of licences issued by the
Copyright Licensing Agency. Enquiries concerning
reproduction outside those terms should be sent to
the publishers.

Library of Congress Control Number: 2015938457

British Library Cataloguing in Publication data

A catalogue record for this book is available from
the British Library

ISBN 978-1-4462-5883-5
ISBN 978-1-4739-1355-4 (pbk)

Contents

About the authors vii
Preface ix
Acknowledgments xi

PART 1 GETTING READY **1**

1 The foundations of qualitative research 3
2 The aims of qualitative research 19
3 From topic to research design 31
4 The politics and ethics of qualitative research 45

PART 2 DOING THE RESEARCH **59**

5 Sampling 61

THE RESEARCHER ASKS QUESTIONS 73

6 Interviewing 75
7 Focus groups and group interviews 93

THE RESEARCHER OBSERVES 107

8 Observing people 109
9 Observing things 121
10 Observing texts 129

THE RESEARCHER ASKS THE PARTICIPANTS TO PROVIDE THEIR OWN ACCOUNTS 141

11 Narrative inquiry 143
12 Making sense: data management, analysis and reporting 157
13 Combining approaches 177

References 181
Index 189

About the authors

Vivienne Waller is a Sociology Lecturer at Swinburne University of Technology, Melbourne, Australia, with research interests in the areas of knowledge, the environment and technology, as well as research methods more generally. Viv holds a PhD in Sociology from Australian National University, and a BA and a BSc from the University of Melbourne. Prior to entering academia, she worked as a consultant conducting social research and in policy and evaluation areas of the Australian government.

Karen Farquharson is Associate Dean (Research & Engagement) and Associate Professor of Sociology at Swinburne University of Technology. She is a sociologist with research interests in the areas of sport, race and the media, and on issues of belonging and social inclusion more generally. Karen holds PhD and MA degrees in Sociology from Harvard University, and a BA in Social Science from the University of California, Berkeley. She was also the recipient of a Fulbright International Dissertation Research Fellowship to South Africa.

Deborah Dempsey is Senior Lecturer in Sociology at Swinburne University of Technology. She holds a BA and MA from the University of Melbourne, and a PhD from La Trobe University. Deb's research interests are in the sociology of families, relationships, personal life and ageing, particularly relatedness in the era of assisted reproductive technologies and the socio-legal aspects of same-sex relationships. Before becoming an academic, Deb conducted social research in the community and social marketing sectors.

Preface

The idea for this book was born out of our enthusiasm for teaching together on an undergraduate course in Qualitative Research Methods. Although there are many excellent textbooks on the market, there were none that quite met our students' needs. It was serendipitous to be then approached by SAGE to write this book.

Many of the examples we use in this book are based on our own experiences as researchers as well as those of our research students. When combined, this experience is vast. Viv first became a social researcher working in policy and evaluation areas of the Australian government. She then worked as a social research consultant and in market research before finding her home in academia.

Karen started off in public health before moving into sociology. Her PhD looked at race relations in post-apartheid South Africa. This was followed by a stint examining tobacco control policy for a non-government organization, and then a position as a lecturer in sociology.

Deb's interest in doing qualitative social research began in the community services sector when she was a project worker in a women's crisis service. While completing her PhD on lesbian and gay parented families, she worked in a university research centre and for a commercial social research and marketing company before joining the sociology group at Swinburne.

Reflecting our varied backgrounds in academic, commercial, community and government research settings, this book will, we hope, be useful to students and other academic researchers, as well as practitioners working beyond university settings.

Acknowledgments

Writing this book together has been intellectually stimulating as we clarify our ideas through debating them with each other. It has also been a lot of fun, especially the conversations over fine meals during our writing retreats.

We would like to thank the many people at SAGE who have assisted us: Chris Rojek, for initiating the project and getting it off the ground; Jai Seaman and Lily Mehrbod for their helpful editorial advice; and all of the production staff who made the publication process such a smooth one. We would also like to thank the many people who have been on research teams with us over the years, and our own research students who continually inspire and challenge us with their ambitious projects. Some of the research discussed in this book was conducted as part of Australian Research Council Projects (DP0451524, LP077215 and LP110100063). We would like to thank our colleagues at Swinburne University and elsewhere for their support, and the support of Swinburne University for qualitative research.

We would also thank all the people who have been participants in research that we have conducted over the years. It is our hope that this book will go some small way to promoting useful and ethical research.

On a more personal note, we each thank our friends and families for their ongoing love, care and support.

PART 1

GETTING READY

There are a variety of issues that a prospective researcher needs to be on top of before designing and actually conducting a qualitative research project. It is important to be clear about how values and beliefs enter the research process, and how these then underpin different approaches to research. It is also important that you have a well-articulated research question that is framed appropriately for qualitative inquiry. Lastly, it is vital to think through the ethical issues and the politics of undertaking any piece of research before you get started.

The first four chapters of this book are intended to get you ready for undertaking qualitative research. They are designed to help you think critically about these issues, formulate a research question, and structure a research proposal.

ONE

The foundations of qualitative research

CONTENTS

- What is qualitative social research?   4
- Qualitative vs quantitative research – a series of trade-offs   5
- Approaching qualitative research   6
- Research paradigms – values and beliefs about research   7
- What is reality and can it be known?   9
    - Positivist   9
    - Post-positivist   9
    - Criticalist   10
    - Constructivist   11
- What is the relationship of the knower to the known?   12
    - Positivist and post-positivist – the dispassionate researcher   12
    - Criticalist – the researcher as advocate   13
    - Constructivist – research as a 'non-innocent conversation'   14
- How do we find things out?   15
    - Positivist and post-positivist   16
    - Criticalist   16
    - Constructivist   17
- Conclusion   17
- Going further   18

WHAT IS QUALITATIVE SOCIAL RESEARCH?

How does it feel to be long-term unemployed? What is the relationship between ethnicity and individual health? Why do people waste food?

It is possible to attempt to provide an immediate answer to these questions based on your own understanding of the world. This type of answer may be based on your past experiences and learnings, books you have read, what you have heard other people say, what you believe or your intuition. Another way of obtaining answers to these questions is through conducting social research. This may involve observing people, listening to them talk, asking them questions, or it may not involve any direct contact with people at all. You may instead be studying what people have written, buildings, objects people have made, the traces people leave behind.

At a minimum, social research involves applying empirical research methods to investigate and increase our understanding of some aspect of the social world. In an academic setting, social research is explicitly informed by theory and results in a contribution to theory to help explain what is going on. This book will equip you to conduct high-quality qualitative social research appropriate to the situation and will help you to make best use of digital technologies in your research. We also hope to inspire you when conducting qualitative research to look beyond the obvious taken-for-granted reality to arrive at a new understanding of what is going on.

Box 1.1

Looking beyond the obvious taken-for-granted reality

Have you ever seen fruit fall from a tree? According to legend, the scientist Isaac Newton (1642–1727) was sitting under an apple tree when an apple fell onto his head. Whereas some of us may have rubbed our skull and watched where we sat next time, Isaac Newton got to thinking about why the apple had fallen rather than remained on the tree or gone upwards. He settled on the idea of some force that pulled everything towards the Earth. Now, the point here is that although many people had seen apples fall from a tree, it was only Isaac Newton who came up with the idea of gravity causing the apple to fall.

This book is designed to teach you how to question your own assumptions about the world so that in interpreting the social world through the conduct of qualitative research you may arrive at a new explanation for what is going on. The term 'qualitative social research' encompasses a range of approaches to social research that are conceptually distinct from those for quantitative social research, although in practice the two are often used together and the distinction between the two is sometimes subtle. Before delving into qualitative social research, the following section explains what distinguishes *qualitative* social research from *quantitative* social research.

QUALITATIVE VS QUANTITATIVE RESEARCH – A SERIES OF TRADE-OFFS

Any research into an aspect of the social world is fundamentally addressing one of the following two questions:

1. What is going on?
2. How widespread is this?

In crude terms, qualitative research involves investigating the first question, that is, the quality or nature of something, while quantitative research aims to quantify it through addressing the second question. You can only answer the second question if you know the answer to the first, and very different research approaches are required to finding out answers to these two questions.

The following example should make this clearer. When home Internet connections first became available, no one knew what the Internet was being used for at home. Until researchers had done some qualitative research into how people were using the Internet and the meanings that it had for them, it was not possible to find out how widespread particular uses or meanings were, and how these related to particular groups of people. To discover how widespread something is, you need to research everybody or everything, or at least a representative sample of people or things.

This example illustrates another important difference between qualitative and quantitative research. With quantitative research the researcher usually needs to have an idea or a theory about what they think is going on and this means that quantitative research, conducted in an academic setting, tends to be about testing theories. While qualitative research can also be used to test theories, it can be particularly useful when the researcher has little or no idea what is going on with regard to their area of interest. In this case, qualitative research can be conducted to generate theories about what is going on. Another way of saying this is that quantitative research tends to be deductive, whereas qualitative research tends to be inductive.

In the 1960s Robert Bogdan conducted a famous qualitative study of just one person. The goal of his research was to understand what it is like to feel that you are a woman trapped in a man's body. The result was a book called *Being Different: The Autobiography of Jane Fry* (Bogdan, 1974). Here the emphasis was on understanding the experiences of 'Jane Fry', and the meanings she gave to those experiences, to generate theory about what it is like to feel that you are a woman trapped in a man's body. As is typical of qualitative research, this research gave voice to 'Jane Fry's' lived experience through narrative (in this case, Jane's own words). In contrast, quantitative research tends to reduce people's lived experience to numbers to enable the identification of patterns among large groups. In quantitative research, complex experiences such as gender identity are likely to be reduced to a number on a scale to enable a comparison to be made between different groups of people. For example, a quantitative research project might look for patterns between gender identity and any other aspect of a person's life that can be measured and reduced to a number for the purposes of identification (e.g. sexual orientation, ethnicity, childhood experiences, attitudes towards religion, as well as any combination of these).

The *Jane Fry* example above illustrates one of the trade-offs in qualitative research, namely that a depth of understanding is often achieved at the expense of representativeness. Bogdan does not claim that 'Jane Fry's' experience is at all representative of those who feel that they are a woman trapped in a man's body. However, what Bogdan's study does provide is a depth of understanding of 'Jane Fry's' lived experience of being a woman trapped in a man's body, which at that time involved being treated as having a mental illness. As Chapter 5 explains, the findings of this research, although not representative, can still be generalizable.

By now it should be clear that neither qualitative research nor quantitative research is better than the other, but that each approach has its own advantages and disadvantages. At a deeper level, different approaches to research are based on different values and different beliefs about the purpose of research. The aims of this chapter are twofold: first, to enable you to distinguish between the foundations of *quantitative* research and various approaches to *qualitative* research, and second, to help you identify the values and beliefs, including your own, that underpin different approaches to research. This will enable you to be conscious of the implications of the research method you are using, as well as the implications of everyday decisions about how you conduct the research.

APPROACHING QUALITATIVE RESEARCH

Before you even think about how you will go about doing a piece of qualitative research, you will need to be clear about the purpose of the research and what you hope to achieve from doing it. We illustrate the importance of this clarity before you start the research by drawing parallels with a more everyday decision (i.e. which bicycle to purchase).

Suppose you want to buy a bicycle but you are not sure which one is the best for you. In order to decide, you will need to think about what you want the bicycle for and how you want to use it. Will you be the only one riding it? If you want to be satisfied with your purchase, you will need to think carefully about why you want a bicycle. What do you want to use it for? Is it to do high-speed road training? If so, then a road bike may be best. Is it to explore some of the forests near where you live? A mountain bike is best suited for that purpose. Do you want to use it to ride to work each day or just for occasional rides to the shops and the odd longer recreational ride? A hybrid may be best or even an electric bike. Or perhaps you just want a certain type of bike to fit in with a certain type of crowd? You may choose a cruiser or a fixed-wheel bike. It should be obvious here that there is no best bicycle. It depends what you want it for. Whether or not you have made a good purchase decision can only be assessed by taking into account what you want the bicycle for. Buying a high-quality road bike at a bargain price for the purpose of careering down dirt tracks is not a wise move.

Similarly, with qualitative research there is no best method or approach. There are a variety of methods and approaches, each with their own merits and their own disadvantages.

To make a good decision about these, you have to look at why you want to undertake the research and what you hope to achieve by doing so. This involves values. Different approaches to research are underpinned by different values as well as different beliefs about knowledge and the nature of reality.

Even once you are clear about what you want to get out of the research, there is still no one best way to actually do the research. Again, it depends on a combination of values and beliefs about the nature of reality and the gaining of knowledge. We will ease into this more philosophical terrain with an everyday example of how our beliefs and values guide our *ideas*, followed by an everyday example of how beliefs and values guide our *actions*.

It is clear that there is no one best way of living a good life. Ideas about what is the best way to live will depend on one's values and beliefs. For example, someone who values money above all will have a different idea about the best way of living a good life from someone who places the greatest value on relationships with other people, or someone who places the greatest value on health or the teachings of their religion. It is only within each of these value and belief systems that it can be judged whether someone has lived a good life. Similarly, ideas about the best way to conduct research are based on values and beliefs.

The following example shows even more clearly how beliefs and values combine to guide not only our ideas but also how we act. How do you travel to work or your place of study? If you cycle, you will probably believe that there is some advantage to cycling rather than walking, driving, or taking public transport. You may believe that it will help you get fit, that it will be quicker, that it will be relaxing, that it will be cheaper, or that it will help reduce air pollution. Will it really be more relaxing? It depends on how you perceive cycling and how you perceive the alternatives. While one person perceives riding on a train as relaxing or a good opportunity to read, another person perceives it as uncomfortable or a waste of time. As well as beliefs, you can see that there are values mixed in with the beliefs about cycling, the valuing of fitness, speed, relaxation, cost and clean air. Similarly, how much you spend on the bicycle will depend not only on how much money you have to spend, but also on your values, your idea of how much a bicycle is worth.

Just as there is no one 'best' way to live a good life, and no one 'best' way to travel to work, there is no 'best' or single correct way to approach or conduct qualitative research, although there are plenty of bad ways of doing qualitative research. For example, there is no 'best' way of investigating the relationship between ethnicity and individual health (an example we will return to later). The specific approach that you will prefer to take will depend on a combination of your values and beliefs.

RESEARCH PARADIGMS - VALUES AND BELIEFS ABOUT RESEARCH

We can be more explicit about how values and beliefs enter research by using the idea of a social research paradigm. A paradigm is a set of basic beliefs about how the world is and values about how the world should be. Just as a combination of beliefs and values will guide how you act, a research paradigm is a combination of basic beliefs and values that will guide how you do your research. The beliefs can't be proved but have to just be accepted on faith. These beliefs and values can be difficult to identify because, unless explicitly challenged, we tend to take for granted both our beliefs about the world and our values.

In the academic literature, you may come across a bewildering array of research paradigm typologies and terminologies. In this chapter, we will guide you through a far simpler way of identifying the beliefs and values that underpin different approaches to social research, by means of the following three questions:

1. What can be known?
2. What is the relationship of the knower to the known?
3. How do we find things out?

Taken together, the answers to these questions characterize the research paradigm which underpins any piece of research (Skeggs, 1994; Denzin and Lincoln, 2000). Answers to the first question 'What can be known?' depend on our beliefs about what exists, that is, ontological beliefs, as well as our beliefs about knowledge, that is, epistemological beliefs. Hence this question could be rephrased as 'What is reality and what can be known?' Answers to the second question involve our beliefs about knowledge and our values. The third question relates to methods and methodology, informed by the answer to the first two questions.

We will use these three questions to explain and contrast four major research paradigms. The research paradigms we will investigate are those identified by Guba and Lincoln (1994) in their well-established typology: positivist, post-positivist, critical, and constructivist. We have selected this typology as it is both comprehensive and elegant, although we follow others in using the term 'criticalist' rather than 'critical' to avoid confusion with the ordinary meaning of 'critical'. We continue to use this typology throughout this book, as we relate our discussion of each method back to its philosophical foundations. It is, however, important to note that there is a huge array of typologies and terminologies and various scholars have different understandings of particular terms. For example, Guba and Lincoln themselves added another category (participatory/cooperative) in their 2011 revision (Lincoln et al., 2011), and some scholars distinguish between constructionist and constructivist (Crotty, 1998) while others group together non-positivistic approaches as interpretivist (Blaikie, 2007).

The key point is that you are able to see clearly how different approaches to research are underpinned by different values and different beliefs about knowledge and the nature of reality. This will enable you to consciously undertake research that is consistent with your beliefs and values, when you are in a position to do so. It also means that if you are working on a research project that you did not design, you will be conscious of the implications of the research method that you are using as well as the implications of everyday decisions about how you conduct the research. Regardless of what terminologies or typologies you come across in the future to describe research paradigms or methodological approaches, you can use the three questions to go beyond the labels given and access the core of what is being discussed. Underlying philosophical differences translate not only to our methods of data collection and analysis, but also to how we write up the research, how we present 'the worlds and experiences that have been witnessed' (Smart, 2009: 303).

WHAT IS REALITY AND CAN IT BE KNOWN?

Can we know the experience of multiple personality disorder? Can we know divine intervention when we see it? Tied up with the question of what can be known is the question of what exists. Our answer to the question 'Can we know reality?' depends on what we think reality is. Would the world exist if there were no people left? This is a question that philosophers have argued about for centuries and it is different beliefs about reality that underpin many of the conflicts in the world. Although you may not have thought much about the question of whether we can know reality, it is important to look more closely at how the various possible answers to this question underpin different approaches to research. Throughout this book, we will be relating everyday decisions about method back to the beliefs and values underpinning the research.

Positivist

Usually associated with the development of Science and the Scientific Method, the positivist belief is that the one reality exists. The world would continue to exist even if there were no people left, as things are believed to exist independently of human consciousness about them. The positivist view on gravity, for example, is that it has always existed and Isaac Newton was the first person to discover its existence.

According to this view, the task of science and social science is to know, understand and describe this reality. It is possible for us to obtain perfect knowledge using rigorous methods of inquiry. This means that the positivist view does not acknowledge the reality of abstract or mystical phenomena, and includes scepticism about whether certain medical conditions, such as chronic fatigue or dissociative identity disorder, actually exist. Reality is only composed of phenomena that we can sense or detect by deduction. As an example, social class is, according to the positivist view, an objective phenomenon with observable properties.

Post-positivist

Like the positivist view, the post-positivist view is that reality exists independently of human consciousness. However, post-positivist research concedes that we can never really have perfect knowledge of this reality. We can only try to gain approximate knowledge through well-designed research. Even statistical methods are only approximate, and sampling procedures and weightings are used to minimize the distance of research results from the truth. Much quantitative research is post-positivist, but, as you will see, it is possible, though less common, for qualitative research to be undertaken from within this paradigm.

Criticalist

In contrast to positivist and post-positivist understandings of reality as existing independently of human consciousness, researchers operating within the criticalist paradigm understand reality as being a product of human consciousness. Social reality is shaped by a whole range of human values and biases which sediment over time. These include social, political, cultural, economic, ethnic, and gendered aspects of reality. Researchers operating within the criticalist paradigm view existing social realities critically (that is, they think about their implications, rather than take them for granted). Throughout history, there have been people who have seen beyond the current state of human affairs to a world where no person is exploited by another. According to these visionaries, the reality that is experienced is a product of particular human values becoming normalized over time, so that the current state of affairs is simply taken for granted as reality. Karl Marx is famous for his analysis of class in the late nineteenth century. At that time, the differences between the propertied class and the landless working class were stark. The propertied class accepted that they should be the ones to make money and prosper, while members of the working class typically thought that to work long hours for low pay was their lot in life. Any explanation of social reality at that time would not be complete unless it included an analysis of class. What was striking about Marx was that rather than accept class difference as part of the natural order of things, he argued that such acceptance was a false consciousness. He considered a classed society to be a transitory state of affairs. In future, there would be a classless society where everyone had as much as they needed and no one had the power to dominate others. Similarly, Martin Luther King had a dream of an America where people were treated equally regardless of their perceived race. In America, sociologists find that, on average, white people have a much higher educational attainment than black people. However, rather than thinking that this is an essential feature of race, criticalist researchers (Ladson-Billings and Tate, 1995; Decuir and Dixson, 2004) understand that this situation is the result of decades of exploitation, discrimination, and reduced educational opportunities.

Hence researchers operating within the criticalist paradigm do not consider that social phenomena such as gender, race, heteronormativity, class, and power exist independently of human consciousness. Rather, they argue that when we accept existing manifestations of these social phenomena as part of our reality, these are 'as limiting and confining as if they were real' (Guba and Lincoln, 1994: 111).

One final example illustrates the various realities that have existed at different times concerning gender. In certain cultures at certain times, the reality is that women are *inferior* to men in terms of opportunities and treatment. There are other cultures where the reality is that women are *equal* to men, and despite the prevalence of patriarchy there have been cultures where, in terms of opportunities and treatment, the reality is that women are *superior* to men. Rather than any of these realities reflecting some universal truth about women in comparison to men, they are the product of specific values and practices.

We can go further than this, however, and argue that even these different realities depend upon the idea that there are two sexes, male and female, and that this 'reality' is not a universal truth either. In his book *Making Sex: Body and Gender from the Greeks to Freud* (1990), cultural historian Thomas Lacquer traces how in Western civilization the reality that there are two sexes, male and female, was constructed some time in the seventeenth century. Previously, the 'reality' was that medically there was one sex. In 2014, in Australia, 'intersex' was legally recognized as a third sex, changing the 'reality' yet again.

Constructivist

This brings us to the constructivist view of reality as local and specific. According to this there are many realities, each based on shared perceptions. For example, for many Western doctors the reality is that chemotherapy stops the growth of cancer, whereas for a different type of healer the reality is that meditation stops the growth of cancer. There are also groups of cancer sufferers who have experienced as reality that a changed diet stopped the growth of their cancer (Pekmezi and Demark-Wahnefried, 2011).

According to the constructivist view, reality can be actively constituted through representations and discourse as well as practices. In Western countries, the ideal woman's body is a reality that is actively constituted through representations in the mainstream media. The ideal woman's body now is much thinner than that of sixty years ago. However, even the concept of an ideal woman's body is a social construct that is not present in all cultures.

Now for an example of reality actively constituted through discourse. The dominant discourse in Australia is that marriage is between a man and a woman. This discourse is currently competing with an alternative discourse that marriage can be between any two people. In many other countries, such as Canada and the United Kingdom, the discourse that marriage can be between any two people has become dominant. This change in discourse has led to changes in the law so that same-sex marriage has become an observable reality.

While the criticalist view of reality tends to be limited to social reality, the constructivist view of reality as local and specific can include the view that the reality of *objects* is local and specific. This can be a difficult concept to grasp, as no matter what era you are in and where in the world you are, you ignore the existence of a horizontal pole blocking your path at your peril. But let us look more closely at that pole. Is it really a pole or is it part of a sculpture? Perhaps it is just the boom of a gate and it will lift as you approach it? The materiality of the object in front of you is not in question. There is definitely something solid blocking your path. It is its status as an object which is a human construction. According to this type of constructivist view, the definition of what constitutes a particular object is a human act of drawing a boundary. This idea may seem counterintuitive as in everyday life the definition of objects is so taken for granted as to often appear natural and universal. However, to take another example, there is nothing natural or universal about what is understood to be a dwelling. Many court cases involve developers, planners and government officials arguing whether or not a particular building is a dwelling. In this way, human interaction with the material world produces what we usually take for granted to be a dwelling.

This idea extends beyond humanly constructed objects to the physical world. For example, there is nothing natural about the definition of what we will call a particular patch of grass. One person may define this particular patch of grass as an oval and use it to play football. The same patch of grass may be considered to be part of a sacred site by another person, while to a third person just one part of that patch of grass is worthy of definition, being host to a rare species of ant. In this way, humans interact with the material world to produce objects, an idea sometimes referred to as the social construction of reality (Luckmann and Berger, 1971). Of course, this does not mean that we can bring any reality into being just by imagining it. All but the most radical constructivist view recognizes that aspects of these interactions between humans and the material world are beyond the control of human imagination. Rather than throwing out the idea of reality altogether, the constructivist view is that there are many realities, each locally produced. This means that the constructivist researcher goes into the field particularly alert to the possibility of encountering a world radically different from their own.

The idea of reality as being actively constructed by humans brings us to the second question characterizing a research paradigm. This is the epistemological question 'What is the relationship of the knower to the known?'

WHAT IS THE RELATIONSHIP OF THE KNOWER TO THE KNOWN?

The nature of this relationship between the researcher and the researched will depend on beliefs about the purpose of the research as well as values. Here we focus on the differences across the paradigms regarding the relationship of the researcher to the researched.

Positivist and post-positivist – the dispassionate researcher

The task of positivist or post-positivist research is to find objective truth or, in the case of post-positivist research, as close as possible to objective truth, an unmediated slice of reality. The researcher aims to see things as they really are. Furthermore, the researcher is like a scientist looking through a one-way mirror, able to conduct the research without having any effect on what is being researched. Emile Durkheim, one of the founders of

Sociology, was keen for it to have the same legitimacy as the physical sciences. Hence, he advocated that the methods used to study the social world should not differ in any important way from the methods used to study the physical world. Furthermore, Durkheim considered that social research should be value-free.

Many social researchers take issue with Durkheim and consider that it is neither possible nor desirable for social science methods to mirror those used to study the physical world. While scientists routinely conduct controlled experiments, it is rarely possible to conduct controlled experiments with human subjects. Unlike a soil sample or a slice of tissue on a slide, people may change their behaviour when they know they are being researched.

Regarding the issues of values in research, it is very difficult to sustain the argument that social research can ever be value-free. Is it ethically desirable to conduct controlled experiments with human subjects? The answer depends on one's values. As will be demonstrated throughout this book, which topics are considered to be worthy of study, the framing of the topic, the research design, the way in which the research is conducted, the way in which the research participants are treated, the way in which the findings are presented and who they are presented to, all reflect the values embedded in the paradigm underpinning the research.

Criticalist – the researcher as advocate

As we will see in the next chapter, researchers working within the criticalist paradigm are very upfront about the values they hold. Their values explicitly guide their choice of topic, research approach, relationship with research participants, analysis and presentation of findings. They are often deliberately aiming to empower the research participants, using the research to raise their consciousness or give them voice.

Both those operating within the paradigm of criticalist research and those operating within the paradigm of constructivist research hold that it is impossible to see things as they really are. Who the researcher is makes a difference. What we see depends on who we are, and who we are is the culmination of our identity as a researcher, our life experience, our previous education, what we have read, who we have met, what we believe in, how we relate to our subjects/objects of study, and so on. To give a simplified example, imagine we are observing the exchange of presents at Christmas time. The extent to which we understand this exchange as an expression of affinity, of obligation, or of competitiveness as each person vies to have bought the best presents, will be coloured by whether we have experienced this phenomenon ourselves and the nature of these experiences. As another example, compare the following two researchers investigating mothers' experiences of childbirth. One is a 26-year-old woman who recently had a difficult pregnancy. The other is a 65-year-old male researcher who has never had children. We can expect differences in the way that they interact with the research participants, and in the way that the research participants respond to them. As discussed further in the next chapter, who we are affects not only our relationship with the research participants, but also our interpretation of what they do and say. For example, when interviewing someone, whether and how we interpret their body language will depend on our cultural norms and our relationship to that person, as much as the exact postures they take.

Good researchers within both the constructivist and criticalist paradigm are reflexive about their involvement in the research. This means that, as a researcher, you are aware of who you are as a researcher and the power relations between you, the researcher and the researched, as well as how your own experiences, values and expectations shape and affect your research. For example, if you work for a community housing organization and are interviewing housing tenants, you will need to be aware of what this means for the well-being of the research participants and for the research results. You will also need to be aware of how this colours your approach to the research, any preconceptions or prejudices you have from working in the community housing organization. Examples of ways in which one can be reflexive in the communication of findings are to include yourself as an actor in the transcripts of dialogue, to use the first person and outline your own experience that is relevant to the topic of study.

Reflexivity includes acknowledging that the very act of conducting research is often an intervention into the lives of the research participants. As Hitzler and Keller put it, the qualitative researcher is 'permanently in the dilemma of being at the same time co-actor, observer and reporter' (1989: 100). The following is an example of how one of us (Viv Waller) was a co-actor in our own research. She asked a child who was an avid reader whether the thought of reading stories on the Internet appealed to her. It then became obvious that the child had not realized there were books available on the Internet. For whatever reason, her father tried to downplay this newly revealed fact, but by the next interview the girl had actively searched for books on the Internet.

Constructivist – research as a 'non-innocent conversation'

Within the constructivist view is the idea that it is both the researcher and the research participants who co-create the findings. According to the constructivist view, research is like a conversation with the participants – a two-way process. However, research is not an innocent conversation as the researcher has an agenda. How much voice the participants are given is up to the researcher. They then need to decide on a balance between privileging their own position as researcher and taking seriously the perspectives of the research participants. On the one hand, the researcher may be doing the research with the express objective of giving voice to the research participants. On the other hand, they may not want to privilege the stories of their research participants considering that this limits the analysis to their partial perspectives. For example, a research participant may say that the reason that he can't get a job in hospitality is because no one wants people with brightly dyed hair. The researchers may have heard competing explanations from potential employers or even formed their own view on why this man can't get a job in hospitality (for example, some potential employers may say it is because he has an abrupt manner). When faced with competing perspectives, the researchers need to consciously decide how much weight they will give in their analysis to the perspectives of the various research participants. Some constructivist research makes a point of actively involving the participants in any or all of the research design, data collection, data analysis, and presentation of findings.

Whether it is the voice of the researcher, the voice of the researched, or a mixture of these, the research findings are an account of the result of the researcher's interactions with the world. No researcher has a 'gods-eye' view of the world. The constructivist view recognizes that the vision of anybody, whether researcher or researched, is partial, situated and embodied. Any data collected are by their nature incomplete and selective. Further, the assembling of these data into an account of the research involves the filter of the researcher's interpretation. In other words, the way in which a researcher observes or deciphers their subjects/objects of study is mediated through their partial and specific abilities for observation and understanding. Moreover, the conduct of the research may transform the researcher. To extend the previous example, they may change their views on unemployment as a result of doing the research.

The fact that the researcher is not dispassionate, all-seeing, or all-knowing does not mean that the research has no value or no relation to the world. As Haraway (1991) puts it, the research is 'a view from somewhere', a 'non-innocent conversation' with the subjects/objects of study. A caricature of constructivist research is that it is just made up by the researcher and research participants. However, the presented research is more than just a free-floating narrative because it is anchored to people and a material world that exist quite independently from the account of the research. In this way it achieves 'embodied objectivity' (Haraway, 1991), a concept discussed in more detail in the next chapter.

HOW DO WE FIND THINGS OUT?

The third question 'How do we find things out?' can refer to both methodology and methods. In casual use, the words 'methodology' and 'methods' are often interchanged as if they are referring to the same thing. However, while a research methodology is a theoretical approach taken to finding things out, something akin to a set of principles, research methods are the specific strategies for finding things out, such as interviews or observation. There are a variety of methodologies used by qualitative researchers, including symbolic interactionism, phenomenology, and participatory research. A discussion of these methodological approaches is beyond the scope of this book, but we would direct you to the suggestions in the Going Further section at the end of this chapter for a fuller treatment of these. The chapters making up Part 2 of this book are devoted to outlining specific strategies for finding things out (i.e. specific methods). We can, however, make some general comments here about how the research paradigm is relevant to how researchers find things out by returning to our example of investigating the relationship between ethnicity and individual health.

Positivist and post-positivist

Both positivist and post-positivist research are trying to capture an objective, measurable truth about the real world. Hence, for example, the researchers are likely to work with established categories of ethnicity that they think reflect real ethnic differences. They are likely to assign people to ethnic groups on the basis of established criteria, such as first language spoken at home, country of birth, or mother's country of birth. Similarly, established measures of health will be used to measure individual health. The researchers will be trying to uncover social facts about the relationship between ethnicity and health, and will endeavour to be emotionally detached from their research. As mentioned, most positivist and post-positivist research is quantitative rather than qualitative.

Criticalist

Researchers operating within the criticalist paradigm are motivated by a desire to 'create change, to the benefit of those oppressed by power' (Lincoln et al., 2011: 102), and understand that power relations determine what counts as knowledge. This means that categories that are commonly taken for granted as self-evident or natural are actually the result of a particular alliance at a particular time. For example, 'gender' can be understood as a political category, acting to regulate sexuality within a regime of heterosexuality (Butler, 1990). As another example, Jane's narrative of her life in *Being Different: The Autobiography of Jane Fry* illustrates the specific networks of power that operate to define someone as 'mentally ill' (Bogdan, 1974). As yet another example, since 1995, the two categories used in Australia to identify indigenous Australians are Aboriginal and Torres Strait Islander. These categories make visible Torres Strait Islanders, who were previously subsumed under the category Aboriginal. However, at the same time, they render invisible the South Sea Islanders who, unlike the Torres Strait Islanders, were unsuccessful in their attempts to gain official recognition by the Australian government (Australian Bureau of Statistics, 1998).

For those working within the criticalist paradigm, it is important to have accounts of the world that do not take existing power structures, including existing categories, for granted. Indeed, the very act of articulating possibilities for alternatives destabilizes categories or structures that have a regulatory effect on people's lives through exposing their constructed nature. Referring back to our example of the relationship between health and ethnicity, rather than simply accepting the category of 'ethnicity', a researcher operating from within the criticalist paradigm might look at the historical construction of categories of ethnicity, observe how ethnicity is performed and the meanings invested in that category. Similarly, rather than simply accepting the category of 'health', researchers working within the criticalist paradigm may look at how health is performed and the meanings invested in that category. This involves explicit recognition of the cultural specificity of what constitutes health in the Western world. Western understanding of, and measurements of, health include ideas about a 'healthy' weight and the absence of specific conditions understood as diseases. This is different from the meaning of the category 'health' within traditional Chinese medicine, which relates to a balance between yin and yang, and 'health' within the Ayurvedic tradition, which relates to a balance of the three doshas.

Rather than start with a fixed idea of what is meant by the category 'health', researchers working within the criticalist paradigm are likely to look at how different meanings of the category 'health' benefit or disadvantage particular groups of people. Categories are a double-edged sword for those working within the criticalist paradigm, as for all their shortcomings it is categories like ethnicity (and gender, class and race) that help us identify and explain large-scale inequalities.

Constructivist

As with those in the criticalist paradigm, researchers working within a constructivist paradigm are unlikely to use a top-down structural approach that relegates people to particular social categories. Rather, they are likely to privilege people's own understandings of their ethnicity and health over common sociological understandings. They are also likely to pay particular attention to the meanings that people give to their lived experience and are less likely to find any use for categories. For example, it may be that many people have their own idiosyncratic understanding of what health means to them. For example, one person's understanding of health may incorporate some aspects of Western medicine, some ideas from traditional Chinese medicine, and some ideas that draw on Buddhist ideas of karma. The mixing of these ideas may not be coherent or logical according to external standards of rationality, but still make perfect sense to the person. Hence, rather than investigate Durkheim's observable 'social facts' relating to health and ethnicity, constructivist research is likely to include what Maffesoli calls societal facts, namely 'whatever warmth and disorganization existence possesses' (Maffesoli, 1989: 14). The resulting thick descriptions of constructivist research defy neat categorical analysis.

CONCLUSION

Human beings are complex and contradictory beings. Although we may have an identifiable set of beliefs and values about something, it is rare that we always live according to these beliefs and values. For example, we may value taking care of the environment and believe that rising greenhouse gas emissions are destroying the planet. The way we live our lives may reflect this, making our homes energy-efficient, choosing to source renewable electricity, use public transport, eat what is in season, compost, and so on. However, we are interested in travel and every year or two we take a long-haul flight to another country, even though such flights are one of the fastest-growing contributors to greenhouse gas emissions in the world. For example, simply flying business class return from London to Sydney once a year doubles the annual greenhouse gas emissions of the average British person (World Bank, 2010; Jarrett, 2012).

With regard to doing research, our behaviour is likely to be similarly inconsistent. Our beliefs and values may accord with a constructivist paradigm but we are involved in quantitative research that assigns people to established categories. In order to make sense of this, you need to understand that the terms 'post-positivist researcher', 'criticalist researcher' and 'constructivist researcher' are ideal types. In practice, one researcher may conduct research in each of these paradigms. Even a single research project may include various pieces of research that were designed according to different paradigms, for example a quantitative survey (post-positivist) and interviews conducted and interpreted within a constructivist paradigm. However, the key point here is that even though a particular piece of research may not fit neatly into these categories, the aspects of one paradigm are emphasized more than others. As the rest of this book demonstrates, in order to make appropriate decisions about how to conduct research, a researcher needs to be aware of the beliefs and values that underpin the research. Similarly, in order to assess the quality of the research, you need to understand what the research was trying to achieve, and, as the next chapter demonstrates, this varies across the paradigms.

Going further

Blumer, H. (1969) *Symbolic Interactionism: Perspective and Method*. Englewood Cliffs, NJ: Prentice-Hall.

Symbolic interactionism is a common methodological approach to qualitative research. This is the classic text on this approach.

Brown, B. (2010) 'The power of vulnerability'. Audio available at www.ted.com/talks/brene_brown_on_vulnerability?language=en.

In this highly personal 20-minute account of doing qualitative research and the process of dealing with copious amounts of data, Brené Brown describes how doing qualitative research transformed her. Implicit in her account is how her values and beliefs about research shifted from a positivist paradigm to a criticalist paradigm.

Guba, E.G. and Lincoln, Y. (eds) (1994) 'Competing paradigms in qualitative research', in E.G. Guba and Y. Lincoln (eds), *Handbook of Qualitative Research*. Thousand Oaks, CA: Sage. pp. 105-17.

This chapter is the source for the typology of research paradigms used in this book.

Spencer, R., Pryce, J. and Walsh, J. (2014) 'Philosophical approaches to qualitative research', in P. Leavy (ed.), *The Oxford Handbook of Qualitative Research*. New York: Oxford University Press. pp. 81-98.

This chapter includes a brief discussion of a variety of methodological approaches, including symbolic interactionism, phenomenology, and participatory research.

Williams, M. and May, T. (1996) *Introduction to the Philosophy of Social Research*. London: UCL Press.

This book is for those who want to delve deeper into the philosophical foundations of qualitative research.

TWO

The aims of qualitative research

CONTENTS

- What's going on – selection and interpretation 20
- What the research tries to achieve 20
  - Generating theory from the data 20
  - Useful and ethical research 21
- Judging the quality of research 22
  - Reliability and objectivity – the elephant in the room 22
  - The aim of validity 24
  - Validity in how data are generated 24
  - Validity of the interpretation of data 26
  - Reflexivity in constructivist research 27
- Conclusion 28
- Going further 30

You saw in the last chapter that there are a range of approaches to research, with no one approach clearly superior. Values and beliefs underpin all research and we can identify and label systems of values and beliefs as positivist/post-positivist, criticalist and constructivist. As was suggested in the last chapter, the purpose of the research, and hence how its quality is judged, differs across each research paradigm or system of values and beliefs. Before examining these differences, we will look more closely at the general aim that is common to all qualitative research, that of finding out what is going on.

WHAT'S GOING ON - SELECTION AND INTERPRETATION

Qualitative research can be about understanding any aspect of what is going on in the social world. However, as you will see, there is never only one correct answer to what is happening in any social situation. As mentioned in the last chapter, all descriptions and observations involve both selection and interpretation.

Say I am researching how people use the physical space of a library. I observe that a young man is sitting in a public library reading – a simple description of what is going on, but notice that even this simple description involves interpretation. I have interpreted the sex of the person as male, his age as young, and his activity as reading. Is that an adequate interpretation of what is going on? Perhaps this 'young man' is there because he doesn't want to go home. Perhaps he has no home. Perhaps he is trying to keep warm and the library is warm. Perhaps he is trying to impress the librarian. Perhaps he is filling in time before his bus leaves. Perhaps he just enjoys being there. Perhaps he is reading the same page over and over, barely taking in a word as he tries to process the devastating news he has just received. Perhaps he is a detective pretending to be reading while he observes the activities of various patrons. Did I mention that he has a large suitcase with him and that his right hand is wrapped in a blood-soaked handkerchief? All qualitative research involves selection and interpretation – selection of what to observe and interpretation of the observation.

WHAT THE RESEARCH TRIES TO ACHIEVE

Generating theory from the data

Interpretation of the observations may lead to the generation of theory, that is, a way of explaining what's going on at a more general level than a particular case. This type of theory is induced from the data rather than logically deduced. An example should help to illustrate this.

When Waller studied the early days of home access to the Internet, an existing theory circulating at the time was that men used the Internet for functional purposes and women used it to communicate. However, rather than starting with this theory and then looking for data to support it, Waller started with the data. She observed how a diverse group of males and females used the Internet and how they talked about their use or non-use. For example, she observed that male research participants who exhibited a 'blokey' masculinity, and associated technical mastery with masculinity, were at pains to describe themselves as being skilled at using the Internet, even when it seemed obvious to Waller that they were not. She also observed that some research participants told her that chat rooms were frequented by strange and unsavoury characters, and that these same research participants also expressed distaste at the idea of visiting chat rooms. She interpreted this as research participants using their non-use of chat rooms as a way of presenting themselves as 'normal'. From a wide range of individual examples observed in the rich and complex data gathered, Waller induced the theory that people invest particular meanings in their use or non-use of the Internet as a way of performing their self (Waller, 2012).

When applied to gender, Waller's theory is the reverse of the theory that men use the Internet for functional purposes and women use it to communicate. Rather than understanding the meanings that people gave to the Internet as patterned or predictable by gender, Waller theorized that people actually perform gender through the meanings they give to aspects of their use or non-use of the Internet. This allowed for explanation of those cases that didn't fit the existing theory.

Theory generated from qualitative data is a way of conceptualizing or thinking about what is going on which describes and explains much of what is observed. Was Waller's theory the correct one? This question may be misguided. According to Glaser and Strauss (1967), the criteria for judging theory that is induced from data are that it needs to fit the data, be understandable to a lay person, be general enough to apply to other situations, and allow the user partial control over the situation under study.

While the aims of understanding and explanation are common to all qualitative research, the extent to which qualitative research tries to generate theory varies. So what else does qualitative research try to achieve?

Useful and ethical research

Most researchers hope that their research is useful and ethical, yet ideas about what constitutes useful and ethical research differ across the research paradigms. The aim of positivist research is to try to find out the truth of what is going on while post-positivist research attempts to get as close to the truth as possible. As described in the last chapter, this is like trying to have a 'gods-eye' view of what is going on and it is less common for qualitative research to be undertaken from within this paradigm.

Criticalist researchers conduct research in order to achieve social change. Denzin and Lincoln succinctly express the aims of qualitative research associated with the criticalist paradigm: 'We want a social science committed up front to issues of social justice, equity, nonviolence, peace, and universal human rights' (2011: 11). The choice of research topic reflects this: for example, criticalist researchers might research the working conditions of outworkers in the garment manufacturing industry, or indigenous people's access to the labour market. A criticalist researcher looking at the relationship between ethnicity and people's health would want the research to improve the position of those ethnic groups who are most socially and economically marginalized. As well as conducting research, the criticalist researcher is often an advocate or activist on behalf of the research participants.

Researchers operating within the constructivist tradition may be motivated to do research in order to give voice to people who are not usually heard. For example,

David Karp's (1996) study of depression doesn't look for the causes of depression or cures. Instead he is interested in how people suffering depression make sense of what is happening to them and around them, what they think about psychiatry and medications, and how they deal with family and friends. Sometimes the conduct of this research is almost an end in itself, as involving participants in telling their own stories can be an incredibly empowering experience for them. A constructivist researcher researching the relationship between ethnicity and people's health is likely to want to give voice to the experience of people from minority ethnic groups suffering little-known health problems.

JUDGING THE QUALITY OF RESEARCH

Qualitative research is often criticized for not being reliable, valid, or objective. As you will see, criticisms about not being reliable or objective often reflect confusion about what different types of research are trying to achieve. Should a piece of abstract art be judged by how realistic it is? Of course not. Note that we said we can only judge whether someone has lived a good life with respect to a particular system of values and beliefs. Similarly, the quality of research can only be judged with respect to a particular set of values and beliefs about research (i.e. a research paradigm). All qualitative research needs to be valid, and in the chapters that follow we will discuss good practice in conducting particular methods of qualitative inquiry as well as in data analysis. At a more general level, however, ideas about what makes qualitative research valid differ across the paradigms. This should be intuitively obvious. A post-positivist researcher who wants to get as close to the truth as possible is going to have a different conception of quality research from that of a constructivist researcher who wants to give voice to people's experience and understandings.

Reliability and objectivity – the elephant in the room

The criticism that qualitative research is not reliable tends to miss the point. In social research the term 'reliable' has a very specific meaning. It means that the same results would be obtained if the research was conducted by somebody else, or conducted with a new but similar group of participants. Of course, this makes sense if your aim is objective truth. You want the research to uncover the objective truth regardless of who conducts the research or which particular participants are involved. Hence positivist and post-positivist research aim to be reliable in both the collection and the interpretation of the data. With respect to the collection of data, this means that the researcher has a transparent and dispassionate approach, rather than one that depends upon the nature of the relationship established between researcher and participant. The examples given in the interviewing chapter should make this clear. With respect to the interpretation of data, reliability involves coding the data, for example, interview data, according to transparent rules. Intercoder reliability is a quantitative measure of the extent to which the data are coded the same way irrespective of who codes it. For example, if the way that Karen codes an interview coincides exactly with how Viv codes the same interview 90% of the time, the intercoder reliability is 90%.

For research operating within the critical or constructivist tradition, reliability is not an appropriate aim as the idea that objective truth exists is a myth. In critical and constructivist research it is acknowledged that different researchers will have different partial perspectives, according to who they are, their life experiences, and so on. According to this view, if the research is replicated by someone else it is to be expected that the results will not be exactly the same. With respect to data collection, different researchers will establish a different type of relationship with the research topic and research participants. With respect to data analysis, it is acknowledged that the coding of qualitative data tends to involve some degree of subjective interpretation rather than adherence to transparent rules. This makes a quantitative measure of intercoder reliability inappropriate. Unless the data are already structured, for example as answers to questions, and each answer is being placed into one or more categories according to tightly specified rules, calculating a numerical measure of the extent of similarity within coding is incredibly difficult. Qualitative data are seldom this structured. When researchers are working together as a criticalist or constructivist team, what is required instead of reliability is negotiation of a common and consistent approach to the research, both in collecting the data and interpreting these. The consistency of coding within a team can be increased through cross-coding, team coding, and regular discussions about coding.

With its dependence on notions of an objective truth, you can see that reliability is closely related to objectivity. Another common objection to qualitative research is that it is not objective. It is only positivist/post-positivist researchers, however, who believe that we can know something objectively. Those operating within a constructivist paradigm believe that how we know something depends on where we are looking from and who we are.

You may have heard the Indian story of the six blind men describing an elephant through touch (www.jainworld.com/literature/story25.htm). Each one had a different description of what the elephant was like, because each of them had touched a different part of the elephant's body. Their descriptions of the elephant varied from a pillar, a rope, a thick branch, a big hand-fan, and a huge wall, to a solid pipe. It was the blind man who could only reach the trunk of the elephant who described the elephant as like the thick branch of a tree. It was the blind man who could only touch the tail of the elephant who described the elephant as like a rope. It was the blind man who could only reach the belly of the elephant who described the elephant as like a solid wall.

The story finishes with the arrival of a wise man who can see all these different aspects of the elephant and explains that each perspective is true because each of the blind men has only a partial perspective on the elephant. Does such a wise man with an all-seeing, objective view exist? It is only those operating within a positivist or post-positivist tradition who believe so. Those operating within a constructivist tradition aim for 'embodied objectivity' (Haraway, 1991: 188). This is an understanding of objectivity and validity that acknowledges there may be many valid and objective versions of the research. What gives them legitimacy is that they are 'a view from somewhere' (Haraway, 1991: 196). In the case of the story, none of the competing descriptions of what an elephant is like is more true than the others. Each is true given the location of each blind man. In other words, each account demonstrates 'embodied objectivity'.

Now imagine that when the blind man touched the trunk of the elephant it leaned down and picked up the man in its trunk. The blind man would no longer describe the elephant as like a thick branch of a tree. He might instead describe it as like a python. As discussed earlier, constructivist research is both a dialogue and an intervention – the researcher's perceptions are contingent not only upon how they collect the data (in this case, through touching the trunk) but also on the interaction between the researcher and the subject of study.

Trustworthiness is more appropriate than reliability as an aim of qualitative research. In order for your research to be considered trustworthy, you will need to be able to demonstrate that you have been rigorous in applying the standards of the research paradigm in which you are operating. For example, trustworthiness of coding in post-positivist research involves intercoder reliability, whereas trustworthiness of coding in criticalist or constructivist research involves consistency of approach.

The aim of validity

As mentioned, qualitative research is often criticized for not being valid. Now all qualitative research does aim to be valid, but there are different understandings of what this means. In *quantitative* research the simplest definition of validity is that it actually measures what it intends to measure. This idea becomes less straightforward in *qualitative* research. Following Mason (2002), we can distinguish between the validity of the way the data are generated and the validity of the interpretation.

Validity in how data are generated

With regard to the validity of the way the data are generated, the methods used to generate the data, such as observation or interviews, need to make sense given the specific aims of the research and the beliefs and values underpinning it. Using the example of research on the relationship between ethnicity and health, and in particular obesity, we will look briefly at what this means for each research paradigm before returning to the issue of the validity of the interpretation. (We will discuss in more detail how to choose a valid sample for your research in Chapter 5.)

With rare exceptions, post-positivist research explicitly builds on existing knowledge, which involves using established categories of knowledge. Post-positivist researchers investigating the relationship between ethnicity and obesity would select their research participants using established categories of ethnicity and established categories of obesity. Each category would involve a set of rules or procedures for determining the ethnicity or obesity status of any research participant. For example, ethnicity may be determined from characteristics such as country of birth, country of parents' birth, first language learnt, or participation in particular cultural practices. Validity would require that the characteristics of the research participants assigned a particular ethnicity matched established ideas about that category of ethnicity. Whether or not the assigned ethnicity matched with the participant's own ethnic identification would not affect the validity. Similarly, obesity status would be determined through reference to established criteria, perhaps by asking the respondent to fill in a questionnaire or undergo a physical assessment. Having determined the ethnicity and the obesity status of the research participants, the research could then focus on aspects of the relationship between obesity and ethnicity.

The next aspect of validity for the post-positivist researcher would be that the method of data collection (for example, observation, interviews or focus group) generated an accurate picture of what was actually going on. It would be important that the data collection strategy allowed participants to speak honestly and freely. In the case of focus groups, for example, it would be important that all the research participants felt equally able to participate. It would probably not be a good idea to combine teenage girls and boys in the one focus group to talk about obesity, as given the pressures on teenage girls and boys to look a particular way it would be likely that some participants would feel uncomfortable, or would withhold certain relevant information in order to present themselves in a particular way.

In contrast to the approach of post-positivist researchers, where validity is increased through correctly matching participants to established categories of ethnicity and obesity, the approach of the criticalist researcher is not to take the appropriateness of these categories for granted. Rather, validity in the approach of the criticalist researcher is increased by interrogation of these categories. So the criticalist researcher may examine how the research participants understand and experience ethnicity, and how this intersects with the understandings, perceptions and lived experiences around obesity. For example, teenage girls strongly identifying with cultures where larger bodies are the desired norm may have a different understanding of what constitutes obesity from that of a teenage girl who immerses herself in North American celebrity culture. The criticalist researcher may even deliberately combine teenage girls and boys in the one focus group to talk about obesity. Rather than considering that this may distort the data generated, a criticalist researcher may consider that how the two sexes interact around the issue of obesity is as telling as what individuals say or don't say about obesity.

Validity in the generation of data for constructivist research is increased by actively involving participants in the research process, including in deciding what is considered to be data. The generation of data for constructivist research should be an empowering experience for the research participants. For example, it would be important not to inadvertently label participants in ways that may reduce their self-confidence.

Across the paradigms, it can increase the validity of the data generated to ask respondents to confirm its accuracy. This works best with interview data where transcripts can be provided back to the respondents to check that they have been heard correctly and that they are happy with what they said. This is not always possible, however, as respondents may not be interested or able to do this.

Validity of the interpretation of data

In general, the validity of the interpretation of the data relates to the rigour of the process in which you have engaged and your capacity to make this intelligible to others. As Mason says, ' ... you should be able to, and be prepared to, trace the route by which you came to your interpretation' (Mason, 2002: 191). If you are generating theory, ' ... you should not be satisfied until your generalization is able to apply to every single gobbet of relevant data you have collected' (Silverman, 2011: 379). You need to be satisfied that you have canvassed all possible alternative explanations and can justify what makes yours stronger.

Some scholars advocate the idea of face validity (Babbie, 2007) or apparent validity (Kirk and Miller, 1986). This is basically the idea that the interpretation of the research should seem, at a glance, to be plausible. However, although this may seem to be common sense, relying on face validity can blind researchers to unexpected interpretations. Regardless of whether the interpretation of the data has face validity or indeed goes against conventional wisdom about the topic, a researcher needs to be able to demonstrate how they arrived at their interpretation of the data.

In addition to Mason and Silverman's advice about being rigorous in arriving at and being able to justify your interpretation of the data, there are some aspects of the validity of interpretation that are relevant only to research within a particular paradigm. In order for the interpretation of data in post-positivist research to be considered valid, the evidence must be available for scrutiny by people other than the researcher.

Some post-positivist researchers will triangulate in order to demonstrate validity. The term 'triangulation' originally referred to a technique that made use of the mathematical properties of triangles to pinpoint a precise location. In social research, within the positivist paradigm, triangulation of methods means the use of a variety of methods to pinpoint the precise answer to a research question. In other words, if the variety of methods yield the same findings, this is then taken as increasing the validity of the findings. However, the reverse is not true. A variety of findings do not negate the validity of the research. Rather than being a problem, contradictions or conflicting data indicate the need for further investigation of how contradictions are experienced and lived. As Pierre Bourdieu has said:

> ... to be able to see and describe the world as it is, you have to be ready to be always dealing with things that are complicated, confused, impure, uncertain, all of which runs counter to the usual idea of intellectual rigour. (Bourdieu et al., 1991: 259)

Hence, in triangulating, post-positivists use multiple methods to get closer to the truth. In contrast, while research conducted from a constructivist or criticalist perspective may also use multiple methods, the intention is to gain a variety of perspectives. This use of multiple methods is not triangulation, as there is no intention to triangulate, namely to use the variety of perspectives to get closer to the one true perspective, the 'gods-eye view'.

Interpretations of data in criticalist research need to explicitly take into account the social structures in which the activities of research participants are situated. Returning to our example, the interpretation of the criticalist researcher would be unlikely to be considered valid unless it had taken into account the cultural, political, and economic factors around obesity.

Validity for the constructivist researcher also means that the interpretation of the research needs to align with participants' own interpretation of what is going on, and that this interpretation should empower the participants and improve understanding. So, for example, in interpreting what is going on, the researcher should pay attention to the cultural meanings that participants give to different body types. A typical strategy that the researcher could use to ensure the validity of her interpretation would be to ask the subjects of study to write stories, or draw pictures, about what is important to them in relation to the research topic. Another example relates to reporting on a study of men's sexual practices. Using the term 'homosexual' when reporting on male research participants who have sex with men would be invalid if those research participants understood themselves as heterosexual men who had sex with men.

Researchers operating from within the constructivist paradigm may also ask the research participants to confirm the validity of the researcher's interpretation of the data. This practice is known as respondent validation. Usually this is done through providing each research participant with what the researcher has written about them to see if they agree with the interpretation.

However, as Silverman (2011) outlines, it may not make sense to undertake respondent validation in criticalist or post-positivist research. Participants may not understand the sociological framing, they may not be interested, and what the researcher has written may not fit with the participant's image of themselves. This last point can present a dilemma for the criticalist researcher who has an agenda of reducing the disadvantage suffered by certain groups in society and explicitly takes power structures into account in their analysis. This means that a criticalist researcher may have an unflattering interpretation of behaviour that is valorized within a certain group. In other words, the group for whom the criticalist researcher is intending to expose and reduce structural disadvantage may themselves reject the research and feel disempowered by it.

Reflexivity in constructivist research

An integral aspect of validity for those operating within both the constructivist and criticalist tradition is for the researcher to be reflexive about their involvement in any particular research. This means they need to pay attention to how their experiences, values and expectations shape and affect their research. As with the story of the six blind men describing the elephant, this does not imply that such research is less true. Rather it is a recognition that all research presents a view from somewhere – the disembodied 'objective' view does not exist. Reflexivity involves being aware of who you are as a researcher as well as the power relations between you, the researcher, and the researched, and how these may affect the conduct of the research, the type and quality of data generated, and your interpretations.

An example from Waller's research on household use of the Internet illustrates how who you are as a researcher can affect what data are generated. Waller, then a young female researcher, did not feel comfortable pursuing the issue of pornography on the Internet, particularly with male interviewees, some of whom were using the Internet in private for several hours each night. As a result, the only data that Waller collected on use of the Internet to access pornography were in terms of parental concern about children's use of the Internet.

Another example relates to the obvious difficulties associated with an adult researcher trying to enter into a child's world. In particular, there is an unequal power relationship between adult researcher and child in the research situation. One consequence of this unequal power relationship is that children may try to give the adult researcher the answers that they think that person wants. Of course, this can occur when researching adults as well.

An example from Schatzman and Strauss's (1991) study of a community that had just experienced a tornado illustrates how who we are can affect our interpretation of the data. Assigning class on the basis of education and income, Schatzman and Strauss found that middle-class people were more able than working-class people to use a variety of perspectives to describe what had happened. However, they also admitted that, as middle-class researchers themselves, they may have not understood some of the cultural codes embedded in working-class ways of talking.

Being reflexive means paying attention to how aspects of ourselves affect the data collection and analysis, even though it is never possible to fully know what effect we, as researchers, have had.

CONCLUSION

While only some research aims to generate theory, all qualitative research should aim to be useful, ethical, trustworthy and valid. In this chapter we have shown how understandings of what it means to conduct trustworthy and valid research differ across the research paradigms.

Table 2.1 summarizes the fundamental philosophical differences between the research paradigms, indicating how the broad aim of the research varies according to these basic beliefs and values.

Table 2.1 Underlying philosophical differences in research

RESEARCH PARADIGM	Positivist	Post-positivist	Criticalist	Constructivist
View of social reality	Social structures have an independent existence	Social structures have an independent existence	Social structures are a product of human consciousness, values and biases, and unequal power	Social reality (may include 'objects') is local and specific, actively constituted through representations and discourse and practices
Relationship between researcher and findings	Objective	Aim for objectivity	Researcher has progressive political agenda (justice, equity etc.) in topics, aims, design, execution and use of research	Who the researcher is affects what they find out
How to find things out	Measuring and deduction Objective and reliable methods Expertise of researcher Collect social facts	Measuring and deduction Objective and reliable methods Expertise of researcher Collect social facts	Reflexive Interrogate existing structures	Reflexive Expertise and voice of participants Researcher and researched co-construct findings Societal facts
Aim	Capture objective, measurable truth	Get as close to objective truth as we can	Create positive change Articulate possibilities for alternatives	Give voice to participants Empower participants

Table 2.2 shows how these underlying philosophical differences translate into everyday decisions about how to conduct the research. Note that positivism is missing from this table as it is incompatible with qualitative research.

Table 2.2 Defining aspects of the paradigms for everyday decisions in qualitative research

RESEARCH PARADIGM	Post-positivist	Criticalist	Constructivist
Power of researcher vis-à-vis participants	Researcher in charge	No defining aspect	Equal – and empower participants
Level of voice of participants	Researcher interprets what's going on	No defining aspect	Participant voice paramount
Use of categories	Assign people to established categories	Critique established categories Investigate people's lived experience	Investigate people's lived experience – categories perhaps not relevant Societal facts
Relationship between researcher and participants	Dispassionate	Advocate	Equal

(Continued)

Table 2.2 (Continued)

RESEARCH PARADIGM	Post-positivist	Criticalist	Constructivist
What counts as data	Researcher decides	May be researcher or participants	Participants help decide
Validity in interpretation	Correct matching of participants to categories	Interrogation of categories Take power into account	Matches participants' interpretation Researcher reflexive about their role
Validity in data generation	Researcher doesn't affect outcomes	Participants empowered	Participants empowered View from somewhere

Going further

Charmaz, K. (2004) 'Premises, principles, and practices in qualitative research: revisiting the foundations', *Qualitative Health Research*, 14 (7): 976–93.

In this transcript of a keynote address Charmaz offers insights about the purpose and conduct of qualitative research, drawing from Goffman and her own work as a qualitative researcher operating within a social constructionist paradigm.

Denzin, N. (2013) 'The death of data?', *Cultural Studies ↔ Critical Methodologies*, 13 (4): 353–6.

In this short but provocative piece, Denzin challenges post-positivist assumptions about data.

Patton, M. (1999) 'Enhancing the quality and credibility of qualitative analysis', *Health Services Research*, 4 (5), Part II: 1189–1208.

This article is written from the perspective of a programme evaluator and contains much practical advice.

Shenton, A. (2004) 'Strategies for ensuring trustworthiness in qualitative research projects', *Education for Information*, 22: 63–75.

This article offers clear practice and advice on improving the trustworthiness of qualitative research, contrasting positivist approaches to reliability and validity with what might be appropriate in qualitative research.

Skeggs, B. (1994) 'Situating the production of feminist ethnography', in M. Maynard and J. Purvis (eds), *Researching Women's Lives from a Feminist Perspective*. London: Taylor and Francis. pp. 72–92.

This chapter demonstrates reflexivity as the author situates herself with respect to an ethnographic study of working-class women doing a further education course.

THREE

From topic to research design

CONTENTS

- Timely and feasible research — 32
- Topics and questions — 33
    - Developing good qualitative research questions — 33
- Role of the literature in developing research questions — 36
    - Writing a literature review — 39
- Linking research questions to methods — 40
- The research proposal — 41
- Conclusion — 42
- Going further — 42

A research question should express the essence of your enquiry. Therefore, you need to have done a great deal of thinking about the essence of your enquiry in the sense of its ontology, its epistemology and most importantly its intellectual puzzle in order to be able to formulate research questions sensibly and coherently. [Research questions] ... are the formal expression of your intellectual puzzle. (Mason, 2002: 20)

Qualitative research must be well designed. Whether the research is explanatory, exploratory or descriptive, it is important that it should be based on one or more clear research questions that have been framed appropriately for qualitative inquiry. Sometimes researchers working in applied research settings, such as market research companies or government departments, are given their research questions. In academic settings, consulting the existing literature on your topic is critical and you are usually expected to develop your own questions. In this chapter, we discuss the difference between a topic and a well-crafted research question along with strategies for developing a coherent research design. We also reflect on the role of the literature in helping you transform conceptually vague research topics into concise qualitative research questions that express your 'intellectual puzzle', to use Jennifer Mason's turn of phrase, and discuss ways to ensure a good fit between research methods and questions in research design. We finish the chapter by outlining a structure for a research proposal. This proposal can be thought of as the road map of your research design.

TIMELY AND FEASIBLE RESEARCH

Before we consider the characteristics of good qualitative research questions, it is necessary to think through what makes for a good social research project in general.

In the first instance, it is important that the social research topics you pursue are intellectually and socially substantial enough to be worthy of a research study. There must be identifiable benefits that stand to arise from you seeking to answer these questions, either to the participants or to social knowledge more broadly. Asking yourself why the research is relevant, who stands to benefit from the knowledge, and whether the benefits arising from this knowledge are likely to outweigh the harms that could accrue to people who take part, is vital. These kinds of considerations about research involve ethical and moral concerns, and are dealt with in more depth in Chapter 4.

Beginners and experienced researchers alike must consider the timeliness of their research, particularly if they want to attract research funding. Sometimes priority areas for research are developed by research funding bodies, and knowing what these are can help you identify the kinds of research topics likely to receive financial support. Whether or not obtaining funds to carry out your research is necessary, or whether or not you are interested in fitting in with research agendas that the government deems a priority, it is worthwhile considering if there is a compelling reason for pursuing your research idea here and now, or whether a different priority is more worthy of your attention.

Your research design should also be feasible, meaning it must be appropriate in scope relative to the resources available or obtainable. 'Resources' here include money, time and access to the population you are interested in, and all three are crucial considerations. When it comes to financial resources, expenses that may need to be factored into research will include building and maintaining a project website, travel for researchers or participants, transcription of interview recordings, costs associated with hiring additional staff to help you and phone calls, room or equipment hire, and disseminating the results to relevant communities in written or electronic form. Your time is an equally valuable resource, and the complexity of the project needs to take this into account. There is no point in designing a project based on 20 group interviews, for example, if you know you will only have two days to carry out your data collection and you can't afford to pay someone to help you. Similarly, the degree of access to your desired setting or participants requires forward thinking and planning. If you are interested in doing research that involves schoolchildren during school hours on school premises, what kind of permission will you need and is it likely to be forthcoming? And if that permission is not forthcoming, what is your back-up plan?

TOPICS AND QUESTIONS

When beginning work on developing a new project, students and experienced researchers alike will often have only a broad idea about what their research needs to cover. They may be able to articulate their idea in one or several words as a topic, but not with much more precision than that. For instance, you may know you are interested in sexuality and ageing, or women and work, or international students' experiences, or family formation using assisted reproductive technologies. These are all perfectly sound topics for qualitative social research. However, these broad topics are only a starting point, and without a more fully-formed question or set of questions the focus of the inquiry will flounder, and it will then be difficult to pursue the research project to its successful completion.

Developing good qualitative research questions

In the first instance, it is necessary to ensure that your questions are actually answerable via social research. This may seem like an obvious point to make, but a common mistake made by beginners is to design questions that do not lend themselves to investigation through empirical techniques. For instance, a researcher may decide they want to design a project based on the question 'Should abortion be legal?' While this is a research question of great social relevance, it cannot be answered by a researcher asking people what they think about abortion or looking at how abortion is represented in the news media. Analysis of these sources will tell them how people's views about abortion are similar or different, or whether abortion is represented more favourably in certain kinds of media commentary, but it will not enable them to decide on the more ethical, philosophical question of whether and why it should be legal. 'Should' questions in general invite answers that are based on more abstract kinds of reasoning rather than the data obtainable from social research.

Qualitative research questions typically begin with 'how' or 'what', in keeping with the concerns of inductive social research. Inductive research generates theory, knowledge and propositions about the social world rather than testing well-formulated, pre-determined theories or hypotheses. It is useful for assisting us to explore social processes or meanings, how things happen and what sense people make of their experiences. Well-designed qualitative research questions typically help us find detailed descriptions or accounts of social phenomena in context. Qualitative research questions tend to be more open and exploratory, and will generate more conceptual work in the analysis than the design phase of the research. By contrast, quantitative research questions often imply a hypothesis about the social world that is being tested. Quantitative research questions tend to have a narrower focus and be more specific. This contrast is well expressed in the following questions about assisted reproductive technologies:

Quantitative question: Is religiosity or trust in science a better predictor of attitudes to family formation using assisted reproductive technologies?

Qualitative question: What motivates gay men to become sperm donors for lesbian or single heterosexual women?

Sometimes you will need more than one research question, in which case it is important that your questions be logically linked and complementary. Often researchers will pose an initial broad research question within which other more specific questions are nested. For instance, a health researcher may be interested in knowing what it is like for women or men to find out that they are carriers of the genes for the rare kinds of breast cancer known as BRCA1 and BRCA2. But they may want to go further. Three related research questions guiding this kind of study might look something like this:

1. What motivates women and men to be tested for BRCA1 & BRCA2 genetic mutations?

Among people who test positive:

2. What considerations inform the treatment choices made?
3. How do they reconcile being 'genetically at risk' with living in an otherwise healthy body?

In the above example, the first question is more of a general question about why people get tested, and the secondary questions are specifically related to the consequences that follow on from a positive diagnostic test result.

Even though qualitative research questions are generally more open and exploratory than quantitative research questions, this does not mean they should be conceptually vague. Box 3.1 discusses two research questions which were both developed by students taking part in a qualitative research methods course.

─────────────── Box 3.1 ───────────────

Two research questions developed by students

- How do international students feel about permanent migration to Australia?
- How do women in management positions negotiate time use strategies for combining motherhood and paid work?

> The first student began with the topic 'international students' experiences', and the second with a broad interest in 'gender and work'. At face value, both of these students developed their topics into research questions that were much more precise than the topics they began with. Both their questions qualify as 'how' questions that explore social processes, and are thus suitably phrased for a qualitative research study. Both are also empirically researchable, in that they can be answered through research methods such as interviews or focus groups.
>
> However, the phrasing of the first question is very ambiguous if we compare it to the second in that the scope of the inquiry is not immediately apparent. For instance, is it a project about international students' views about the prospect of personally migrating to Australia, or is it seeking to understand how they think about migration in a broader social context beyond their own plans or desires to migrate? Is it a question aimed at international students who have come to Australia to study and subsequently become permanent residents? A further problem with the question is its use of the word 'feel', which is a very vague concept to be working with in a research question. Is this word trying to get at the attitudes, beliefs or experiences the students might have? Also, what aspect of 'permanent migration' is of interest? We might also question the concept of 'permanent migration'. Is this a phrase that refers to a legal category of migration that would be commonly used by policy makers or migration scholars? Does it refer to people who are permanent residents of Australia or only those who have taken out Australian citizenship? The fact that this research question begs so many other questions about its meaning indicates that there is work to be done on improving its clarity.
>
> The second question could also be improved upon. While it is clear that the specific area of interest about mothers who work in management positions is 'time use', the word 'negotiate' is ambiguous. Does it mean how do mothers personally organize their time so as to fit in their care responsibilities and paid work, or how do they have difficult discussions with partners and employers about issues such as divisions of household labour and working hours? After feedback from her supervisor, the student who wrote the second question adapted it further to read: 'How do women in management positions and dual-earner relationships organize and prioritize their time use when combining motherhood with full-time paid work?' When asked to think about what she really meant by 'negotiate', the student realized she was more interested in knowing about women's personal strategies for managing their caring and working lives, than in the question of how negotiations with partners and employers transpired. She also further clarified that she was interested in mothers in management positions who were in relationships with partners who were also in the paid workforce, rather than those whose partners were the stay-at-home primary carers of the children.

We can't emphasize enough that qualitative research questions should be conceptually clear and precise, as well as intellectually interesting. This is in keeping with Mason's (2002) observation in the quote prefacing this chapter that doing social research is akin to solving an 'intellectual puzzle'. For researchers working in academic settings, in order to move from a topic to a clearly conceptualized and intellectually interesting question usually means making considerable inroads in the scholarly literature, and we now turn to how the existing literature can help in formulating research designs.

ROLE OF THE LITERATURE IN DEVELOPING RESEARCH QUESTIONS

Depending on the context in which you are designing research, you may be given a question or questions that you are expected to answer with little or no reference to any pre-existing literature. This would often be the case if you are carrying out policy-oriented market or social research for a private company or government department.

Usually, though, there will be a number of reasons why reading widely and early in the life of your project will assist you in creating intellectually interesting and well-conceptualized research questions and a cohesive research design. If you are carrying out your research in an academic setting, a comprehensive review of the existing scholarly literature will be expected of you. By 'scholarly literature' we primarily mean published books, book chapters, and peer-reviewed journal articles on your topic. While Wikipedia and other web-based resources can be useful in getting a feel for your topic or understanding its parameters, you will need books and peer-reviewed journal articles to obtain a broad range of theoretical and empirical work relevant to your topic from which to develop your ideas into more focused questions. Graduate students and academic researchers need to become very familiar with the online databases in their campus libraries, and utilize various keyword searches to find relevant material.

Immersing yourself in the literature helps you recognize how different paradigms underpin different research designs. As discussed in Chapter 1, our assumptions about what exists and what can be known have implications for research questions and design because these encompass political, philosophical and moral questions that we may bring to bear on the issue we are investigating. The following example shows how our assumptions about social reality guide our research questions.

Imagine you are interested in conducting research on the topic of gestational surrogacy. This reproductive technology enables a woman to become pregnant through an IVF procedure, with the intention of giving the baby to someone else to raise. Commercial surrogacy clinics have been operating for many years in some US states, and are now a lucrative commercial enterprise in less developed countries such as India and Thailand.

Your research questions will depend upon, and require thinking through, your views about the ontological status of pregnancy and motherhood. For instance, do you understand pregnancy, birth and motherhood as fundamentally natural processes that are tampered with in commercial surrogacy, or do you understand these as social processes that are mediated by technologies but not necessarily in negative ways? Assumptions that pregnancy is or should be a natural process are far more likely to give rise to research questions that are implicitly or explicitly critical of commercial and gestational surrogacy.

We continue with this example to show how your assumptions about the relationship between researcher and findings will also affect your research design. If you read widely in the literature on surrogacy you are likely to find a range of epistemological assumptions both implicitly and explicitly expressed by writers and researchers in this field. You would also find that feminist epistemologies are often relevant but that there are a number of ways of understanding the issues from a feminist perspective.

If you approach the topic of surrogacy with criticalist feminist assumptions, this is likely to result in a very different kind of research design from those assuming a more constructivist feminist perspective. A project on surrogacy informed by criticalist feminist assumptions may seek to liberate Indian or Thai women from needing to earn money through this kind of reproductive labour. The research questions may imply some kind of intervention or political strategy with Indian surrogates or the medical professionals who recruit them, with the broader social goal of improving the women's quality of life and control over their reproductive labour. Conversely, a researcher informed by more constructivist feminist assumptions about surrogacy may not assume the practice is harmful, or see the goal of the research as one that requires effecting social change in the women's lives. The research question may be phrased in a way that seeks to understand how women come to be surrogates, and why they prefer or make use of this way of earning money to other kinds of jobs available to them locally.

Reading the existing literature will help you clarify your ideas about why the topic you are tackling is interesting or important and to whom. Here we are talking not only about the scholarly literature, but also about the 'grey literature' that comprises the reports, literature reviews and policy documents generated by policy makers and researchers working in applied research areas for government. As we discussed earlier in the chapter, there is no point in undertaking research that is only of interest to you: there must be a wider audience for the work, and it should be of some social benefit. Reading widely will help you understand the broad social context of your topic, and the legal and policy issues that are associated with it, as well as shed light on which aspects of the topic would be worthy of consideration at that point in time.

Academic researchers often work within the parameters of an intellectual discipline or field of expertise, and so reading the literature will inform you about disciplinary distinctions in your area of interest. For instance, legal scholars, sociologists, medical doctors, psychologists, anthropologists and social workers have all published research on gestational surrogacy. Although funded research studies are often 'interdisciplinary' in their concerns, understanding disciplinary differences can also be an important way of finding a manageable focus. Whereas a social worker or psychologist researching gestational surrogacy may be interested in research questions about how to counsel intended parents and/or intended surrogates in clinical interviews, this kind of focus is unlikely to be of interest to a sociologist or anthropologist whose expertise lends itself more to exploring how reproductive technologies influence the expression and conceptualization of family relationships more broadly. Finding relevant concepts that have been used within your discipline to explore the issues raised by your topic, and the variety of ways in which these concepts are understood, will assist you in developing intellectually interesting research question(s) that are within your area of expertise.

Finally, a key reason for accessing the scholarly literature is that this enables you to ensure you are making an original contribution to knowledge. Social research builds, where possible, on work that has gone before it, and it is important not to knowingly duplicate work already completed without a good reason for doing so. This is not only a waste of resources, it could also constitute an unnecessary intrusion into the lives of the people who take part. At the same time, being original does not mean you need always produce work that is completely novel or radically different from what's gone before, and there are many modest ways in which it is possible to develop original research questions.

Reading the literature will help you identify a range of ways in which you can make an original contribution. Articles published in academic journals are usually a good place to start because in these you will often find explicit mention of 'gaps' identified in the literature. In many social science disciplines it is customary for researchers to discuss the limitations of their own study with regard to who took part, the research questions explored, or the sample of people they recruited, along with suggestions for future research topics or questions. Sometimes researchers will publish comprehensive or 'integrative' literature reviews in which they will survey the state of knowledge in a given field and point out fruitful avenues for future research. Reading journal articles also often provides ideas about how you might do things differently, even if the specific gaps or limitations of previous work are not identified for you. For instance, close reading of the existing literature may leave you feeling dissatisfied because you think the researchers asked the wrong questions, or you may be unconvinced by the way they interpreted their data, and such feelings can spark your own imagination.

If very little has been published on your specific topic, you may need to think quite creatively about how you will find relevant literature. Sometimes research questions and designs will emerge out of a process whereby researchers have decided to apply a different body of theory to a social setting/problem of interest, or extend an existing conceptual/theoretical framework to cover a new topic or setting.

To summarize, you should read the pre-existing literature to:

- firm up your ideas about why the problem posed by the research question is interesting or important;
- refine your research questions;
- find or devise the main concepts;
- make sure that your question has not already been answered to your satisfaction;
- clarify how different approaches to the issue are underpinned by different philosophical positions.

Writing a review of the literature will often be an integral part of the proposal in which you will outline your research design, and we suggest a possible approach to this below.

Writing a literature review

The first part of your literature review can be thought of as the 'background' section. It is here that you will explain the social context for your topic and the general area of inquiry in which your work is situated. Information included in the background section usually addresses the following questions:

- Why is it important to study your topic?
- What are the main bodies of theory that will be useful in developing your research?

When you have the answers to these questions you will probably also have an idea about the way in which the topic is linked to broader intellectual and practical concerns. This section may also expand to become your introductory/background sections later on when it comes to writing a thesis, report or article based on the completed research.

The next part of a literature review discusses the pre-existing social research studies in your field and how these relate to each other. The literature review usually ends with a paragraph explaining the 'gap' highlighted from your consideration of the literature, leading into your own research questions and proposed methodology or strategy for the research study.

The background and literature review sections of a proposal should develop a persuasive argument based on the pre-existing literature for why your own research is needed, rather than their simply listing and describing other research studies that have been conducted in your field. It is necessary to indicate clearly how the pre-existing studies you discuss relate to each other when writing your review. Your own 'voice', or viewpoint on the literature should come out clearly when writing the review, as in the following sample paragraph.

Box 3.2

Sample literature review paragraph

> First sentence of the paragraph gives a clear indication of theme and the author's point of view.
>
> Studies that express variations on that theme are grouped and discussed in the paragraph.

The patriarchal precedents for contemporary surname conventions are well established in the literature. Historically, married women in Anglo-Saxon and some other European cultures have taken their husband's surname, and children their father's surname, as an extension of their status as his property in law (Gittins, 1993). As Janet Finch (2008) reminds us, name-changing by women upon marriage was very much challenged by second wave

(Continued)

(Continued)

feminists in the 1960s and 70s as a powerful symbol of women's oppression. For instance, Jessie Bernard (1973) claimed that for a woman to change her name after marriage indicated her structurally inferior position to her husband. For Women's Liberation-era feminists of radical and more liberal persuasions, name-changing represented a willingness to sacrifice one's individual identity as a woman and person on the altar of patriarchal convention. More recently, Nugent (2010) has argued that for women and children to assume the husband, father or male partner's name firmly instantiates the 'patriarchal dividend' (Connell, 2005) in delivering a range of social and symbolic advantages to men as a group.

Note that the literature review in Box 3.2 has been deliberately structured to build a persuasive argument for the need for research on the meanings women give to surnames.

LINKING RESEARCH QUESTIONS TO METHODS

Once you have done enough reading to have formulated clear questions, and written a draft of your literature review, you will need to think about where and how you will obtain the data you need to answer your questions. Can you answer your research questions with data that are already obtainable from other sources? Or do you need new data? The numerous data sources that already exist include biographies, historical archives, policy documents, newspaper articles, diaries, blogs and social media data such as public Facebook posts. It can be very convenient and cost effective to use these kinds of data sources if they are appropriate. Data that you collect or observe, or ask your participants to collect or observe, include in-depth or group interviews, focus groups, observational fieldwork, and visual methods such as taking photographs or making short films.

Your research questions will 'drive' the methods you need to answer them rather than the other way around. Recall the final version of the research question we discussed earlier: 'How do women in management positions and dual-earner relationships organize and prioritize their time use when combining motherhood with full-time paid work?'

The logic of this research question demands that mothers in management positions be asked about their organizing and prioritizing strategies. There are a number of ways in which you could do this. You could interview the women one-on-one, or you could conduct a focus group. Getting them to tell you what they do will rely on their memories, so you may decide that asking them what they do in general is OK, but getting them to keep diaries would be more accurate for detailed information about organizing and prioritizing from day to day. Combining interviews and diaries could also prove useful.

Feasibility is another factor in deciding on the method or methods to use. Managers who are also mothers are very busy. Even if you think there might be benefits to interviewing them in groups, would this be too complex to administer for this group of women? And how are you going to get them all in the same room at the same time? Choosing the right methods often means weighing up the kind of information you need with how convenient it will be for your participants to provide you with this.

THE RESEARCH PROPOSAL

Your research design will usually be documented in a research proposal which will serve as a kind of road map for your research. In a qualitative research study the road you take may change a bit along the way, but without plotting a course beforehand you are unlikely to get to your desired destination. The following sample format is suitable for undergraduate and postgraduate students' research proposals and certain kinds of research funding grant applications. Proposals written for grant applications are typically shorter than those prepared by higher degree students, and give more detail about how research will be disseminated as well as conducted.

Box 3.3

A sample research proposal

1. **Title of the project.** This should be descriptive of the project but reasonably short. Often people will chose a brief evocative title followed by a colon and a subtitle. A clear title (and a clear research question; see point 4) can do wonders to focus your work.
2. **Introduction.** A short paragraph or two giving an overview of your field of research and aims. This is to orient the reader before they explore your ideas in depth.
3. **Background and literature review.** As well as providing background, if possible, the literature review should be structured so as to clearly identify your proposed research as filling a gap in the existing literature.
4. **Research questions.** Here you will identify the particular research question(s) you will be trying to answer in your research. Stating your research question clearly is crucial to this.
5. **Ethical considerations.** If you are carrying out research using data from human participants, you will need to consider relevant ethical issues. Your research is also likely to require clearance from an institutional review board or human research ethics committee, if you are based in a university or other academic institution, or working with participants in institutional settings such as schools, prisons or hospitals. How does the research affect your participants? Could it harm them? What procedures will you take to minimize the risk of this? We discuss these issues in depth in Chapter 4.
6. **Methodology.** How do you plan to find answers to the research question you have posed? Give details of the specific research methods you plan to use to answer your research question. Here you should be specific about the scope of the project. For example, what

(Continued)

> *(Continued)*
>
> historical material will you consult? How much time will you spend in the field as a participant observer? Who will you interview, why, and approximately how many interviews do you plan to include?
> 7. **Timelines.** Indicate how long each of the activities will take and when each of these will need to be completed.
> 8. **Budget.** If you are applying for research funding in a commercial or academic environment, a detailed budget will usually be required.
> 9. **References.** List the key sources you've cited under the points above with full bibliographic details.

CONCLUSION

Qualitative research designs tend to be open, exploratory and inductive, but this does not mean they are vague or sloppy. In well-designed qualitative research there will be clear questions, the feasibility of methods and access to other resources will have been taken into account, and there will be a good fit between the research questions and the chosen methods.

Researchers will read pre-existing literature for a number of reasons: to firm up their ideas about why the problem posed by the research question is interesting or important; to refine their research question through reading previous studies and theory related to their topic; to make sure that their question has not already been answered to their satisfaction. That said, it is also possible to conduct research in more applied commercial and policy settings without referring to the pre-existing literature.

Ideas for qualitative research can come from many places. It can often be helpful to talk over your project ideas with others, and ask them for suggestions about good keywords to search on or key people in the field. Peers can also make good suggestions that you will not necessarily have thought of yourself. Their tips and questions may help provide you with a new angle on a topic, and your discussion of research topics can both stimulate and focus your thinking. Keeping an eye on news media/popular culture/policy developments for new topics that lend themselves to empirical inquiry can also prove fruitful.

Going further

Denscombe, M. (2012) *Research Proposals: A Practical Guide*. Maidenhead: Open University Press.

See especially Chapter 3, 'Selling an Idea'. A good resource for students and more established researchers, the book assists with structuring research proposals for different research contexts and clearly discusses other aspects of research design.

Gabb, J. (2008) *Researching Intimacy in Families*. Basingstoke: Palgrave Macmillan.

Gabb's work is a telling reminder that research design needs to be tailored to the sensitivities and complexity of the topic. She provides a rich and comprehensive account of considerations in designing research about family relationships. Researching children and families can include a creative range of methods that will enable young people and adults to express their views and emotions to researchers despite varying degrees of literacy.

Mason, J. (2002) *Qualitative Researching* (2nd edition). London: Sage.

Chapters 1 and 2, 'Finding a Focus and Knowing Where You Stand' and 'Designing Qualitative Research', are helpful for thinking about how to develop a topic into a question, and also explore the philosophical issues involved in developing qualitative research projects.

Murray, R. (2011) *How to Write a Thesis* (3rd edition). Maidenhead: McGraw-Hill/Open University Press.

Chapter 3, 'Seeking Structure', provides a good discussion of the role of literature and tips for writing literature reviews. The book is aimed at graduate students but is also useful for researchers working in other contexts.

www.literaturereviewhq.com/

This website began in 2011 and has a range of useful strategies for writing literature reviews in various disciplines. It also tackles some of the common issues that academics and students face when writing these, such as procrastination and being overwhelmed by the amount of material.

FOUR

The politics and ethics of qualitative research

CONTENTS

- Ethics　　　　　　　　　　　　　　　　　　　　　　46
  - Respect　　　　　　　　　　　　　　　　　　　　46
  - Beneficence (do no harm)　　　　　　　　　　　50
  - Research merit, integrity and competence　　　53
  - Justice　　　　　　　　　　　　　　　　　　　　53
- Politics in research　　　　　　　　　　　　　　　　54
  - The researcher and the researched　　　　　　54
  - Politics and research funding　　　　　　　　　55
  - Politics and reporting research findings　　　　56
- Conclusion　　　　　　　　　　　　　　　　　　　　56
- Going further　　　　　　　　　　　　　　　　　　57

Social research is rarely value-neutral. We are interested in particular topics, and approach them in particular ways, based on who we are, where we are socially located (our class, cultural, gender, ethnic and spatial positioning), and what is important in our world. We are also influenced by what funders will (or will not) pay for, and often shape our research in accordance with those priorities. So the very topics of research vary by our social location and the resources we have access to. Those resources include people we might be able to research with, such as colleagues and participants.

Ethics refers to whether the research is honest, has integrity, is not harmful, and is – on balance – beneficial. The chapter discusses these and other elements of research ethics, including whether a qualitative project needs to go through an ethics review process, and when covert research is warranted. It incorporates real examples from our own and others' previous research to explore the issues. In our discussion of ethics we distinguish between honesty/integrity and risk, and how researchers need to be aware of and balance both. We also discuss researching controversial and illegal topics.

The chapter discusses both the politics and ethics of qualitative research. The politics of research is about the power relationships between the researcher, the researched, and the context of the research, including its funding, location and consequences. The politics is closely related to the research paradigm underpinning the research. We discuss power relations in research by looking at specific examples where those relations will shape the research process. These will include issues around funded research, where the funder has interests in particular findings, researching vulnerable communities, and researching elites. We also discuss ongoing relationships with research participants, and how to negotiate what can be tricky power dynamics.

Ethics is about conducting honest and accurate research that is beneficial to society and does not cause harm. However, what is deemed 'beneficial' and 'harmful' is socially constructed and subject to debate. It is related to how society itself is structured, and how power is distributed.

ETHICS

Social researchers are and should be concerned with the ethics of their research. Power and ethics are very much interrelated. The exercise of power often raises ethical issues. There are a number of ethical aspects that are considered essential. These largely emerge from the social values underpinning the research. Although values vary by locale, research in Western societies is generally underpinned by respect, beneficence (including do no harm), research merit, and justice (National Commission for the Protection of Human Subjects of Biomedical and Behavioral Research, 1979). We discuss each of these in turn.

Respect

Respect involves respecting the rights, dignity and self-determination of others. It means giving research participants enough information for them to make considered decisions about whether to be involved in the research. It also means protecting the vulnerable. Valuing respect means that participants should voluntarily consent to take part in research, should be informed of how long their data will be retained, and for what purposes those data may be used in the future. Research participants should be accurately informed about any potential harm that may occur to them as a result of their participation, and should be allowed to withdraw from the research at any time.

Respecting participants means that those participants should, for the most part, know that they are taking part in a research project. The process of informing participants about the project and acquiring their consent to take part is called the informed consent process. Most research ethics review committees (also called internal review boards or IRBs) will require that researchers provide details of the research project to potential participants, and that potential participants give their consent to participate. Informed consent means that research participants are aware of the goals of the research project. It means that covert research – namely research where the people being researched do not know the research is taking place – should not occur.

There are possible exceptions, such as observing behaviour in a public place where it would be difficult to identify individuals. We might imagine a study of how people interact at a train station, for example. One notable (or notorious) study was conducted by Laud Humphreys in the 1970s. Humphreys' research was of men's sexual behaviour in public restrooms ('tearooms') (Humphreys, 1972). He was able to observe the men's behaviour by playing the role of a voyeur – a person who enjoyed watching other men have sex – and who also watched out for the police. The men were initially observed anonymously, but Humphreys then followed up by noting their licence plate numbers and getting their contact details. He then put on a disguise, went to their homes, and asked them to fill out a health survey.

We might argue that Humphreys' covert study was justifiable as men who have sex with men in public are a hard-to-reach population for researchers and it is important to learn about their sexual practices for public health reasons. As long as the men were not identifiable, we could argue that the benefits of such a study would outweigh the harms. However, covertly collecting identifying information about these anonymous men and interviewing them later, without disclosing that he had seen them before, goes against the principle of respect. Power relations play a role here too. Humphreys had the power to identify the men by name. Most were married and may not have elected to participate had they known that he had knowledge of their illicit sexual behaviour. However, the study raises a number of issues if we value respect. In particular, were the findings so important that they warranted violating this principle? Would the study have been ethical if it merely observed men in the tearooms? Here, the ethical issue was not the research topic but getting the participants' contact details and locating them without their consent.

There are also grey areas, such as online spaces, which may seem public to an outsider but may be experienced as private by the people interacting within them (Markham and Buchanan, 2012). The issue hinges around whether online communications that persist as publicly accessible text should be treated the same as any other publicly accessible text, or whether in some cases the communities' discussions should be treated like private conversations. Barbara Sharf (1999) experienced one such grey area when researching a breast cancer support email list in the 1990s. A participant observer on the list, Sharf disclosed her research intentions when she joined and posted, but her main source of data was posts by other list participants whom she quoted when she wrote up the research. She attributed the quotes to pseudonyms rather than members so that individual posters could not be identified. After writing up the findings, she felt it was important to contact the people quoted and get their permission. So she contacted them all and asked their permission, which she eventually received. In reflecting on her experiences Sharf argues that it is important to protect online communicators' privacy, particularly when studying vulnerable populations. To do this, it is important to get people's permission to use their words, even if ostensibly they seem to already be in the public domain and even when pseudonyms are used.

Sharf's experiences are an example of a cautious approach to online research ethics. Other researchers take the view that anything published online is a text, not a conversation. In this view, anything published online that is used for research should be properly attributed to its author like any other text. An email list such as the one used by Sharf is more private than an open online forum as it can only be seen by members, and participants would have a reasonable expectation that only members would have access to their words. In this case, it is ethical to treat this as a private conversation. But what of the case where an amateur blog writer is studied? Is it reasonable to use their words with attribution but without permission? In thinking about this we might consider whether a blog is more like a private journal or more like a text that is intended for public consumption and engages with commenters. The value of respect would suggest that the blog writer's and commenters' permission should be sought, but this is very much debated by academic researchers.

The debate between whether online posts constitute published texts or instead are like private conversations reflects real tensions that researchers must navigate. We would advise being cautious and careful to respect potential research participants. There is a qualitative difference between posting a comment to a newspaper website and posting a message to an online support group. There is a reasonable expectation that your post to a newspaper website would be widely read and engaged with, whereas there is a reasonable expectation that your post to an online support group will only be read by group members. Even if the support group you are posting to is public, you might reasonably expect there to be only a few readers. As researchers, we need to be aware of this difference in reasonable expectations on the part of people publishing online and act accordingly. However, there are no hard-and-fast rules.

Respect also suggests that if confidentiality is promised, then that promise must be kept. Confidentiality refers to keeping participants' identifying information out of the research report. The researcher will know who the participants are. In contrast, anonymity is when the researchers do not know who the participants are. For example, a researcher studying a group engaging in illegal activities might interview people at a nightclub without asking for, or collecting, their names or any identifying information. Those participants would remain anonymous.

Researchers will often promise research participants that they will keep their identity confidential. This means that each participant's words will not be associated with their identity. Researchers offer confidentiality because they believe it will encourage participants to be candid and will protect them from harm. If you promise not to use someone's name, you are intending to protect them in case their words are embarrassing or may put them at some sort of risk. As the researcher you have the position of power. The participants will trust that you will keep their identity private.

It is relatively easy to promise a participant that their identity will be kept confidential, that they will be referred to by a pseudonym and that any identifying characteristics of their story will be altered. However, the extent to which a story can be altered without losing its meaning is somewhat limited. There is also the issue of internal confidentiality. Internal confidentiality (Tolich, 2004) is the promise that a participant's identity will be unknowable, even to their close confidants. Internal confidentiality is an issue when participants who know each other are being studied, as in the case of participant observation. It is much harder to maintain and researchers need to develop novel strategies to manage it.

Box 4.1

Internal confidentiality and the risk to participants

In her study of entrepreneurs and their spouses, Dina Bowman (2007, 2009) interviewed male and female entrepreneurs and their spouses. The entrepreneurs and spouses were interviewed separately and promised confidentiality. Spouses know each other intimately, including the way in which their spouse is likely to phrase their comments. This meant Bowman had to work out a way to accurately report the findings while protecting the participants' confidentiality. As the study was about negotiating intimate relationships, some of the information could be damaging to the participants' relationships should their spouse have been able to identify them. What Bowman did was to analyze each category of participant as a group. The male entrepreneurs were considered together, as were the female entrepreneurs, the husbands and wives. Spouses were never paired. Although this was an effective strategy, the downside of it was precisely that the spouses were never paired, so the husbands' and wives' narratives were not able to be analyzed together, potentially preventing Bowman from reporting some of her most interesting findings.

Offering confidentiality as a way to encourage participation and protect participants is a norm in social research. It is almost as though it is generally expected that people will not want to participate in research if they are not offered confidentiality. However, it is unclear whether promising confidentiality actually encourages research participants to be more candid or not. There is some evidence that complete anonymity can lead to fewer socially desirable responses, meaning that participants are less likely to say what they think the researcher wants to hear, but it has also been associated with a lack of accountability, leading to less care taken with providing careful and accurate responses (Lelkes et al., 2012). As researchers, we do not have to promise confidentiality. If we believe that our participants are active agents in the research process, as is the case with research conducted within criticalist or constructivist paradigms, we can expect that they will choose to participate, or not, and share their views candidly, or not, themselves. This puts some power back into their hands. In these approaches, sharing power with research participants can be an important consideration.

As researchers, it is vital that we are careful about what we promise, and that respect for participants is our guiding principle.

Beneficence (do no harm)

The value of beneficence means that the potential benefits of the research should outweigh any potential harm. This means taking into account the risks – assessing the likelihood that harm may occur. The construction of risk is related to the research topic and the population being studied. We can think of three types of risk that need to be considered: risk to the researcher; risk to the researched; and risk to the institution. Potential harms can include physical, emotional and psychological, and legal harms.

Risks to the researcher

In some studies a researcher may find themselves in a risky situation. For example, when studying illegal activity a researcher may find out the names of people who are criminals. Researchers are not protected categories of people: if subpoenaed they must testify. This type of risk to the researcher makes it difficult to undertake research into illegal activities. An example of this type of risk was Sudhir Venkatesh's PhD research (Venkatesh, 2008). Venkatesh studied the economics of poverty in Chicago, including the structure of a gang's drug dealing activities. Venkatesh knew the drug dealers and who they dealt with. His account was not published until many years after the fieldwork, and after the main participants had moved on.

One way that researchers can get around this risk to themselves is by conducting anonymous interviews – that is, interviews where they do not know the participants and do not collect their names. Here the participants give verbal consent. This risk shapes the kind of research data that can be acquired. The type of participant observation that Venkatesh (2008) undertook, for example, is particularly risky, even though the quality of the data is likely to be very high. Most institutions would not approve such a project.

Researchers may also be at physical risk. Kathleen Blee (1998) studied organized racist movements through interviews with white supremacist women in the United States. The participants in her research openly threatened her with violence. In her discussion of the issue, Blee argued that the participants used fear to shape the kind of rapport that they developed with her and to assert power over her in the interviews. Nevertheless, she was in genuine fear for herself, and this shaped her research findings.

These risks to the researcher are possibly less common now that most academic research must be approved by institutional ethics processes. However, we must acknowledge that these processes shape the types of research we are able to do. They make it difficult to conduct qualitative research with marginalized groups who may be involved in illegal acts. One way to get around this issue is to interview people in the field, but without collecting any identifying information about them.

Risks to the researched

Research participants may also be at risk as a result of participating in research. Risk in this instance is most often associated with vulnerable participants, although it needs to be considered for all projects. Participants may be vulnerable because of their age, whether they have a disability, or other social factors such as being a refugee or a prisoner (Remenyi et al., 2011). For example, prisoners may feel pressured to participate while refugees may participate because they feel indebted to the researchers. Vulnerability may also be due to a perceived inability to fully consent (this may be the case for children and people with a mental disability).

Most social research is not high risk for participants. The idea behind requiring that participants be informed about the project and provide their consent to participate means that people must be informed of possible risks and choose whether or not to participate. Research participants, in this view, are seen as active agents who are able to look out for their own well-being.

In some cases, though, the research participants may not be aware of the potential risks. In Bowman's (2009) study of entrepreneurs, discussed in Box 4.1, Bowman recognized – after she had completed the interviews – that some of the responses from the spouses could potentially damage their relationships if they were to get back to the entrepreneurs. Some participants had been very candid about the shortcomings in both their spouse and their marriage. Because they had been promised confidentiality, Bowman had to ensure that their words were disguised enough so that their spouse would not be able to recognize them, thus ensuring that internal confidentiality was maintained (Tolich, 2004).

Researchers need to be aware of the possible negative outcomes from participation and mitigate the risks. Where risks are likely, the benefits of the study should outweigh these and the researchers should take as much care as possible to minimize them. Whether or not the benefits seem to outweigh the risks depends on value judgements. These value judgements will be made according to the beliefs and values, or paradigm, underpinning the research.

While not qualitative research, Stanley Milgram's (1963, 1974) obedience studies highlight the issues of benefits versus harm to participants in social research. Milgram's (1974) study was an experiment that investigated how people would react to authority. Each participant was asked to administer an electric shock to another person, one whom they believed was also a participant, but was actually an actor playing a role. A researcher figure, in a lab coat, asked the participants to administer increasingly strong electric shocks, even when the person pretending to be shocked was screaming out in pain. The experiments were a way of trying to understand how the Holocaust could have happened, how normal people could be made to perform horrific acts of violence (Milgram, 1963). The research found that people would respond to authority even when it went against their beliefs. This was an important and useful finding, but participating in the studies had long-term negative effects on some of the participants. Whether the harm outweighed the benefit depends on the weight you give to the benefits to society of the findings versus the harm to participants.

Risks to the institution

The institution where a researcher is based is also a stakeholder in its research projects and liable for that research, and is therefore interested in minimizing the risks to the researcher, the researched, and the broader community.

If your research is being conducted under the auspices of a university or other institution that has an ethics review process, you must comply with that process. The institution's ethics processes are designed to ensure that risk is minimized. This entails applying for permission from the institution to conduct the research. Each institution will have its own process. In the case of qualitative social research, this process usually entails outlining the proposed research, who or what is being researched, how the research will be conducted, and providing copies of the participant information document, the informed consent document, the interview schedule/list of issues to be covered, and any other consents or clearances required. In general, if the research involves people it will need to comply with the institution's ethics review processes. These processes aim to establish that the principles for ethical research discussed are being adhered to.

Because the institution is liable for the research, it may resist approving research that is inherently risky. For example, any research into child pornography – even a simple analysis of images – will be very difficult to get approved. A researcher must have a solid reason for doing the research and a solid research method. Then they must first get access to the images, which may be monitored by the police. One Australian researcher who was doing research on child sex tourism in Southeast Asia recounted that they were interested in understanding the dynamics of child sex tourism. The research involved looking at websites where child sex tourism was advertised. Once they started to access the images their computer was monitored first by their university, and then by the federal police as it is illegal to view child pornography online in Australia. In the end it was decided by the authorities that it was a legitimate research project, but that they needed a senior government minister to approve the research before they could even start. Despite this approval there were too many ongoing obstacles and in the end the project was suspended.

Humphreys' (1972) study of tearooms raises questions about risk and beneficence. By identifying men who participated in illicit sex, he potentially put them at risk. Had their identities been discovered, there could have been terrible consequences for some participants. However, a counter-argument could be that if Humphreys had not observed the men in the tearooms beforehand, the research would not have captured that seemingly heterosexual men participated in gay sex. He also did not out the men, so it could be argued that despite the risks no harm was done and the benefits were substantial.

In summary, beneficence means that the benefits of a research project must outweigh the risks to the researcher, the researched, and the institution.

Research merit, integrity and competence

Valuing research merit is related to beneficence and means that there must be some potential benefit from the research. If there is no potential benefit, there is no justification for undertaking the research (National Health and Medical Research Council, 2007). Research merit can be broadly defined. Doing basic research – for example, learning how social processes work – is certainly worthwhile. The research does not need to benefit the participants themselves if there is a likelihood that it will benefit others in the future.

Related to research merit is research integrity: being honest, respectful and fair in carrying out and reporting the research findings. Integrity includes maintaining confidentiality if that is promised, and reporting negative findings as well as positive ones. Research merit is sometimes raised in the context of online research. Critics argue that it is impossible to know who is participating in an online interview. The same criticism could also be levelled at postal interviews or even face-to-face interviews with strangers, as there is no guarantee that they are being honest either.

Research integrity has to be balanced with beneficence. In Bowman's (2009) study she had to shape the reports of her findings to protect her participants. The need for beneficence meant that some findings could not be reported. This is not uncommon and is part of the research process. That is not to say that negative research findings should be withheld as a matter of principle. Quite the opposite is the case if we are to value research integrity. Nonetheless it is naïve to think that researchers should and/or do not consider the contexts for their studies and reports. The reporting of negative findings in particular can be political and is discussed further later on in the chapter.

Having the appropriate skills to do the proposed research is also an important ethical value and is central to research integrity (American Sociological Association, 1999). Researchers should be sufficiently competent to carry out their research, and if they are not they should upskill before they start the project. Related to this, research practice should be based on well-established principles, and it is incumbent on researchers to stay up to date with developments in their field.

Justice

Finally, valuing justice focuses on the fair treatment of participants and means not excluding particular groups from either participation or benefit. If particular groups are to be excluded there should be a compelling reason to do so. This is important because all groups are important. Medical research for a long time did not include either women or children in its work. The consequence of this has been that many medical protocols and drugs have not been tested on women or children, despite being used by both (Taylor, 2009). The justification for excluding women and children was based on the principle of beneficence – the concern they might be harmed in the research (Merton, 1993). However, the outcome of their exclusion is that their use of the drugs or other medical protocols is a large natural experiment, one that occurs outside controlled circumstances and which may or may not be tracked. It would have been fairer if they had been included in the studies initially.

POLITICS IN RESEARCH

Qualitative research necessarily involves power relations or politics. We can understand power as the ability to get what we want and/or to get another person to do what we want them to do, and it is related to status and hierarchy. Even the most junior researchers will have some power in the research relationship (i.e. the power to report findings).

There are three aspects of politics that are important to consider. First is the politics of the relationship between the researcher and the researched. Second is the relationship of the research to its funding bodies. Third is the politics of reporting research findings.

The researcher and the researched

The power relations within a given research project will depend partly on factors such as the type of project (its goals, who initiated it and for what purpose), the participation elicited, and the broader context for the research.

How we approach the issue of power relations between the researcher and researched is related to the epistemological position underpinning the research. If we are coming from a criticalist perspective, we may have a particular social justice goal that we would like to achieve which would involve the active participation of the participants. In this case we would need to design a project that facilitates the participants sharing the power. However, from a post-positivist perspective we may see the participants as information providers and believe that the researcher's role is to interpret and report the findings as objectively as they can. If this is the case, beyond ensuring that the participants are willing, as researchers we are unlikely to implement strategies that seek to empower the participants through their participation. In constructivist research, such as action research, power is shared by the researchers and the participants as a core research value.

A researcher generally has the power to define the research question, determine who should participate, and decide how to report the findings. In general, the participants have the power to decide whether to participate, and if they do participate, what information to share with the researcher.

Box 4.2

Training and research participation

Karen Farquharson gives an example of a case where the researchers and the participants had different agendas. She was part of a research team that implemented and researched a media intervention (Marjoribanks et al., 2013). The goal of the project was to see whether providing journalism training for Sudanese Australians would enable them to develop their own media voice, so the research was action-oriented. In order to access the training, participants had to also take part in the research, which involved participant observation, focus groups and interviews. Power was exercised by the research team in that all participants in the training had to agree to participate in the research. On the other hand, participants could elect to use the training however they saw fit. There was no requirement for them to use it to engage in media participation.

For many of the participants, the reason for participating was to be able to engage directly with the mainstream media. However, some participants were involved in the training as they hoped it would lead to work. The need for gainful employment was an ongoing issue within the community. Job training was not, however, a part of the agenda of the research team or an intention of the journalism training. The research team was very focused on the research outcomes that were required as part of the research funding agreement. This does not suggest that the participants were unhappy about participating in the research, just that their goals around the project did not involve the research outcomes. Thus the funding of the project had material effects on the intervention and hence on the participants.

The researcher and the participants, then, can each have their own agenda regarding the research (see Box 4.2). The researcher should be reflexive about their agenda, critically considering why they are involved in the research and what they want to get out of it. These power issues are also related to research ethics, in particular valuing respect for research participants.

Politics and research funding

As the example in Box 4.2 shows, if the research is externally funded, you will need to manage the expectations and political interests of the funders, who will have their own reasons for providing that funding. Funders can range from being intimately involved in the research design to being completely hands-off once the funds are awarded. It is important to know beforehand where your funder lies on that spectrum.

When working with funding agencies, there are a number of issues around politics that should be considered. These will include what is the funder's interest in the research (why do they want to fund it)? How much input will they expect to have into the research design? How much control will they have over the reporting of the findings, and what will happen if the findings are not what they had hoped for? And if it is academic research, will they be able prevent publication of the findings?

Depending on the answers to these questions, funders can fundamentally shape the results. Politics and ethics are intertwined here. If you believe it is your obligation to report the research findings regardless of what these are, you may come into conflict with the research funder, particularly if the findings are not in their interest. How you manage this will depend on how much power you have in the relationship and the arrangements you have put in place beforehand. Working out beforehand whether or not the funder has, for example, the right to quash the results is important. Note that some of these issues can be sorted out in the research contracts that will provide the parameters for the project.

Politics and reporting research findings

One of the most important powers a researcher holds is that they control how the findings are reported and to whom. There is an implicit contract between the researcher and the researched that the researcher will report the findings accurately and that they will not harm the participants. Indeed this is embedded in the values that shape research ethics processes. In real life, though, there will be grey areas in the reporting of research findings that will bring into play issues of power and valuing respect, beneficence, justice, and research merit and integrity.

For example, imagine you were conducting research from a criticalist perspective into the circumstances leading to disadvantage for a particular group. In that research you found that although there were social structures that kept the group you were studying disadvantaged, the group itself also carried out some practices that helped to maintain their disadvantage. How would you report the research? If you report the negative practices, the group may be blamed for the disadvantage, but if you do not, you are not reporting accurate research findings. The decision you make will depend on your assessment of the risks for the group of disclosing the findings versus the benefits of actually knowing what is going on, and possibly developing strategies to reduce the disadvantage.

CONCLUSION

This chapter has discussed the ethics and politics of qualitative research. While the values listed should underpin social research in general, the epistemological position underpinning the research will shape your approach to managing power dynamics. The research paradigm will also shape your sampling decisions, which we discuss in the next chapter.

In qualitative research there are often no straightforward rules about managing power dynamics and ethics. We would strongly advocate that the principles behind your research should reflect ethical practice regardless of who your participants are, and whether they are online or face to face.

Going further

Hammersley, M. and Traianou, A. (2012) *Ethics in Qualitative Research: Controversies and Contexts*. London: Sage.

A comprehensive text on ethics in qualitative research.

Markham, A. and Buchanan, E. (2012) *Ethical Decision-making and Internet Research: Recommendations for the AoIR Ethics Working Committee* (Version 2.0), Association of Internet Researchers. Available at: <aoir.org/reports/ethics2.pdf>.

Provides comprehensive guidelines for decision making regarding online ethics.

National Commission for the Protection of Human Subjects of Biomedical and Behavioral Research (1979) *The Belmont Report: Ethical Principles and Guidelines for the Protection of Human Subjects of Research*. Washington, DC: Department of Health and Human Services.

National Health and Medical Research Council (2007) *National Statement on Ethical Conduct in Human Research*. Canberra: National Health and Medical Research Council.

These statements provide comprehensive overviews of bioethics and guidelines for research with people.

Research Ethics, available at <rea.sagepub.com>.

This journal publishes contemporary studies on research ethics and is a good resource for the latest research.

'The Deadly Experiment', documentary film available at:

< http://documentaryaddict.com/the+deadly+deception-9274-doc.html>.

This film analyzes the Tuskegee syphilis study, a government-sanctioned experiment that aimed to see what would happen to someone with untreated syphilis. Disadvantaged African-American men infected with syphilis were denied treatment, even after an effective treatment became available. The men were never told that they were infected.

Tolich, M. (2004) 'Internal confidentiality: when confidentiality assurances fail relational informants', *Qualitative Sociology*, 27 (1): 101–6.

Researchers often do not consider internal confidentiality when designing their project. This article provides compelling reasons why we should pay attention to this important issue.

PART 2
DOING THE RESEARCH

There are three main ways in which a researcher can find things out, each involving a very different type of relationship between the researcher and the researched. Probably the best known way in which people conduct qualitative research is to ask questions. However, alternatively, a researcher may choose to remain silent and just observe what's going on, or even ask their research participants to provide their own accounts of what's going on. As you will see, a researcher can use one or all of these approaches in a variety of ways.

This part of the book is devoted to providing a critical account of these specific data collection strategies, such as interviews, content analysis and narrative inquiry. These methods chapters are meaningfully grouped according to the type of relationship that exists between the researcher and the researched. We will make explicit the links between the everyday decisions around doing qualitative research and the social research paradigm underpinning the research. In other words, we will make explicit the link between epistemological issues and practical, ethical, political, and methodological issues. We hope that you will find this grouping of methods useful when making your own critical assessment of the issues involved in using any qualitative research method not covered by this book.

FIVE

Sampling

CONTENTS

- What is sampling and why do we care about it? — 62
- Sampling a population — 62
- Theory, epistemology and sampling — 62
  - Starting with theory — 63
  - Starting without theory — 64
- Sampling and recruitment strategies — 66
  - Theoretical sampling — 66
  - Snowball sampling — 66
  - Purposive sampling — 67
  - Convenience sampling — 68
  - Recruitment — 69
- Generalizability — 69
- Non-respondents — 70
- Sample size — 70
- Sampling, hard-to-reach populations and research ethics — 71
- Conclusion — 71
- Going further — 72

WHAT IS SAMPLING AND WHY DO WE CARE ABOUT IT?

Sampling is the process of selecting participants, cases and/or location(s) for your study. Your sampling strategy is intimately related to the goals of your research and the paradigm within which it is operating.

Deciding where and with whom to conduct your study has important consequences. You will need to select an appropriate location and appropriate participants if you are going to be able to answer your research question with care and rigour. If, for example, you want to understand how a community uses a particular public park, you will need to select this as the location for your research. While insights into park usage in general could possibly be made from observing other parks, if you would like to know how this particular park was being used you would need to locate your study there. Similarly, if you would like to understand how people who smuggle drugs transnationally become involved in the smuggling trade, you would need to look at people who had participated in transnational drug smuggling. The local park and its users are unlikely to provide insights into transnational drug smuggling, and the transnational drug smugglers will not provide insights into local park usage unless they happen to be part of that community which uses the local park.

This chapter explores issues of sampling. We first discuss the relationship between theory and sampling and the philosophical assumptions underpinning the research. This is followed by an overview of the popular approaches to sampling in qualitative research and issues of generalizability. We conclude with a consideration of sampling in the context of hard-to-reach populations.

SAMPLING A POPULATION

When we think of doing social research we are interested in understanding a social phenomenon involving a population of some sort. A population is all the people/things within a particular category or group of categories. Women may be a category, as might gravestones, parks, or children aged between one and four in a particular neighbourhood. It might even be a single workplace. Your population category or categories will be determined by your research question. Any people you research should be part of the target population.

Since it is not usually feasible to include all the members of a population, researchers will select some members to participate in their study. How we go about doing that is called our sampling strategy. This strategy is determined by our research approach (the underpinning values and beliefs) and our research question(s).

THEORY, EPISTEMOLOGY AND SAMPLING

In Chapter 1 we discussed the necessity of being clear about the philosophical underpinnings of any research with which we are involved. We argued that the values and beliefs underpinning the research would shape the kind of research that is conducted. This extends to sampling.

A key decision you will need to make is whether you are going to start from a theoretically informed position or whether you intend to let your theory emerge from the data. We will discuss each of these in turn. In practice, all studies are informed by theory to some extent as it is impossible to have a completely 'empty head' (Stanley and Wise, 1990: 22). However, in some studies the researcher will be open to, or will intend to develop, theory through the course of their analysis.

Starting with theory

Theory can shape qualitative sampling in three key ways. First, it informs the research questions and interpretations of the findings. Second, although not very common, some qualitative research, particularly from a post-positivist perspective, involves testing theory. Third, it can provide practical assistance with sampling strategies. We shall discuss each of these in turn.

The first way theory might influence our sampling strategy is by informing the research question and the approach taken. Qualitative research is often expected to generate theory, so it is somewhat against popular wisdom to go into it with a particular theoretical approach in mind. Nonetheless, in preparing our research question we will read the existing findings in relation to our topic and assess the key points and where the gaps are. Previous studies will likely have developed explanations (theories) for what they have observed. These earlier findings should inform our study in terms of helping us understand what to expect and make sense of what we might find. We may intend to build on existing theory, propose adaptations, or develop new explanations through our study. In any case we will want to assess how our research fits into the broader existing body of the literature.

Previous studies can help us to identify which categories to sample for. For example, if our proposed topic has already been investigated, previous theory can help us assess which elements would warrant further investigation. Most social research does not investigate completely new topics. Rather, it provides new insights into previously studied topics. By carefully assessing the previous research, we can identify what has been overlooked or where it would be useful to extend the investigation.

Existing theory will likely, thus, inform our study, but what we do with it will depend on our approach to knowledge. If we are operating from within a post-positivist paradigm, we may use a qualitative approach to test theory. For example, if we think the local park is being used for illicit activities, we might design an observational study to test the theory. The method, observation, is qualitative, but it is being used in a positivist way. Theory testing is a deductive approach to research. Deductive approaches start with theory and then see whether they can explain what is observed. If the theory does not explain the data observed, then it can be altered and tested further.

We may also use an existing theoretical framework to help us identify our participants and setting. This is an approach advocated by Yin (1994) in the context of case study research. Yin likens case studies to experiments rather than 'sampling units' (1994: 31). Each case is seen as equivalent to a separate experiment, so if a theory explains each case, and counter-theories do not, that theory can be thought to be robust. He argues that choosing a 'critical case' that will test your theory enables you to refine it (1994: 35). Additional cases can be sought to test and further develop it.

Finally, previous research findings can guide our sampling strategy in a practical sense. For example, studies of lesbians and gay men have found that there is a tenuous link between participating in same-sex relationships and identifying as gay or lesbian (Weeks, 1995; Weeks et al., 2001). This suggests that it is important for you not to limit studies of same-sex relationships to self-identified lesbians and gay men because you will most likely be excluding a large proportion of your population.

Qualitative researchers will use theory in a variety of ways that will then shape their studies. This is most explicit for those conducting research within a post-positivist paradigm, but is also present to a lesser extent in criticalist and constructivist approaches. Criticalist approaches which seek social change may use theory to shape their sampling in such a way that it will most effectively achieve its advocacy goal. Even constructivists will want to know what types of things have been found about the research topic, and they will use a previous theory to assist with sampling strategies. However, most qualitative research aims to develop theory inductively. The following section discusses starting without a well-developed theory.

Starting without theory

The work of most qualitative researchers is located in the criticalist or constructivist paradigms, which lend themselves to a more situated and exploratory approach. In exploratory approaches, the research question often takes the form of 'what is happening here on this topic?' With this type of approach, careful sampling is important because your sampling decisions will shape your findings. If you want to find out how lesbians and gay men approach parenting, it is necessary to locate lesbians and gay men who are parents. It is not enough to ask any parents about their experiences.

Starting without theory does not necessarily mean starting without an awareness of the previous research on your topic. Rather, it means beginning this with an eye to developing a theoretical explanation based on the data gathered. This is called an inductive approach to research. In contrast to the deductive approach already mentioned above, theory developed inductively will necessarily explain the findings because the theory emerges from the findings. The key question with inductive approaches is whether the findings will be generalizable to other contexts.

Developed by Glaser and Strauss in 1967, grounded theory provides a systematic way to select samples that will enable theory development. This approach is called theoretical sampling.

In the grounded theory approach researchers start with a topic and identify a sample based on that topic. This might be something like 'how do people use a public park?' Based on this, a researcher would identify one or more public parks and a strategy for investigating how they were used. For example, they might interview park users, exploring how they use the park and why. They would aim for a broad range of users to try to identify all of the various reasons for people using the park. The selection of the park would be based on its 'theoretical purpose and relevance' (Glaser and Strauss, 1967: 48). To see whether the theory that emerged about park usage from the first park was robust, the researcher may choose to investigate other parks for comparison purposes.

Trying to identify and interview a wide range of participants is called sampling for maximum variation, and this means purposely trying to locate the widest range of people in the category as possible. The idea is that if the theory developed can account for the range of responses gathered with this type of sample, it is a robust theory and likely to be generalizable. Generalizability in qualitative research is discussed in greater detail later in this chapter.

In the grounded theory approach you would collect and analyze your data simultaneously, revising your sample and your interview questions based on what you are finding. Your data would suggest areas for further exploration, which you would then proceed to undertake. As you develop your theory, you will be constantly testing and revising it. You would then keep going until you achieved informational redundancy and theoretical saturation (Glaser and Strauss, 1967). Informational redundancy is achieved when you are no longer getting new information from the participants. At this point you would have enough information to describe the range of experiences in your sample and hopefully your population. When you have reached this point you can stop interviewing. Depending on how broad or how narrow your population is, this may take less or more time to achieve. Theoretical saturation has been reached when all new data can be coded in to your identified categories. This means that your explanatory framework works for all the cases you included. For theoretical saturation to be achieved, you will need to have sought a range of diverse cases.

Because of the importance of the principles of both informational redundancy and theoretical saturation, the grounded theory approach can be both time-consuming to achieve and difficult to get approved by institutional ethics committees. For this reason many qualitative researchers who are undertaking exploratory research would use an approach to sampling that utilizes previous research findings to guide sampling decisions. To elaborate on an example used above, if we know that men engage in homosexual behaviour who do not identify as gay, and we want to study the range of men in homosexual relationships, then we would need to adopt a sampling strategy that would build on this information and specifically seek men who do not identify as gay but are in same-sex relationships. It would not be a case of starting without theory, it would be a case of using existing theory to shape our sampling strategy.

Ethnography is another type of qualitative research method that starts without theory. In ethnography, however, the goal is to describe and explain what is happening with a group or in a locale in a comprehensive way at a particular time and space rather than to specifically develop theory about a social phenomenon (Atkinson and Hammersley, 1994). There are many debates about the nature of ethnography (see Atkinson and Hammersley, 1994, for a discussion). Unlike with grounded theory, it does not suggest a particular approach to sampling.

Starting without a theory does not mean entering into the project without having done background reading. Instead, it generally means having an open mind about what is going on, and developing an explanation based on what is being observed. We would argue that it is vital to be familiar with previous research on your topic, particularly as it may provide assistance with honing your sampling priorities and supporting your sampling choices.

SAMPLING AND RECRUITMENT STRATEGIES

The previous section discussed some of the philosophical aspects of sampling. In this section we outline the main approaches to identifying and recruiting samples in qualitative research. Decisions around sampling, about who or what should be selected to participate, come before decisions about which recruitment strategies to pursue, although there is some overlap between the two. Qualitative researchers usually use non-probability sampling techniques. Probability sampling refers to selecting a sample from a population in such a way that each member of the population has an equal chance of being part of the sample. In order for the sample to be representative of the population, the sample needs to be a certain size and also fulfil certain other conditions.

Like quantitative researchers who use probability samples, qualitative researchers are also trying to find a sample that will generate findings that are broadly applicable. However, qualitative studies are usually small in scale and in depth. The approach to sampling is quite different in that care is taken to select cases and participants that will provide relevant information for the research questions. The four ways that qualitative samples are selected are: theoretical sampling; snowball sampling; purposive sampling; and convenience sampling. Some researchers will decide to adopt more than one sampling method. We will explore each of these before turning to a discussion of recruitment strategies.

Theoretical sampling

As was discussed earlier, theoretical sampling is a specific approach to sampling that aims to develop theory. Once a research topic is identified, appropriate groups are selected through which to investigate the research question. However, the researcher will not know which groups or how many until the end of the research because that research continues until the new data are no longer emerging and theoretical saturation has been achieved (Glaser and Strauss, 1967).

Snowball sampling

Named with reference to the image of a rolling snowball increasing in size, snowball sampling is where participants are asked to suggest further participants. It is a very common approach in qualitative research. Once a research question is selected and the target population identified, the researcher looks to one or more members of this target population to increase the sample. These key informants should be able and willing to refer the researcher to further participants. Snowball sampling necessarily only involves people who share a social network, so it is appropriate for research questions where that is likely to be the case. Where this is not the case, the researcher can start more than one snowball with unrelated key informants, enabling the inclusion of people in separate networks. For example, a study might be interested in exploring the workplace experiences of skilled migrants to Australia. After reading the previous research, the researcher might expect that ethnic background and English proficiency might influence migrants' workplace experiences, so they would then decide to interview people from different ethnic backgrounds. To do this they might start with migrants from several ethnic backgrounds with the expectation that the participants will know others from their own ethnic background. The snowball technique would then lead to participants who came from from a variety of different ethnic backgrounds. If the study had started with just a single migrant from one ethnic background, the sample might not have much ethnic variation.

Snowball sampling is particularly useful for doing research with hard-to-reach populations. Disadvantaged people, people engaged in illicit activities, or stigmatized groups such as injecting drug users, can sometimes only be studied through snowball sampling. However, because all the participants are in the same or adjacent social networks, the variation within a sample chosen through snowball sampling can be limited. A researcher would need to take this into account in their study design.

Purposive sampling

Purposive sampling refers to selecting participants with particular criteria that will enable the researcher to answer their research question. Here participants are selected because they have particular attributes that the researcher wants to study. These are known as inclusion criteria. Criteria for inclusion are attributes the participants in your study must possess (Robinson, 2014). For example, in a study of mothers' experiences of housework, the participants must be mothers (motherhood is the inclusion criterion). Exclusion criteria are attributes that would disqualify someone from the study. In our hypothetical housework study, having paid help with the housework might be an exclusion criterion, as might being a father. Yet they also may not be, depending on the scope of the study. Obviously, the more inclusion/exclusion criteria adopted, the narrower your population.

Purposive sampling is often used when there is only a limited number of potential participants based on the selection criteria. For example, Hadi Sohrabi (2013) studied Muslim public figures for his PhD research. To identify his participants he searched for Australian Muslims contributing to and being quoted in mainstream and alternative media sources. Once he had identified these Muslim public leaders, he approached them for interview.

Purposive sampling is common in qualitative research and can be used with other methods. Sometimes snowball sampling is a type of purposive sampling, as with the reputational snowball described in Box 5.1. The reputational snowball is a way of identifying a purposive sample where the researcher wants external confirmation that their identification of elite participants is accurate. Alternatively, a researcher may identify a few participants purposively and snowball from there.

---------- Box 5.1 ----------

Peer-nominated reputational snowball

A modified version of snowball sampling is the peer-nominated reputational snowball which is used to identify elites. In the reputational snowball a range of people is asked to nominate people by reputation. The returned nominations are then collated and the individuals with the most nominations are included in the study. This was the approach Karen Farquharson (2005) took in a study of health and tobacco control policy elites in Victoria, Australia. In that study seven people thought to be in those elite networks were asked to launch the snowball. Each person nominated the 10 to 15 individuals they thought were the most influential in each of the two policy networks. Once the nomination forms were returned, all the individuals nominated were then sent a nomination form and asked to complete it. The snowball ran for five rounds until almost no new names were being elicited. The technique successfully identified a population of policy elites. By counting the number of nominations each person received, Farquharson was able to identify those who were perceived to be the most influential in that population.

Convenience sampling

Convenience sampling refers to selecting participants who are easily available. A common convenience sample is university students, who are frequently studied by academics because they are accessible and often interested in taking part. Indeed, at many universities students are required to participate in research as part of their course of study. However, student samples have significant limitations: they are usually of a narrow age band, and they are often not representative of broader populations in terms of ethnicity, social class, or other characteristics that might be relevant to a study.

A convenience sample is not necessarily bad in qualitative research. It can be an important starting point for a study. This does not mean that you should be less than rigorous about your data collection. Convenience sampling is frequently criticized and needs to have a solid rationale if it is to be used. Some would consider it to be a sample of last resort. As with other sampling strategies, it needs to be appropriate to your research design.

Recruitment

Your recruitment strategy is how you will operationalize your sampling strategy, that is, how you will get actual participants to participate in your project. At some point you will have to directly ask people if they would like to participate. Snowball and convenience sampling are recruitment strategies as well as sampling strategies as they help to identify all the people you will ask.

An additional recruitment strategy would be to advertise for potential participants. While not frequently discussed as a means of finding a qualitative sample, advertising is actually often used. Researchers may advertise online, in newspapers, by putting up flyers, through word-of-mouth, or otherwise. Advertising may also be used in concert with snowball sampling to identify non-related sub-samples. For example, Sue Malta (2013) advertised on an online dating site for her study of older adults' romantic relationships. After being interviewed, participants suggested other people, thus initiating several snowball samples.

Formal advertising for participants with particular criteria is helpful for finding participants not connected to the researcher or to each other and can help to increase variation in the sample. However, relying on advertising can be risky if there is a chance there will be no responses. Advertising also only attracts people who are interested in participating in the project. This group may be systematically different from people who are not interested in participating, and this needs to be considered when interpreting the research findings and assessing the study's generalizability.

GENERALIZABILITY

It is frequently thought that qualitative research is not generalizable to broader populations. However, the goal of grounded theory is generalizability. If the sample has been selected to maximize variation, and theoretical saturation has been achieved, it is plausible that the theory developed is generalizable. Hence theoretical saturation can be linked conceptually with generalizability (Becker, 1988) precisely because once saturation has been achieved no new insights will be emerging from the data. This indicates that it would likely not be helpful to go beyond the existing sample. This type of generalizability is different from the type achieved through statistical techniques, but it is genuine.

Studies that are not organized around the principles of grounded theory may also be generalizable, but their generalizability would need to be justified. Yin (1994) argues that research using his case study approach is generalizable in the same way that scientific experiments are generalizable. In this view, research findings should be generalized to theory rather than to other cases. There is no need to locate 'representative' cases, just as scientists do not try to conduct 'representative experiments'. Each case is an experiment that is contributing to theory (Yin, 1994: 37). The lesson from Yin is that careful case selection is important for generalizability of this sort.

NON-RESPONDENTS

It is important you select a sample that will be able to answer the research question(s) in a way that satisfies your aims. However, in doing so it is necessary to consider how you manage people who refuse to participate. Those who refuse may be systematically different from those who agree to participate, leading to bias in your sample and limiting the generalizability of your findings. This issue was encountered by Farnaz Zirakbash (2014) in her study of professional women who had migrated to Australia from Iran. Zirakbash was interested in whether and how migration affected the lives of highly educated women who had grown up in the Islamic Republic of Iran and had a Muslim background. She wanted to interview both religious and non-religious women, but found that non-religious women would not participate if the study was seen to be for religious women and vice versa. Her study ended up being composed almost entirely of non-religious women, and so it is plausible that the findings are not generalizable to professional Iranian women migrants to Australia who are religious.

SAMPLE SIZE

How big should a sample be? This is one of the key questions that qualitative researchers have to grapple with. In grounded theory the answer is 'big enough that both informational redundancy and theoretical saturation can be achieved'. In real life this answer is not that helpful as many of us do not have the resources to undertake a well-developed grounded theory approach: we cannot keep going indefinitely. However, the criterion of informational redundancy is a lower hurdle than that of theoretical saturation, and might be reasonable to consider when deciding how many is enough. Informational redundancy occurs when no new information is forthcoming and the researcher is hearing the same information over and over. In practice, though, we also often need to specify the sample size and composition beforehand to institutional ethics committees, so it may be difficult to achieve either informational redundancy or theoretical saturation.

A second criterion that could be considered is sufficiency (according to Seidman, 1991, who also argues for informational redundancy as a key criterion). Sufficiency means that participants represent the range of population members and sites in terms of whatever social categories are considered relevant, for example ethnicity, class, gender, or region. Seidman (1991) also suggests that it is important to interview more than one person in each category.

Our view is that your sample size needs to be large enough to answer your research questions and provide plausibly generalizable findings. There is no magic number of participants that can be identified to indicate when this has been achieved, and you may not know beforehand how many you will need. For more complex research questions a larger sample may be required. However, an in-depth case study can also provide important insights into social phenomena, as with Robert F. Murphy's (1990) auto-ethnographic account of disability. One of the first studies of this kind, Murphy used his experiences as a man with a progressive disability to shed insight into the lived experience of disability. He had a sample size of one, but the impact of the study has been so widespread that over twenty-five years after its publication it is still in print.

SAMPLING, HARD-TO-REACH POPULATIONS AND RESEARCH ETHICS

The transnational drug smuggler study mentioned at the start of this chapter was not hypothetical. Roslyn Le (2015) has recently completed a PhD looking into the behaviour of Vietnamese women who smuggled illicit drugs across borders, also called drug mules. Drug mules are difficult to identify because the behaviour is illegal. Our university's human research ethics committee does not generally permit students to conduct research into illegal behaviour because it may put them in danger as a result of their knowledge, and it may also put the participants at risk of prosecution. For Le to do her study she had to devise a strategy that would enable her to identify the drug smugglers and also not put herself or them at risk. To accomplish this she interviewed women who had been convicted of drug smuggling and were incarcerated. This novel strategy enabled her to complete a very interesting study. However, this sampling strategy had an important limitation: it only captured smugglers who had been unsuccessful at least once. There might be a systematic difference between drug smugglers who are never caught and those who are. Nevertheless, incredibly useful insights into the ways Vietnamese drug smugglers became involved in the illicit activity were gleaned from Le's study.

Vietnamese drug smugglers are one example of a hard-to-reach population. Other hard-to-reach populations would include stigmatized groups like drug users and the homeless, among others. Qualitative methods are one of the best ways to capture hard-to-reach groups. In particular, once a researcher has the trust of a key informant or two who are willing to help, snowball sampling can lead to rich studies. Because hard-to-reach groups are often this way for a reason, researchers need to take into account not only issues concerning research ethics, but also their own personal safety. The three questions you should consider if you are planning to study a hard-to-reach group are:

- How can I access the group safely?
- What are the possible consequences for me and the participants if my findings are not positive?
- What are their vulnerabilities?

CONCLUSION

This chapter has explored sampling in qualitative research. In particular, we have highlighted the relationship between the philosophical assumptions underpinning the research and sampling and examined how existing theory can influence the decision making around sampling. The chapter has also provided practical issues to consider and general guidelines. There are no hard-and-fast rules about how to locate a sample or how large it needs to be for qualitative studies. Decisions around these should emerge from the research question and the research approach.

Going further

Denzin, N. and Lincoln, Y. (eds) (2011) *The Sage Handbook of Qualitative Research*. Thousand Oaks, CA: Sage.

A comprehensive discussion of all aspects of qualitative research, with strong chapters on sampling and generalizability.

Flyvbjerg, B. (2006) 'Five misunderstandings about case study research', *Qualitative Inquiry*, 12 (2): 219-45.

Flyvbjerg argues that well-constructed case studies are certainly generalizable.

Glaser, B.G. and Strauss, A.L. (1967) *The Discovery of Grounded Theory: Strategies for Qualitative Research*. New York: Aldine de Gruyter.

This classic text discussing grounded theory is key for anyone interested in understanding this approach.

Halkier, B. (2011) 'Methodological practicalities in analytical generalisation', *Qualitative Inquiry*, 17 (9): 787-97.

This article discusses the various ways that qualitative research is generalized.

McCormack, M., Adams, A. and Anderson, A. (2013) 'Taking to the streets: the benefits of spontaneous methodological innovation in participant recruitment', *Qualitative Research*, 13 (2): 228-41.

This article describes the unconventional but successful approach of the researchers when their initial recruitment strategy failed to attract participants.

DOING THE RESEARCH

THE RESEARCHER ASKS QUESTIONS

SIX
Interviewing

CONTENTS

- Interviews: structured and semi-structured — 75
- Designing the semi-structured interview — 77
- How to interview effectively – the interview guide — 78
- Modes of communication – practical considerations — 82
  - Synchronous interviews — 83
  - Asynchronous interviews (email interviews) — 85
- To see or not to see – a trade-off between anonymity and visual cues — 86
- The appropriate mode for your research interviews — 87
- Effective communication – establishing a rapport during the interview — 88
  - Presentation and disclosure — 89
  - Establishing a rapport in real-time text interviews — 90
  - Establishing a rapport in asynchronous email interviews — 90
  - Establishing a rapport when interviewing in immersive digital environments — 90
- Conclusion — 91
- Going further — 91

INTERVIEWS: STRUCTURED AND SEMI-STRUCTURED

'So how were your holidays? When did you get back? Where did you go? What was the weather like?'

Interviewing is essentially asking someone questions, and it is one of the most common ways of finding out what's going on. In this sense, it is a technique that all of us are familiar with using as part of conversation, and indeed interviews have been described as a conversation with a purpose (Berg, 2001). Ann Oakley suggests, somewhat provocatively, 'Interviewing is rather like marriage: everybody knows what it is, an awful lot of people do it, and yet behind each closed front door there is a world of secrets' (Oakley, 1981: 30). In this chapter, we hope to open the doors to some of the secrets of effective interviewing.

A research interview can be usefully understood as a particular type of conversation, the direction of which is guided by the researcher. The extent to which the researcher guides the conversation, the types of questions asked, and even the way that these are asked, can be traced back to the researcher's assumptions about knowledge and about the relationship between the researcher and the researched.

The post-positivist approach to interviewing is that it is a window on to reality and who the interviewer is should have no effect on the data collected. The post-positivist aim of reliability in research means that the same results should be obtained regardless of who conducts the research. What this means for how the researcher conducts the interview is that they will generally stick to a specific set of questions. Regardless of who conducts the interview, the same questions will be asked using exactly the same wording. The underlying assumption here is that the same questions will result in equivalent answers from a participant regardless of who the interviewer is.

The type of interview where the questions are set beforehand is called a structured interview. In a structured interview, the questions are either read out by the interviewer in the set order, or are provided in written form for the research participant to fill in themselves. In cases where the questions are read out and the answers are recorded by the interviewer, the interview may be conducted face to face, over the phone, or in real time via the Internet. Questionnaires for self-completion can be supplied to the research participant by mail or by email. The main advantages of this type of structured interview are that, first, it is easy to conduct a large number of interviews, particularly if they are conducted over the phone or completed by the respondent, and second, if the questions are to be asked by an interviewer, it is straightforward to train that interviewer. What is lost is the ability to establish a rapport with the research participant, follow up on any interesting points that are made, tailor the wording of the questions to suit the style of the interviewer or the respondent, and respond to the respondent's body language. Sometimes a respondent will include the answer to a later question in the answer to an earlier question, and the interviewer will have no choice but to read out the later question as it is written. While all interviews are artificial in that they only exist for the purpose of research, the structured interview can feel particularly stilted and uncomfortable. Have you ever responded to a survey and felt frustrated by the questions you were asked, even though there was space for you to provide the answers in your own words? You might have finished the survey thinking that you didn't have a chance to express how you really felt or what you really thought. You may even have felt that the interviewer wasn't really listening to what you said. These can all be problems with the structured interview as the research participant has no say in the direction of the interview, and the interviewer is unable to modify it to suit the circumstances either.

Table 6.1 The typical amount of structure in an interview

RESEARCH PARADIGM	Positivist/post-positivist	Criticalist	Constructivist
Structured	✓		
Semi-structured		✓	✓

Table 6.1 lists the typical amount of structure in an interview according to the research paradigm in which the researcher is operating.

DESIGNING THE SEMI-STRUCTURED INTERVIEW

One can think of a continuum of the amount of structure in an interview, with structured interviewing at one end and unstructured interviewing at the other end. While the structured interview focuses directly on what the researcher wants to find out, the unstructured interview is almost completely like a conversation. In between these two extremes is the semi-structured interview, which is the focus of the remainder of this chapter. Unstructured interviews are closer to stories generated by the interviewee and are discussed in Chapter 11. There is a wide degree of variation among semi-structured interviews as the term includes both fairly structured interviews and fairly unstructured interviews. The extent to which the direction of the interview is guided by what the research participant has to say, rather than the researcher's questions, depends both on the researcher's interest in giving voice to the participant and in the amount of knowledge that the researcher has about the topic. The more exploratory research is, the less structure is likely in the research interviews.

For example, we can compare the rationale for using semi-structured interviews in the following two cases. In the first Viv Waller was involved in conducting semi-structured interviews with industry leaders about their awareness and perceptions of government programmes relating to industry. Now, the topic of perceptions of government programmes relating to industry is incredibly broad. The researchers had no idea which of these the research participants would know of, and what their experiences and perceptions would be. In this case, because of the broad nature of the topic, it made no sense to formulate predefined questions. The interviewer needed to respond to the industry leader's answers with relevant probes and follow-on questions.

The second case involved Waller also conducting semi-structured interviews, but this time the interviews were with unemployed youth about their experience of unemployment and also of a particular government employment programme. Here, in contrast to the first case, the topic was fairly well defined.

Both pieces of research were conducted for government departments, and formed part of the evaluations of these government programmes. Each of the evaluations was required by law, and in each case the stated overall purpose of the evaluation was to arrive at an objective measure of the success or otherwise of the government programmes. In other words, post-positivist assumptions underlay both pieces of research. So why were semi-structured interviews also included in the evaluation of the youth employment programme? Statistical analyses of youth unemployment could have been used to provide a measure of the net impact of the employment programme, and this approach would have been more in keeping with the post-positivist framework. However, even though the framing of the research under the legislation was post-positivist, the researchers themselves, who were working within this post-positivist framework, had values and beliefs more in line with the criticalist tradition of the empowerment of those marginalized. Unemployed youth are traditionally denied a voice in society. Hence the researchers deliberately included semi-structured interviews in the research design in order to allow the voices of unemployed young people to be heard by the policy makers and politicians responsible for the fate of the programme. This example provides a good illustration of how, in our real and messy world, a particular piece of research may not have a coherent alignment with just one particular research paradigm or set of values and beliefs.

HOW TO INTERVIEW EFFECTIVELY – THE INTERVIEW GUIDE

Once you have decided to conduct semi-structured interviews, you will need to prepare some sort of interview guide, also known as an interview schedule. The opening stage of the interview may involve an explanation of who you are and a recap of what the research is for. You may wish to outline the shape of the interview, thereby indicating to the participant how much you are wanting to direct the flow of this guided conversation. For example, imagine that when interviewing you start with the following: 'There is a range of issues I'd like to cover. First, I will be asking about home-schooling in the media, later I will ask you more about your involvement in home-schooling, and lastly I will ask you about your opinions of any advantages and disadvantages to the student.' By starting the interview in this way, you are indicating to the participant that you have a clear agenda and would like to control the direction of the interview. Contrast this approach with the opening line 'So tell me about home-schooling'. While each of these approaches is legitimate, they each send a very different message to the participant about how you would like the interview to run. For the constructivist researcher, it is important that the interview is an empowering experience for the research participants and so the second approach would probably be more appropriate. If you have not already obtained informed consent for the interview, you will need to do this before you begin the actual interview. Similarly, if you wish to record the interview you will need to obtain prior consent to do so.

Conducting an effective interview involves trying to keep the flow of a conversation. Hence, when preparing the interview schedule, it may be helpful to think of the semi-structured interview as a guided conversation. There will be particular issues you will want to cover. You want the interviewee to cover all of your listed themes with you probing as necessary, but you will also want to disrupt the flow of the conversation as little as possible. We would suggest that the more you condense the written schedule, the more you can focus on your interviewee. Trying to find your place on the written schedule and then reading out a question will really break the flow of the interview. As the interviewee covers the listed issues, you can mark these. In this way, you can discreetly keep tabs on which issues have been covered, regardless of the order in which these are covered. Preparation is key. If you are using a team of interviewers, it will be essential that they have adequate training and clearly understand the meaning of each issue to be covered and the purpose of each question.

To show you an example, Box 6.1 contains an interview schedule that was used in semi-structured interviews that were part of research on the type of information that people seek from home, the ways in which they stay informed, and their engagement with a range of information resources. These individual interviews were held two weeks after the household had been interviewed, and a recording device had been left behind in order for participants to keep an aural diary of their information-seeking activities. This meant that the interviewer had already met the interviewee and did not have to introduce themselves or the research. Note that the interview schedule contains both questions and dot points. If you were to listen to the transcripts of the interviews, you would notice that there was a whole range of different questions asked in each interview depending on the responses. Note also that in practice this schedule was printed with spaces so as to cover the entire side of a page. This made it easier for the interviewer to scan it quickly and mark off the issues that had been covered by the interviewee.

Box 6.1

Sample of a semi-structured interview schedule

- Use and evaluation of different information sources.
- Opinion of recording devices – did it affect anything about how they looked for information?
- Information go-to person?
- Would you ever be looking for a particular book or trying to find out something about a particular book? Where would you go for information on that?
- Use of the Internet – where do you go on the Internet to find information?
- Have you ever used the following to find information? (gauge use and opinion of what they like/don't like about each source)

    o Google?
    o Particular websites? *What?*
    o Wikipedia?
    o Forums?
    o Social networking sites (e.g. Facebook?)
    o Twitter?
    o Youtube?
    o Itunes?
    o Mobile device?
    o Radio/TV as source of information?

- Library – members of local library, use? Librarians? State library? Knowledge? Been?

End of interview – thank respondent.

Box 6.2 shows what the first part of this interview could look like if it was conducted as a structured interview.

Box 6.2

Extract of sample structured interview schedule

Use and evaluation of different information sources:

1. What was your opinion of the digital recorder that we left with you for recording your information-seeking activities?
2. Do you think that having the digital recorder had any sort of effect on how you looked for information in the last two weeks?

IF YES, what effect did it have?

3. I am now going to ask you a series of questions about your use of the Internet. I am particularly interested in how you use the Internet to find information. First, I want to ask you some questions about the search engine Google.

    a) Have you ever used Google to find out information?

If NO, go to Question 4.

   b) What sort of information have you used Google for?
   c) What sort of information do you think that Google is best for?
   d) On average, how often do you use Google?
   e) Are there any sorts of information that you would definitely not use Google for?
   f) Which search results do you click on?
   g) Why do you choose these results to click on?
   h) What, if anything, do you like about Google?
   i) What if anything, do you dislike about Google?

4. Do you ever go to particular websites for information?

... continued.

Some texts advocate asking some ice-breaker questions to start (see, for example, Creswell, 2014). Although it is often a good idea to ease a research participant into a topic and leave sensitive issues until later in the interview, be sure that you only ask questions that are relevant to your research. This is a way of respecting research participants' time. If you are happy for the interviewee to guide the direction of a semi-structured interview, then asking them what interested them about taking part in the research may be a good way to ease into the topic.

As mentioned in Chapter 1, those operating within a criticalist or constructivist paradigm would recognize that conducting an interview is an intervention into the lives of the research participants. The interview may even be a two-way flow of information. For example, an interviewer researching the experiences of newly-arrived refugees may let an interviewee know about relevant services that are available to them. Waller was interviewing a recently arrived refugee when it became apparent that the interviewee's wireless Internet connection was unsecured and that as a result she was amassing enormous Internet bills from unauthorized use. Waller took the opportunity to inform her about the need to secure her wireless connection so that neighbours did not use her connection without her knowledge.

It is also important to be reflexive about your own preconceptions about the topic of research. Are there particular assumptions about the topic embedded in the questions? To return to the home-schooling example mentioned earlier, consider the following interview question:

- Do you think that children are missing out on any important experiences by being home-schooled?

A more neutral way of asking this would be to ask:

- What advantages or disadvantages do you think there are for children who are home-schooled?

You will also need to think about the possible effect of your questions on the research participant. For example, if you are interviewing someone about a topic that involves feelings of anger or sadness for them, you will need to consider how they will feel after the interview. No matter which paradigm you are operating within, it is part of ethical research to try to structure the interview so that the participant does not feel worse after the interview than before it.

When an interviewee has exhausted all of the issues that you want to address, we would suggest you tell that person that they have covered everything you wanted to cover, perhaps ask them if there is anything else they would like to add, and then finish the interview by thanking them and assuring them of the value of their contribution. If you think that you may want to interview that participant again, it would be a good idea to seek permission to contact them again then and there. If you are operating from within a constructivist or criticalist paradigm, you may wish to give the interviewee a chance to comment on the transcript of the interview, or on your interpretations in the final report, article, or thesis.

We would also suggest that you try to audio record the interview unless you think that will have a detrimental effect on the interviewee's comfort and responses. Remember, if you are recording the interview there is no need to take copious notes as well. Taking notes is distracting and makes it very difficult to adequately listen to the interviewee. Allow time immediately after the interview for you to go somewhere quiet and take notes on your impressions and anything that would not have been captured by the audio recording. If you have recorded your interviews, make sure you listen to these all at least once with the express purpose of critically assessing how you did as an interviewer.

It is not just the interviewee who may be negatively affected by the topic under discussion. Interviewers can also be distressed by the content of an interview. This is perhaps to be expected with research into experiences of trauma, violence or abuse. However, even a benign-sounding topic may trigger accounts that will prove upsetting. For example, interviews about migration experiences may include discussion of horrific hardships, and interviewers may also be distressed by the attitudes expressed by an interviewee, for example sexist, racist, or homophobic attitudes. Regardless of the topic of the research, it is important that interviewers have support and an opportunity to debrief. If conducting the interviews is likely to be harrowing for the interviewers, you may consider costing into the research the opportunity for interviewers to debrief with a professional counsellor.

MODES OF COMMUNICATION – PRACTICAL CONSIDERATIONS

It is quite likely that, as you have been reading, you have assumed that the interviews we are referring to are being conducted face to face. Indeed, as little as ten years ago almost all semi-structured interviews were conducted this way, and less often over the telephone. Advances in Internet technologies have enabled new forms of interviewing via the Internet, including interviewing in immersive virtual environments such as Second Life. In this section we will draw on the experiences of some of those researchers who have used these new forms of interviewing.

Table 6.2 summarizes the different types of communication associated with the various interview mediums, grouping these according to whether they are conducted in real-time (synchronous) or not (asynchronous) as well as according to the mode of communication – audio-visual, audio, or text. You can see from the examples in the last column that the term 'online interview' encompasses all of these possible modes. We will discuss some of the issues associated with these various modes before making general observations about using the Internet for interviewing. We will then conclude with some tips on how to establish a rapport with interviewees as the means for doing this will depend on the mode of interview.

Table 6.2 Modes of interviewing

Mode	Timing	Type of connection
Audio-visual	Synchronous	In person, Internet – e.g. Skype, via avatar in 3D immersive environment
Audio only	Synchronous	Telephone, Internet – e.g. Skype audio
Text	Synchronous	Internet – e.g. Instant message, Facebook, Skype, Google Talk, LinkedIn Chat
Text and visual	Synchronous	Via avatar in 3D immersive environment, e.g. Second Life
Text	Asynchronous	Email

Synchronous interviews

Audio-visual

This mode includes both in person (that is, face-to-face interviewing) and real-time audio-visual communication via the Internet (for example, via Skype). Face-to-face interviewing is the most common way of conducting semi-structured interviews. Many people still value that indefinable quality called 'presence' where you can, for example, take in the nervous fidget of the hands or a confident sitting posture, or almost 'feel' the tension in the air around a certain topic. While audio allows you to hear the tone of voice, and video allows you to note the facial expression when answering a particular question, face-to-face allows you to observe, and make use of, the full range of body language. Because an interviewer's body language is also apparent to the interviewee, it is wise to be conscious of any habits you have which are distracting. Even if you are nervous, try to appear confident as nervousness on the part of an interviewer can be extremely distracting to interviewees.

The location of an in-person interview will be significant. It is important for an interviewee to be comfortable with the location of the interview and for it to be convenient for them to get to. In some cases the interview topic will suggest an appropriate location for the interview. For example, Waller was interested in home use of the Internet and so the interviewee's home was the most appropriate location for the interview. This enabled Waller to also observe relevant aspects such as the location of the computer, the size of the TV, and the cultural style of the house. It was also convenient as she was interviewing the assembled household as well as individual members. It may be appropriate to ask an interviewee where they would like to have the interview.

A key practical consideration is that you will need a place that is quiet enough to enable a successful recording of the interview should you be doing this. A café may be a pleasant and neutral place but it may also be noisy. If the topic is sensitive or personal, you should ensure that the location is one where the participant can speak without being overheard.

Audio only

In audio interviews, both the interviewer and interviewee can hear each other's voices but there are no visual cues – the communication is exclusively aural. The interview may be conducted using a fixed line telephone, a mobile phone, or online. This type of interview has the advantage of being able to reach geographically dispersed participants without the costs of associated travel.

Online audio interviews using, for example, Google Talk or Skype audio, are functionally equivalent to telephone interviews but may be cheaper to conduct. The location for the interviewee will still be important as they will need to be free of distraction and in an environment where they can speak without constraint. For example, it would generally be inappropriate to interview someone about a sensitive topic while they are physically in their workplace.

Immersive video environments

Immersive video environments, often known as virtual worlds, include environments such as Second Life. In such environments both the interviewer and interviewee will have an avatar (i.e. a digital graphical representation) through which they communicate. As Salmons (2012: 106) points out, these environments have some unique aspects when it comes to conducting interviews, '... including the ability to visit, explore, demonstrate, or simulate some aspect of the research phenomenon in the context of the research interview'. In these immersive video environments, research participants can also consciously use their avatar's body language to convey additional information about their responses. These are probably best suited for topics related to the immersive video environment in which the interview is being conducted.

Text - synchronous

Synchronous text interviews are those carried out via the Internet using an instant messaging application in a private channel. Text can be particularly useful for those with disabilities who want to be able to communicate without the focus being on their disability (Bowker and Tuffin, 2002). Another major advantage of this mode of interview is that a transcript is automatically produced.

Online text-based synchronous interviews are often used when the researcher is interested in people's use of this mode of communication. For example, Sue Malta (2012) used private chat technology to conduct online real-time interviews to study older adults' romantic Internet relationships. Her population of interest was by definition, familiar with and comfortable using text-based Internet technologies to communicate, although some had not used instant chat before to communicate in real time. Similarly, Couch and Liamputtong (2013) used instant messaging to interview people about using the Internet to meet potential sexual partners as instant messaging was often used by these people when getting to know one another online. Davis et al. (2013) used this in their study of gay men's use of the Internet to obtain sex.

Experience in using online text-based synchronous interviews is mixed. For example, Davis et al. (2013) had a negative experience, finding that the researcher tended to get brief answers, it was difficult to ask for clarification of ambiguity, difficult to probe, and sometimes the dialogue gets out of order as the usual real-time turn-taking conventions cannot be easily applied. They conclude that online real-time text interviews '... don't readily lend themselves to the exploration of meaning' (Davis et al., 2013: 203) but are useful when used in combination with other forms of data collection. In contrast, Malta (2012), as well as Couch and Liampattong (2013), found that instant messaging interviews were a successful method, eliciting quite elaborate answers. A major advantage of this mode of interviews is that a transcript of the interview is automatically produced.

Asynchronous interviews (email interviews)

Whereas all the modes of interviewing so far discussed are synchronous (that is, held in real time) the email interview is asynchronous. The interviewer emails initial questions to the research participant, and follows up on the responses with more questions or comments looking for a response. A single interview can take several months to complete, although of course a number of interviews can be conducted concurrently.

An email interview allows a research participant more time to reflect on their response and shape their answer – a factor that may engender more thoughtful responses. In her study of long-term breastfeeding mothers, Dowling (2012) interviewed her research participants both face to face and with online asynchronous interviews. Although her topic was to do with the body, it was also very sensitive, and she found that the data she obtained from the online interviews were 'richer and fuller' (2012: 291) than those obtained from face-to-face interviews. She noted that this was often the case for sensitive topics relating to the body, citing studies on Alzheimer's disease, cancer, eating disorders, and gay men's use of the Internet to seek sex. Similarly, James and Busher (2013), in their study of the professional identities of teaching academics, considered that the fact that research participants could respond in their own time led to richer stories. In addition, they argued that it led to greater reflection as '… the continuous and visible record of the email interviews in every exchange enabled participants to revisit issues that had slipped temporarily out of view through the course of their interviews' (2013: 241). Other researchers have found the opposite (e.g. Orgad, cited in Dowling, 2012, and Malta, 2012). Malta found that the email interview resulted in very concise email responses, although given that the participant could prepare their email response these were often more focused. One concern expressed by Malta about email interviews was that giving the research participant this time to formulate their responses may result in less honest responses if that participant tries to construct a particular picture of themselves.

An email interview is particularly useful if there are time zone differences. As with instant messaging, a transcript of the interview is automatically produced. Asynchronous interviewing is also useful for interviewing people who would find it hard to schedule a time to be interviewed. For example, Dowling (2012) found that this aspect of online asynchronous interviewing made it particularly appropriate for her research on mothers who were breastfeeding. The mothers could reply at a time suitable to them which usually meant at a time when they were not distracted by their children. Indeed, they '… often commented on how they were writing late at night, or while a child napped' (Dowling, 2012: 283). Dowling considered that this enabled them to give more thoughtful responses than would have been possible in a real-time interview. A side benefit of asynchronous online interviews for the interviewee has been identified by both Deutsch (2012) and Dowling (2012). According to them, it is often therapeutic for the interviewee to have the opportunity to reflect, in their own time, on an issue that is of concern to them.

In practical terms, Kazmer and Xie (2013) identify a trade-off in the benefits to the interviewer of real-time and and asynchronous interviews. Real-time interviews are more challenging when it comes to scheduling a convenient time. Scheduling is irrelevant to asynchronous interviews, but a researcher has the challenge of keeping the participant interested and involved in the interview.

TO SEE OR NOT TO SEE – A TRADE-OFF BETWEEN ANONYMITY AND VISUAL CUES

Text interviews, both real-time and asynchronous, afford a level of anonymity to interviewees. Some researchers have found that it is easier to bring up sensitive topics when the mode of interviewing affords some anonymity for research participants. For example, Malta (2012), who conducted both in-person and real-time online text interviews in her research on online romance, found that it was easier in the real-time online text interviewing to bring up, and get responses on, sensitive topics such as love, sex and intimacy.

There is, however, a trade-off that the researcher has to consider. The more anonymity an interviewee has, the less auditory and visual cues an interviewer has about the interviewee. Granted, the interviewee can *consciously* choose to use emoticons in the text as a stand-in for emotion conveyed through the voice or face. However, it is through tone of voice, appearance and body language that an interviewee also *unconsciously* communicates important context to the interviewer. An additional disadvantage of anonymity for the interviewer is that the interviewee may not be who they say they are.

Seymour (2013), who did online research with people with disabilities, has a response relevant to both these concerns about text-based communication. According to her, we often overestimate the importance of physical presence and body language. She argues that we can understand a lot about an interviewee through their written language, that although we can't see the '... visible expressions of class, gender, prestige, ethnicity, age and notions of ability', these are '"visible" in the discourse' (Seymour, 2013: 275). Malta (2012), provides an example of checking that participants were who they said they were by being alert to the nature of their responses. She recounts how one participant, supposedly an older male, wrote responses that were more like SMSs and ended up asking her more questions than he answered. Suspecting that the participant was not actually an older male, she terminated the interview and excluded this participant from the study.

Researchers should not spend too much time worrying that an interviewee may not be who they say they are. In any interview situation, including in-person interviews, there is always the possibility that an interviewee is manufacturing responses in order to present themself to the interviewer in a particular way. A good interviewer will be alert to this possibility.

THE APPROPRIATE MODE FOR YOUR RESEARCH INTERVIEWS

There is no hard-and-fast rule for determining which is the most appropriate mode of interview for your research. The most critical thing here is that, as a researcher, you have thought carefully about the pros and cons of the various modes for your research. The following general points and observations should assist you in making this decision.

First, it is important for the research participant to be comfortable with the medium used to conduct the interview. In recent years it has become more common to allow participants to choose if they would prefer a particular medium for their interview. For example, Malta (2012) gave her participants a choice of four mediums for participating in the semi-structured interviews: face to face, telephone, online instant messaging, and asynchronous email interview. Most of the online romance group chose online instant messaging as they were already comfortable with this medium and it afforded them some anonymity. As Taylor observes, '… ultimately, some participants may be more comfortable using email, whereas others would prefer a phone conversation, an in-world interview or an offline meeting' (2013: 59).

In deciding whether or not to let the research participant choose the medium, think about whether a particular medium is more appropriate to the context and whether it is likely to increase participation. If you decide on a particular medium, you will need to take into account the topic of the research and the participant's relationship to the topic of research, including whether or not anonymity is likely to be important for the interviewee. If your participants are geographically dispersed, in-person interviewing may be prohibitively expensive.

If you want to use the Internet to conduct the interview, you do need to have a clear rationale for this. For example, this may be in order to save money on travel costs, or because of the sensitive nature of the topic, the attraction of an automatically produced transcript, or because the research topic is related to an aspect of Internet use. You will need to be sure, however, that all the people you are interested in interviewing are comfortable using the technology you will adopt to conduct the interview. Be aware that, depending on your topic, you may be missing out on a particular type of respondent. Not everyone uses the Internet – in Australia, for example, one in six people do not use it (Australian Bureau of Statistics, 2014) and not everyone is comfortable with communicating via the Internet.

You will also need to be cautious if relying on proprietary environments such as Facebook, LinkedIn or Second Life for the conduct of your research. Deegan (2012) used Facebook to contact participants and conduct her research into the development of confidence in young people involved in a creative writing programme. Her progress was severely hampered when for a reason unknown to her she was banned from Facebook.

With regard to choosing between synchronous and asynchronous modes, you will also need to take into account your timeframes for conducting the research as asynchronous email interviews can take several months. Also do be aware that if you are interested in observing participants' thought processes, synchronous interviewing is likely to be more useful than asynchronous interviewing where you will only see the final crafted response (Kazmer and Xie, 2013).

EFFECTIVE COMMUNICATION - ESTABLISHING A RAPPORT DURING THE INTERVIEW

The different modes of interviewing each involve their own unique challenges for effective communication. Before conducting your first interview, you will need to think about and make decisions on how you will listen and respond, and how you will present, including how much you will disclose about yourself. What you decide here will depend on the values and beliefs underpinning the research.

Whether in person or text, synchronous or asynchronous, an interview is, in some ways, a balancing act. Effective interviewing means being clear about and achieving your desired balance of power between establishing a rapport with an interviewee and retaining the researcher perspective. While, on the one hand, you will need a sufficient rapport that the interviewee feels comfortable providing full and honest responses, on the other hand, the only reason you are even having this 'pseudo-conversation' with that interviewee is because you are conducting research. As part of this you will need to be clear about, and try to achieve, the desired balance between steering the 'pseudo-conversation' towards what you the researcher want to ask about and just letting the participant talk about what they want to talk about. On the one hand, you want what the interviewee says to be relevant to your topic. On the other hand, if you want the interview to be an empowering experience for the interviewee you will not want to completely control the conversation. You also do not want to limit the amount of relevant material you get by focusing too narrowly on what you think is important.

For the post-positivist researcher, it is important that the interviewer is emotionally detached from both the content of the interview and from the interviewee. The interviewer should make no value judgements about any of the interviewee's responses, such that the interviewee should not be able to tell what the interviewer thinks about any aspects of the research topic. It is a matter of degree, but in contrast to the ideal of the detached researcher, the criticalist researcher and the constructivist researcher may consciously try to show an interviewee who is recounting a difficult experience that they are 'on their side', offering supportive comments in response to what that interviewee says.

Whether text or audio-visual, synchronous or asynchronous, the principles of active listening apply. These include being interested in the interviewee's responses, acknowledging those responses, and following up on them appropriately.

Presentation and disclosure

Part of establishing rapport is presenting an appropriate identity to the interviewee. Research suggests that we form an initial impression of someone within the first few seconds of meeting them (Slepian et al., 2014). Researchers form impressions of interviewees, while, at the same time, interviewees from their judgements about interviewees. All researchers have to manage their identity and presentation of self, whether the interviews are in person, on the telephone, or via text or an avatar. In face-to-face interviews, the researcher's attire can affect the level of rapport achieved. If we are interviewing in immersive digital environments, it is important that our identity as an avatar is 'credible' (Salmons, 2012: 184). In text-only interviews we will give off a certain impression by the way we frame issues and the words we use. It is also vitally important to be mindful of our presentation of ourselves when scheduling interviews, either by telephone or email. Although not part of the actual interview, this contact is likely to form a research participant's first impression of us.

A research participant will have been selected for interview on the basis of some established criteria relevant to the research topic – for example, they have a particular identity, partake in a particular activity, or have experienced a particular phenomenon. In many cases a researcher is also an 'insider' (Hesse-Biber and Leavy, 2011) with respect to the research topic. A post-positivist researcher will aim to present themself as neutrally as possible, in both attire and language, so as not to distract from the topic of the interview. In contrast, as the following examples show, those within the constructivist or criticalist perspective are likely to want to disclose their 'insider' status or will consciously endeavour to present themselves as sympathetic to the individuals they are interviewing.

The information we disclose about ourselves is part of our presentation of ourselves. As mentioned above, criticalist and constructivist researchers may consciously choose to provide information about their own background as a way of reducing the power imbalance between the interviewer and interviewee. For example, in her online interviews with long-term breastfeeding mothers, in order to put respondents at ease Dowling (2012) disclosed information about herself, including the fact that she herself had been a long-term breastfeeding mother. She considered that, as a result, these interviews felt more equal. Similarly, in her online interviews with older people about online romance, in order to help establish a rapport Malta disclosed information about herself, including the fact that she herself was middle-aged. She writes that she felt '… less as though I was conducting an interview, and more as though I was having a conversation, a feeling which developed more strongly as the interviews progressed. I would liken this to a feeling of equality developing between myself and the participants' (Malta, 2012: 161).

Interviewers need to be sensitive, however, when choosing to actively disclose information about themselves in order to show that they have something in common with interviewees. Whether it is an attribute such as age group, marital status, sexual orientation, ethnicity or religion, or whether it is a past experience, an interviewee may not identify with this supposed commonality. Indeed, they may feel uncomfortable with an inference that, on the basis of this attribute or experience, they are somehow like the interviewer, or that the interviewer has some 'inside' knowledge on them.

Establishing a rapport in real-time text interviews

It takes more of a conscious effort to build a rapport when the mode of the interview is text. Writing about text interviews, Salmons observes, 'When interviews occur online, researchers must devise and learn new ways to build trust and motivate individuals to share thoughts and observations and reveal personal views or experiences' (Salmons, 2012: xvii). This is particularly important with real-time text interviews where the interviewee may be multi-tasking or subject to a range of distractions. In her study of young people, Deegan (2012) found that there were huge time lags when she interviewed participants using real-time online chat. When she found out that the reason for this was that the interviewees were multitasking, she switched to asynchronous email interviews. In general, Malta found that the instant messaging interviews she conducted '… mimicked the normal process of a face-to-face back-and-forth conversation' (Malta, 2013: 159). However, she also reported conversational 'hiccups' in her instant messaging interviews when participants answered the door or attended to another online message. Yet her response was that while patience was necessary, on the positive side these breaks also allowed her space to reflect on how the interview was going.

Establishing a rapport in asynchronous email interviews

Asynchronous interviews are probably the most challenging in terms of establishing rapport. James and Busher (2013) suggest that the researcher should invest time up front in building relationships with the research participants if they are going to use asynchronous email interviews over an extended period of time, as this involves quite a lot of commitment from the research participants. It also poses a challenge to the researcher as there could be weeks between responses and it can be difficult to interpret this silence. Dowling says 'I worried that I might have alienated a participant in some way by what I had written, that I was asking for too much, or was in some way "doing it wrong"' (2012: 288).

Establishing a rapport when interviewing in immersive digital environments

In order to establish a rapport when interviewing in immersive digital environments, it is crucial that the interviewer understands the particular norms and the 'elaborate and meaningful ways of negotiating social relationships and communicating' (Taylor, 2013: 60) within the digital environment they are using. An additional complication is that the interviewee may have more than one online persona. Taylor observes that 'quite often, interviewing a person involves interviewing several' as the interviewee may speak as one of many avatars, as their offline self, or move between them (2013: 54).

CONCLUSION

Interviewing is as easy as riding a bicycle. It is about balance, that is achieving your desired balance between establishing a rapport with interviewees and retaining your researcher perspective, between steering the 'pseudo-conversation' towards what you as the researcher want to ask and letting an interviewee steer towards what they think is important to talk about. Where your desired balance lies will depend on the values and beliefs underpinning the research interviews. As with riding a bicycle, the best way to learn is to get out there and do it.

Going further

Bagnoli, A. (2009) 'Beyond the standard interview: the use of graphic elicitation and arts-based methods', *Qualitative Research*, 9 (5): 547-70.

As this article demonstrates, in certain circumstances an interviewer can gain valuable insights from getting participants to draw their responses to the issues under investigation.

Denzin, N. (2001) 'The reflexive interview and a performative social science', *Qualitative Research*, 1 (1): 23-46.

In this article, Denzin critiques the information-gathering research interview and suggests a new form of interview, which he calls the reflexive interview, which is more of a performance text and a collaboration between the researcher and participants.

Lundgren, A.S. (2013) 'Doing age: methodological reflections on interviewing', *Qualitative Research*, 13 (6): 668-84.

This thoughtful piece from a constructionist perspective analyzes how the interview as method constructs a particular relationship between both researcher and interviewees.

Oakley, A. (1981) 'Interviewing women: a contradiction in terms', in H. Roberts (ed.), *Doing Feminist Research*. London: Routledge.

This classic chapter about the limitations of 'textbook' interviewing was written when positivism and post-positivism were the only legitimate research paradigms.

www.youtube.com/watch?v=KxMlsfTSJ-w

In this video clip several researchers, via their avatars, talk about their experience of conducting qualitative interviews in the virtual world Second Life.

SEVEN

Focus groups and group interviews

CONTENTS

- Group interviews — 94
  - Group dynamic — 94
- Focus groups — 97
  - What a focus group looks like — 97
  - Composition of the focus group — 98
  - How many focus groups to conduct — 99
  - Recruitment – finding the right participants for your focus group — 99
  - Designing the moderator's guide — 100
  - The role of the moderator — 100
  - Online focus groups — 101
  - Strengths — 103
  - When to use focus groups — 104
- Conclusion — 105
- Going further — 105

While focus groups and group interviews are often conflated with each other, a focus group is analytically distinct from a group interview. A group interview is structured around asking questions of participants, while a focus group is a facilitated discussion on a topic of interest to the researcher. The caveat to this is that, in practice, the difference may be one of degree – a group interview can include discussion and a focus group can include questions to participants. By the end of this chapter, however, the differences should be clear. We begin with a discussion of group interviews, bearing in mind that much that has been written in the chapter on interviewing is relevant to group interviewing. Hence, the focus of this chapter is focus groups, as these have some distinctive features.

GROUP INTERVIEWS

Group interviews may be conducted in various ways: a series of questions may be asked of a group of research participants; participants may each take turns to answer a series of questions; or there may be a mix of both of these approaches. Usually the people being interviewed will know each other, and as will be explained below, the rationale for interviewing them together can be either one of convenience or of method.

In some cases, it can be more convenient to interview a group of people all at once. This is particularly the case if the interview is very short and structured and the interviewees all work or study in the one location. Here the benefit of group interviewing is that there is no need to schedule separate interviews – a group of people can be interviewed in less time than it would take to interview each person separately. Of course the disadvantage is that it is difficult for an interviewer to probe the responses of one interviewee while still keeping the attention of everyone else. In addition, depending on the topic and the relationship between the interviewees, some of them may be influenced by the presence and responses of others in the group and tailor their own responses accordingly. This 'disadvantage' with group interviews can prove to be an advantage, however, if the researcher is interested in observing the dynamics of a group. How the interviewees relate to each other around a particular topic may provide useful information to the researcher about what's going on.

Group dynamic

The following example provides an illustration of the rationale for group interviews being one of method. Viv Waller (2001), in her early study of home use of the Internet, was interested in household family dynamics around the home Internet connection. (To understand this example, you need to be aware that this work was carried out at a time when using the Internet tied up the phone line and this was before mobile phones were around.) To explore household family dynamics around the home Internet connection, Waller first interviewed each household family, assembled together in their home, using semi-structured interviews that generally lasted approximately 45 minutes. In these interviews she tried to gauge the general household family environment by asking questions about typical routines, members' main interests, and their activities as a family. She also asked questions about attitudes towards and ownership of technology; how, when, and why the Internet was first connected; the household rules for its use;

the type and level of use, competence and interest; its perceived effect on the family; friendships developed or maintained over the Internet; and the family's general opinions and experience of various aspects of the Internet (such as chat rooms, email, home pages, and the World Wide Web).

It can be argued that in a family interview the presence of other members of the family can stop any individual family member from misrepresenting their activities (Morley, 1988: 33). On the other hand, as might be expected, Waller found that some family members presented differently in the individual interviews regarding matters that they wanted to keep private from the rest of the family (see Box 7.1).

Box 7.1

Example of an interviewee presenting differently when the rest of the family are present

Lyn was 42 years old and married to Andy with two girls. Here is what she said in the group interview in front of the rest of her family:

'I'm very frightened of computers. Andy is the only one who knows the password. He'd go through withdrawal symptoms if the Internet was disconnected [*laughing*]. I don't really have the chance to use it. I come home from work and cook dinner and that's when Andy will sit down and take his turn on the computer. Yes, he used to stay in there until two o'clock in the morning. I'd wake up in the middle of the night and he'd still be sitting there. He does spend a lot of time on it, but we know where to find him if we need him. I take his dinner in there on a plate, so that he can eat his tea there. But we don't stress out about those things, we're very relaxed about it. No, I'm not going to get stressed out about that.

But I think it's totally fascinating, just the thought of all that information. Andy'll look at something and he'll say, you know, he'll know I'll be interested, and he'll call me in to have a look and say come and have a look at this, and while he's here then we'll start going through other things.'

Contrast the above with what Lyn said in the individual interview:

'I really would like to learn more about the Internet. My neighbour who is a school teacher, she's really heavily into it ... I envy her, you know. Andy won't teach me to use the computer. He's quite impatient when it comes to teaching. As I said I ... I lack confidence in myself, I'd probably end up thinking oh I couldn't do that, you know, I'm pretty stupid, oh I wouldn't be able to do it. And to do a course, well, I don't know what the expense of it would be. That would be something I would think of, Hey, can I afford it this month? No, I'll put it off, buy the girls some clothes, and I might go and do it again another time. I'd probably never eventually get around to doing it you know. I sort of get the Internet second hand from Andy I suppose ... Andy would go crazy if the Internet was disconnected. We've had to have a second telephone line put in because it really disrupted, because Andy at first, I mean he became obsessed with it and he was using it quite a lot, and family and friends would just complain and complain that

(Continued)

> *(Continued)*
>
> they couldn't get through to us for sometimes two or three hours at a time. And that ... I used to get quite annoyed with Andy and other people would get upset because they couldn't get through, the kids' friends couldn't ring, and so in the end I rang up and I just said "Right we're having a second telephone line put in" and that made a big difference. But we went for a good two and a half years or so without it. Before we had the other telephone line, I would get very, oh I'd get so frustrated. Just the fact that people couldn't get on to us, and they kept saying if there's an emergency and we can't get through to you, something wrong with the telephone, and that feeling of being isolated because of this thing. We'd been taken over by the computer almost. It was running our life there for a while, but ... the rest doesn't worry me.'
>
> (Source: Waller, 2001: 42)

As mentioned before, contradictions or conflicting data do not necessarily indicate a problem with those data. Waller was able to make sense of the contradictions through her own interpretation of what was going on (see Box 7.2). Her interpretation could well have been within Lyn's repertoire of understandings about herself, but it would not necessarily be one that Lyn would care to reveal to an interviewer, either in an individual or group interview.

Box 7.2

Example of researcher interpretation when data are conflicting

> This is Waller's interpretation of what was going on:
>
> 'Lyn couldn't stand it when Andy was always on the Internet and no one could ring in. She felt so isolated – she knew that something had to give – it was bad enough that Andy never talked to her let alone her friends not being able to contact her. After she got the second phone line, it seemed more manageable. She decided then that if she was to stay with Andy she would need to change her approach to the Internet. Now, she uses the Internet to help them to stay close. She makes sure that she is always interested in what Andy is doing on it and responding to his desire to show her what is on it.
>
> Lyn does not really know much about what Andy does on the Internet. Every night he is in there by himself until late. She can't afford to care about what he is doing in there. She doesn't want to lose him. As long as she is able to sustain the illusion that she is independent and has a healthy relationship with her husband, she can cope.'
>
> (Source: Waller, 2001: 43)

This example highlights the complexity of people's responses in interviews and serves to remind us that responses to questions are always made in the particular context of the relationship between the interviewee and all others present.

An additional limitation of these sort of group interviews, which needs to be recognized, is that the researcher has no way of knowing whether, and to what extent, the interviewer's presence has an effect on how the group interacts.

FOCUS GROUPS

As you will see, focus groups are very different from group interviews. Focus groups are often associated with market research where they are used to test people's attitudes to advertising campaigns, including election campaigns, and their attitudes to products, including proposed endings for Hollywood films. However, focus groups are also a staple of social research. They are particularly useful for exploring people's attitudes and experiences, observing spontaneous reactions, and learning more about a subculture. They are also good for exploratory research when a researcher is not clear about what the issues are likely to be with regard to the topic they are looking at.

Focus groups may consist entirely of a discussion around a particular topic or the moderator may use props to get participants to focus on a particular topic. For example, participants may be shown a video, pictures or things, or will have to play a 'game'. Because the focus group is structured as a discussion rather than as a set of questions, the participants are encouraged to respond to each other. Hence while group dynamics may or may not be of interest to a researcher conducting a group interview, it is the interaction between group members that will be key to the success of a focus group. Focus group participants don't just respond to questions asked by the moderator, they respond to each other and to the group dynamic as a whole. The dynamic of each focus group is unique. As Hesse-Biber and Leavy (2011) describe it, during the focus group a 'happening' is produced that cannot be replicated.

What a focus group looks like

A typical focus group will have six to eight participants and run for one and a half hours. It is difficult to achieve a good discussion with fewer than six participants, and as focus groups exceed eight participants the potential for participation by each member rapidly diminishes. The venue needs to be at a location that is easy for the participants to access. An attempt is made to make the setting informal and relaxed and free of distraction. Participants may sit in comfortable couches positioned in a loose circle or around a table. Ideally, the table would be oval or round so there is no one sitting at the head of the table. Food and drink are often provided to make the experience more relaxing for participants, while many market research companies will additionally provide alcohol. Focus groups on behalf of a company or research team are often undertaken in a purpose-built room where one complete wall is a one-way mirror, behind which will sit members of the company or research team.

Depending on the sensitivity of the topic, it is useful to be able to video-record focus groups as it can be difficult to work out who is saying what from an audio recording. A camera on a tripod placed at one end of the room and trained on the moderator can be an unobtrusive way of video-recording. In cases where video-recording is not possible or will be too intrusive, it may be feasible to include a note-taker who will record people's non-verbal responses, such as their facial expressions, nods of agreement, and body language. The moderator should never take notes as this is likely to interrupt the flow of the discussion, and a good discussion is key to a successful focus group. For this reason, focus groups are almost always conducted in the language of the participants.

Composition of the focus group

When deciding on the composition of the group, it is important to take into account ethical and practical considerations as well as the research topic.

Usually researchers will conduct several focus groups, each containing participants with particular common attributes. Take the example of a researcher conducting focus groups on attitudes to parenting, If that researcher is interested in the intersection of ethnicity and attitudes to parenting, they may conduct a range of groups, each comprised of people with the same ethnicity. If they are interested in gender and attitudes to parenting, they may decide to have separate groups of single mothers, single fathers, mothers in heterosexual couples, fathers in heterosexual couples, gay fathers, lesbian mothers and childless people. Focus groups are commonly analyzed at the level of the group. This means that a researcher can in this case compare, for example, single mothers' confidence in their parenting with that of single fathers, and so on.

As we talked about in Chapter 2, it is particularly important in post-positivist research to establish an environment where research participants can speak freely. This means that they need to feel comfortable with each other and this is more likely to be achieved with groups made up of people who have something in common, for example, similar backgrounds or the same age group. Also in Chapter 2, we contrasted a post-positivist researcher with the example of a criticalist researcher who deliberately combined teenage girls and boys in a single focus group to talk about obesity. In this case observing how the two sexes interacted around the issue of obesity was as telling for the criticalist researcher as what individuals did or didn't say about obesity.

An overriding aspect to bear in mind is that the composition of the focus groups needs to be respectful of the participants and unlikely to cause discomfort. So, for example, if you were conducting groups on experiences of racism, it may be more respectful to participants to group people with a particular ethnicity in the same group. Note also that when focus groups on sensitive topics comprise participants who don't know each other, it can be a good idea to use pseudonyms, as this then affords some anonymity to the participants.

If a focus group brings together participants with a particular interest or members of a small subculture, it is quite possible that those participants will know each other. This is not a problem and some focus groups are deliberately chosen to be comprised of colleagues or members of a club or friendship group. This sort of group is particularly useful for observing the formation and maintenance – through the use of language – of particular worldviews.

How many focus groups to conduct

Ideally, a researcher would keep conducting focus groups until saturation is reached, that is, until they were not finding anything new (Glaser and Strauss, 1967). In practice, a rule of thumb is that a researcher should try to conduct two of each type of group: in the preceding example, this would be two groups of single mothers, two groups of single fathers, two groups of mothers in heterosexual couples, and so on.

Recruitment – finding the right participants for your focus group

How you go about recruiting participants for your focus groups will depend both on the topic and on what sort of participants you want. If you want people who participate in a particular subculture, well-placed notices may be the easiest way to recruit these. For example, if you wanted to run focus groups of skateboarders' attitudes to what they do, you could place a notice at the local skate park, at a skateboard shop, on relevant websites, and at cafés where skateboarders hang out. This method could be used in combination with the snowball method, whereby you will ask those individuals who make contact with you whether they know of any other people who may be interested.

If none of the above methods are going to work to find the type of people you want to include in your focus group, you may have to resort to random telephone screening. This is where people are called at random and asked some screening questions to see if they meet the criteria for the proposed focus group. While effective at obtaining participants that are difficult to access any other way, this is a very expensive form of recruitment.

In general you should over recruit for each group. As a rule of thumb organize ten participants for each group, as it is likely that not everybody will show up. Because of this, it is best to recruit people who are likely to have at least some interest in the topic.

Some researchers will offer payment or rewards for participants, usually termed 'incentives'. Cash payments can range from about $40 to several hundred dollars, while rewards such as music or movie vouchers are cheaper and often used for focus groups with students or young people. In contrast, each participant in a focus group of medical specialists would be paid several hundred dollars, partly to compensate them for the time spent not earning money and partly in order to get them to participate. Sociologists researching disadvantaged groups will often make a point of paying them well as a sign of respect and in recognition that their time is also valuable, even if that time doesn't command a high salary in the marketplace.

Designing the moderator's guide

The word 'moderator' rather than 'interviewer' reflects the fact that the person in charge is 'moderating' the discussion and not just asking questions. Even so, the moderator needs to spend time designing the moderator's guide. They need to work out what is the most appropriate way to introduce the topic or issues for discussion and how best to engage the participants with that topic. In this way, writing the moderator's guide is a two-stage process. First, the researcher identifies the issues that they want to cover in the focus group. Second, the researcher, or the moderator if it is a different person, works out how best to address these issues in the focus group.

A focus group will often start with an activity that is more an icebreaker and a way into the topic than something that would necessarily be analyzed. For example, a focus group on attitudes to HIV/Aids may start with the participants introducing themselves and then saying the three things they think of when they think of HIV/Aids.

Viv Waller was involved in conducting focus groups with Year 10 students about their views of pharmacy as a career. One of the issues covered was the students' perceptions and knowledge of pharmacists and pharmacy as a career. The moderator could have asked the students directly what they knew about what pharmacists did and what they thought of pharmacy as a career. However, in order to engage the students more fully, a more imaginative approach was taken. The relevant extract of the moderator's guide is shown in Box 7.3.

Box 7.3

Example from a moderator's guide exploring Year 10 students' perceptions of pharmacy as a career

Show a picture of a group of people *(a mix of ages and sexes)* and ask which one of them is a teacher, which one a lawyer, which one a computer programmer, which one a pharmacist. *(Discuss the reasons for the selection of the person who is the pharmacist.)*

Has anyone ever thought – I'd like to be a pharmacist? *[reasons?]*

Has anyone ever thought – I really wouldn't like to be a pharmacist? – *[reasons?]*

Pharmacist [WRITE UP THE WORD ON THE WHITEBOARD]

Pharmacist role play: 'everybody imagine that they are a pharmacist for a day' *(allow a couple of minutes)*, then select some students to tell us what their day was like today in the pharmacy. Ask other students to evaluate the likelihood of this being a typical day in the life of a pharmacist.

The role of the moderator

The focus group moderator introduces the topic and facilitates the discussion, encouraging interaction. The moderator has to be able to stimulate a discussion as well as control the group. This means that they must think swiftly and flexibly in order to keep the discussion on topic while not stifling it or interrupting the flow. It is usually up to the moderator to ensure that all the focus group members have a say, and keep any single person from dominating.

In market research the moderator tends to control the group quite tightly, covering all of the issues that the client is interested in and making sure that everyone speaks. In social research, rather than adhering strictly to a list of sub-topics or questions, a researcher is more likely to be interested in the direction the group will take and what that group thinks is important to talk about. Even domination of the group by one or two participants may, in certain cases, be a dynamic that the researcher is interested in observing rather than controlling. This means that in social research the role of the moderator is less that of controlling the group, and more one of asking for clarification.

The principle of achieving a desired balance between encouraging the discussion and controlling that discussion is the same issue discussed with respect to interviewing. However, the consequences when the balance of power goes too far in the direction of the participants may be more severe. In extreme cases, when the moderator loses control of the direction of the group, participants may 'gang up' on the moderator. Wilkinson (1998) cites examples where a female moderator has been sexually harassed by members of the group, in a way that would not have occurred in individual interviews.

It is also possible that members of the group may intimidate or be bullying or disrespectful towards other members. The moderator may be able to use other group members to challenge this behaviour. As Wilkinson notes, however, 'group participants can collaborate or collude effectively to intimidate and/or silence a particular member, or to create a silence around a particular topic or issue, in a way that could not occur in a one-to-one interview' (1998: 116). If the moderator senses that some participants may have been uncomfortable with the behaviour or expressed views of other focus group participants, but felt unable to speak up, they should offer participants an opportunity to make comments privately afterwards or a debrief if necessary.

A researcher may moderate the focus groups, but this is not necessary, and many excellent researchers do not have the skills for moderating focus groups. If they are not moderating, a researcher may observe the focus groups through a one-way mirror or rely on recordings of the groups.

Online focus groups

Running face-to-face focus groups can be expensive, and scheduling the focus group at a time and location convenient to all participants may prove difficult. In addition, some people – and young people in particular – may not have sufficient confidence to meet strangers in an unfamiliar location (Fox et al., 2013). With the advent of new Internet technologies researchers have been experimenting with online focus groups. As with online interviews, the term 'online focus groups' encompasses a range of modes of communication: visual, audio and text, or any combination of these, using technologies such as chat rooms and immersive virtual environments. Many of the issues faced when conducting online focus groups will be the same as those that are relevant to online interviews. In particular, when a focus group is held online a moderator will have to work much harder to keep the group interested. Hence online focus groups should only be used for topics that the participants are likely to be passionate about. These are particularly useful for researching experiences related to medical conditions, as participants may value some anonymity, but at the same time also benefit from interacting with others with similar experiences. A characteristic of online focus groups among people experiencing a similar disadvantage is the forging of a strong group identity. For example, Fox et al. used a real-time text-only focus group to look at 'the appearance-related concerns of young people who have chronic skin conditions' (2013: 320). Participants said they were more confident to meet online than face to face.

Deb Dempsey conducted online focus groups with the clients of sex workers to investigate the problem of trafficking in the sex worker industry. Clients were found through a well-known website that was a forum for sex workers and their clients. The focus groups were conducted through a real-time chat facility on the website which meant that the researcher didn't have to know who the participants were, and the participants didn't know the identity of the other participants.

Real-time text-only focus groups are very challenging: 'Although participants have an equal opportunity to respond and contribute, the participant who is most proficient at typing has the power to say the most' (Fox et al., 2013: 327) in what can be a 'fast, furious, and chaotic' discussion (Tates et al., 2013). The problems experienced with turn-taking in online chat with just one person are multiplied as the numbers of participants involved in the discussion increase. Without visual cues, silences become even more difficult to interpret and the moderator has to make a judgement call as to whether they should intervene because the participants have nothing more to say on an issue or whether they should allow more time for thinking (Fox et al., 2013).

Online focus groups can be run using videoconferencing technology to enable audio-visual communication. In a group setting there is the potential for some participants to be shy of the camera, although researchers have generally found that this uncomfortableness with the medium will disappear once a focus group is in full swing (see, for example, Fielding, 2013).

As with online interviews, online focus groups need not be held in real time. Online asynchronous focus groups are usually conducted using technology like a discussion board where over a specified period participants can post comments and respond to others' posts at a time convenient to them. Although referred to in the literature as focus groups, it is debatable whether these online discussions are actually focus groups. As Fox et al. (2013) point out, researchers lose the spontaneity and immediate emotional reactions that occur in real-time focus groups. It is clear, however, that when participants are passionate about the topic but would like to be anonymous, this type of research method has its advantages. For example, Stewart and Williams (2013) discussed research that used this type of asynchronous online focus group to investigate the employment experiences of inflammatory bowel disease sufferers. Fifty-seven people utilized discussion threads to discuss multiple relevant topics, with little guidance needed from the researcher, who observed how a strong group identity developed.

Tates et al. (2013) ran a similar group with children and adolescents who were having active treatment for paediatric cancer, their parents, and young survivors of this form of cancer. The group ran over a period of a week, with researchers posting one discussion question a day and sending reminders to those not joining the discussion. Participants could start new discussion threads for any topics they considered relevant to the study. The researchers found that this method worked best for adolescents, with the adolescent patients and survivors responding directly to each other's contributions. In contrast, rather than being involved in a discussion, the children and parents tended to respond directly to the moderator. Regardless of the level of discussion generated, evaluations of the process indicated that the anonymity afforded by the online environment meant that participants felt able to bring up difficult issues that they would not have talked about in a face-to-face group (Tates et al., 2013).

Strengths

While the reputation of focus groups has been somewhat sullied by those who have used such an approach as a 'quick and dirty' way to get some research done in a few days, focus groups do have certain unique strengths.

In a focus group it is possible to observe the process by which participants interact, discuss, debate and disagree, or perhaps arrive at a shared meaning. When the members of a focus group are all drawn from a particular demographic or subculture, that focus group can give a researcher insight into that subculture that they are unlikely to gain from personal interviews or observation. A researcher can observe the language participants use, the jokes they share, the level of shared understanding and types of disagreements, the spontaneous reactions to ideas. A moderator can also interject for clarification of any of these aspects. For example, a researcher conducting a focus group with a particular subculture, such as injecting drug users, will have an opportunity to learn a whole new language and come across concepts that are meaningful in injecting drug users' daily experiences, such as how they are treated by the police. The focus group can also uncover group norms around a topic, including group definitions of particular situations.

Focus groups are often an enjoyable experience for participants, especially when they are given the chance to talk with others about a topic in which they are interested. They have also often been successfully used for discussing extremely sensitive topics, as participants may find that others in the focus group can provide support through having undergone similar experiences or by really understanding the experiences. For example, Waller conducted a focus group on turning points in addiction with people undergoing rehabilitation treatment for drug or alcohol addiction. Although each participant had their own unique experience, they all shared the experience of addiction. This meant that they could speak freely about sensitive issues relating to their addiction without the fear of being judged by someone else in the group. Rather, the environment of the focus group was a supportive one. In addition, a focus group can feel less threatening than an individual interview because the spotlight is not continually on just one participant. At times, each participant can take a back seat and listen to the others.

The environment of a focus group can enable greater exploration of a topic by stimulating respondents to think about their views more intensely than would be the case in an interview. Imagine you are conducting a focus group with young men on body image. After one participant says that he feels a pressure to look fit, other participants then respond to this, perhaps adding their own examples or counter-examples. There is also a reduced likelihood that participants would misunderstand the moderator as another member may pick up that a participant has misunderstood. As Wilkinson (1998) points out, focus group participants will often challenge what another participant has said or point out contradictions in a more forthright way than a moderator could.

Focus groups can also be a good way of giving voice to marginalized groups. People who are not usually asked their opinion (for example the homeless) may find that a focus group provides them with a non-threatening way to express their opinions and feelings on issues important to them. As with interviews, focus group participation can be a profound experience for participants who realize, as a result of their participation, that they are not alone in their experiences.

The data generated from focus groups, especially those that are video-recorded, are very rich and detailed. While this is certainly a strength, it can be hard to properly analyze so much data. This brings us to the particular challenges thrown up by focus groups. As would have been apparent in our discussion of the role of the moderator, a focus group's success will depend to a large extent on the moderator's skills. They will need to probe sufficiently to ensure that the discussion is conducted in enough depth to be useful. The moderator also needs to ensure that the group does not get out of control and is not dominated by one or two people. Regardless of the skills of a moderator, there are some weaknesses that are inherent in focus groups. In a group context it may be difficult for a participant to voice an opinion that differs from those of the rest of the group's. Hence a researcher may get a false impression of the level of uniformity of views within a group. Moreover, the views of its participants may not be indicative of the range of views that exists in the population that is of interest to the researcher. Finally, both focus groups and group interviews share with interviews the limitation that what someone says about themselves and what they do may not match with their actual behaviour.

When to use focus groups

Focus groups are particularly suitable for research underpinned by values and beliefs aligning with the criticalist and constructivist tradition.

In getting participants to focus on a topic, focus groups can be used as an intervention. The topic may be one that is relevant to participants, but which they have not thought about before. Being involved in a focus group may help them to explore and clarify their own points of view or they may start to reconsider their own behaviours. For example, imagine you are participating in a focus group talking about why you eat what you do. You sit listening to other people's reasons for why they eat what they do, something you have never thought about before. As several other participants discuss why they only eat free-range eggs, you start to be persuaded by their arguments and resolve to only eat free-range eggs from that point on. This aspect of focus groups can make them very suitable for the criticalist researcher who wants to create a positive change.

Focus groups are particularly useful for teasing out concepts and discussing what these mean. For example, a focus group would be an appropriate method by which to discover what different types of people think about what constitutes a good teacher. Note that how this question is phrased assumes a constructivist understanding that reality is local and specific rather than that there is some universal reality about what constitutes a good teacher.

In a focus group, participants can be given the chance to discuss issues using their own language and framings rather than the language of the interviewer. This then enables a researcher to observe how particular groups actively construct their understanding of the world through their language and framings. For example, in a focus group with university lecturers about technologies for recording lectures, the participants discussed their ideas about what the purpose of a lecture actually was. By the end of the focus group the participants had reached a shared understanding that the purpose of a lecture was not to impart information, but to gather the students together and generate enthusiasm for the subject. In this way a focus group is particularly suited to enabling constructivist researchers to observe how people arrive at shared understandings about the world.

CONCLUSION

By now it should be clear that focus groups and group interviews are distinct in their emphasis and execution. Group interviews are basically interviews with more than one interviewee. In contrast, focus groups are a distinctive method where in place of an interviewer asking questions a moderator facilitates a discussion.

Going further

Adato, M., Lund, F. and Mhlongo, P. (2007) 'Methodological innovations in research on the dynamics of poverty: a longitudinal study in KwaZulu-Natal, South Africa', *World Development*, 35 (2): 247–63.

An honest account of the use of group interviews with households to augment a quantitative longitudinal study into the dynamics of poverty in South Africa.

(Continued)

(Continued)

Boydell, N., Fergie, G., McDaid, L. and Hilton, S. (2014) 'Avoiding pitfalls and realising opportunities: reflecting on issues of sampling and recruitment for online focus groups', *International Journal of Qualitative Methods*, 13 (1): 206-23.

The authors describe their unsuccessful experiences of attempting to conduct online focus groups, with a well-developed discussion of sampling and recruitment issues for online focus groups.

Krueger, R. and Casey, M. (2009) *Focus Groups: A Practical Guide for Applied Research*. Thousand Oaks, CA: Sage.

This comprehensive book is a detailed guide to the practicalities of conducting focus groups.

Turney, L. and Pocknee, C. (2004) 'Virtual focus groups: new technologies, new opportunities, new learning environments', in R. Atkinson, C. McBeath, D. Jonas-Dwyer and R. Phillips (eds), *Beyond the Comfort Zone: Proceedings of the 21st ASCILITE Conference*, Perth, 5-8 December, pp. 905-12. Available at www.ascilite.org.au/conferences/perth04/procs/turney.html.

In this article, Turney and Pocknee argue that online discussion boards should be considered as bona fide focus groups.

Warr, D.J. (2005) '"It was fun ... but we don't usually talk about these things": analyzing sociable interaction in focus groups', *Qualitative Inquiry*, 11 (2): 200-25.

This article about the interactions between focus group participants contains many excerpts from transcripts that illustrate perfectly how valuable these interactions can be to researchers.

DOING THE RESEARCH

THE RESEARCHER OBSERVES

EIGHT
Observing people

CONTENTS

- Definitions   110
- Types of research question   112
- Getting in   113
- Disclosing that you are a researcher and other ethical issues   115
- Collecting the data   117
- Conclusion   119
- Going further   120

To observe basically means to look at or to view. Observation is a key qualitative research technique, and it can refer to looking at and analyzing things, texts and/or people. Observation provides a different sort of data from those gained from interviews, and can be used on its own or in conjunction with other methods. We might include observation as an independent means to find out what is happening in a particular context. For example, people may, when interviewed, say they use a park in a particular way, such as to relax. By observing the park we can see what people actually do there.

In this chapter we will explore the qualitative research method of observing people. We will look at participant and nonparticipant observation, using the term 'observational research' to refer to both these types of observation, and specifying the type only when there are differences. Observational studies are useful for exploring what is happening in a particular social context. Unlike interview-based studies, which find out what people say they do, observational studies can discover what people actually do, how they do it, and the norms that shape their actions. For example, while a lecturer may say they spend most of their classroom time with students standing at the front delivering information, an observer in the classroom may see that the lecturer actually involves students by asking them questions throughout. In the following sections we define participant and nonparticipant observation, discuss the relationship between the research paradigm in which you are operating and the questions you develop, and then outline issues around gaining access to research sites and disclosing your status as a researcher. We conclude with a discussion of the strategies for collecting observational data.

DEFINITIONS

Participant observation is exactly what it sounds like: observing people while at the same time participating in something in which they are also participating. Participant observation is where a researcher participates in activities relevant to what they are studying in order to gain an insider's perspective of these activities. It involves the researcher spending time immersed in their site. While they are participating they are also observing how things work and documenting the observations. For example, in order to understand a student's experiences in a classroom, a researcher may attend the class and participate in classroom activities as though they were a student.

Nonparticipant observation is where a researcher observes but does not interact with the goings-on. For example, in their (1995) study of biker subculture, Schouten and McAlexander started off by observing biker events to examine stereotypes and identify how they could safely access the subculture. These observations at public events gave them insights into the biker culture that then enabled them to identify interviewees and develop a more in-depth study. In this case the nonparticipant observation was an element of a larger study.

We can imagine observational research along a spectrum ranging from a participant researcher completely embedded in a site to a purely observational researcher who is hidden from those at the site, with a range of levels of participation in between. Thinking of observational research as a spectrum between complete participation and complete observation enables us to be creative in designing a study that fits our needs. It suggests that we do not need to fit our research into one category or another. Gold (1958) described this range using four categories that have come to be seen as ideal types: the complete participant, the participant as observer, the observer as participant, and the complete observer. The complete participant involves a researcher becoming fully involved in the site. Because of this in-depth involvement, the complete participant can get holistic insight into all aspects of the site. Gold argued that 'role-pretense' is an important element of being a complete participant: 'The complete participant realizes that he, and he alone, knows that he is in reality other than the person he pretends to be' (1958: 219). In this conceptualization the complete researcher is necessarily covert, which today is not usually within ethical guidelines. (An exception might be police undercover work, which could be considered a type of complete participant observation but is not considered a form of social research.)

The participant as observer does similar things to the complete participant and is what we would think of today as a typical participant observer. The key difference between the complete participant and the participant as observer is that the latter is not covert. An example of this is a study that Viv Waller did at a hospital where she worked as a ward clerk admitting patients for day treatment (Waller et al., 2006). By undertaking this work she was able to gain an understanding of the experience of being a ward clerk in a hospital setting from the ward clerk's perspective. Waller gained experience of what it was like to do the actual work, and she also gained insights into the social life of the workplace. In addition, she gained the trust of staff and patients at the hospital and was able to supplement her observations with interviews.

The observer as participant role, as described by Gold (1958), is more formal than that of either the complete participant or the participant as observer. Gold (1958) describes this as one-off visits to sites where people are observed and interviewed. We would actually not characterize this as a type of participant observational research as in our view participant observational research involves more than one visit. However, if we were to think of a spot between the participant as observer and the complete observer we might imagine a situation where the researcher was present in a largely observational role but still interacted with some participants. An example of this is another study Waller did where she accompanied field officers from the Australian Tax Office on unannounced visits to automobile dealers (Waller, 2007). The goal of the study was to assess the unannounced visits to see how these were enacted and received by the car dealers. She observed what the officers said, how they behaved and how the dealers reacted, but she also interacted with the officers in between visits as she accompanied them, so the study was not completely observational.

The final role is that of complete observer (Gold, 1958), which is what we have termed 'nonparticipant observation'. The complete observer does not become involved with the participants at a site. They might be visibly observing or they may be hidden, but they do not interact with people at the site. Studies of classrooms where researchers sit behind one-way mirrors and observe are an example of complete observation. This type of research is also done in public places.

Depending on your approach, participant observation can be challenging as it involves gaining access to a research site, developing relationships with people at the site, paying attention to the goings-on and documenting them in field notes, and then analyzing those field notes and writing up the findings. It can also be personally challenging as it involves analyzing information gained through relationships developed at the site, which can be an emotionally demanding process in both the data collection and analysis phases, as discussed in Chapter 4. Carrington (1999) found this in his study of domestic labour in same-sex households. His childhood experiences of housework and his personal arrangements in his own same-sex household shaped his initial understandings of domestic labour. These views were challenged during his fieldwork. He writes:

> Much of the fieldwork took place during the week-long time periods when I would dwell with the families I was studying ... I asked each family how they might respond to my presence for a week-long period, and I chose families on the basis of their receptivity. There is nothing particularly representative about these families other than they appeared the most receptive to such observation. I had to cajole and beg several of them. (Carrington, 1999: 23)

Compared to other qualitative research techniques, participant observation is one of the more difficult ones to organize and carry out. However, the data you collect from participant observation can be very rich and provide interesting and relevant insights into the research site that would otherwise be inaccessible.

Nonparticipant observation can be easier to organize because it does not involve engaging with participants. Like participant observation, it is a good way to see what is happening in real life. Nonparticipant observation, however, cannot provide the experience of what it is like to be a part of the field site. Karen Farquharson (Marjoribanks et al., 2013) was a nonparticipant observer in the AuSud Media Project (described in more detail in Box 8.1). In this role she observed journalism training that was being delivered to a group of Sudanese and South Sudanese Melbournians. While she was able to observe the training that was being delivered, as she was not participating she was unable to experience how the training was received or how effective it was in enabling the participants to develop journalism skills.

More generally, both participant and nonparticipant observation can provide insights that you cannot get using other methods: '… the [researcher] has the opportunity to see things that may routinely escape conscious awareness among participants and staff' (Patton, 1990: 204). Through observing you may be able to see what the insiders take for granted.

TYPES OF RESEARCH QUESTION

The research paradigm in which the research is operating will shape the types of question on which an observational study will focus. While the goal of a post-positivist study is to explain what is going on as objectively as possible, a criticalist study aims to create positive change and a constructivist looks at how interactions are socially constructed. All three are compatible with observational methods, but the approaches taken, the things observed and the questions answered will vary.

Sometimes a study will sit within more than one research paradigm. The example below of the AuSud Media Project highlights the ways in which the research paradigm in which one is operating shapes one's research questions, and how the same project can use the same method to answer very different types of question.

──────────── Box 8.1 ────────────

Paradigms and participant observation

Farquharson was a researcher with the AuSud Media Project, a research project that included both observational and participant observation components. The AuSud Project was a multi-pronged media intervention that aimed to enable Sudanese and South Sudanese Australians to develop their own media voice (Marjoribanks et al., 2013). It first provided journalism training to interested Sudanese and South Sudanese Australians. After several groups of people had been trained, the intervention moved to a newsroom format where news stories were being produced and discussed on a weekly basis in a particular location. The formal training sessions were observed by members of the research team, and one of the research team members was a participant observer when the project moved into the news production phase.

If the research team had been coming from a post-positivist perspective, they might have focused their research questions on what types of information the participants were taught, and what types of stories they wrote. They could have explored how the news media engaged with the Sudanese and South Sudanese and vice versa. They may have identified a typology of approaches to story-writing that the Sudanese and South Sudanese Australian news stories fitted within. The research might also have looked at whether and how news reports about Sudanese and South Sudanese Australians changed as a result of the project.

If the team had utilized a criticalist perspective, they might have asked questions that reflected more of a social justice approach: what were the power dynamics of the training programme? How might the training have empowered the participants in their interactions with the media? The research might have focused on how the 24-hour media cycle shaped the kinds of news that was reported, and how that in turn affected the stories about Sudanese-Australians that were likely to be reported. Further, they might have expected the findings to change the power relations: once the dynamics were uncovered they could be shifted. The research, then, would have explored ways to enact changes to the news media that would then alter the ways it portrayed Sudanese and South Sudanese Australians.

If Farquharson and the team had been approaching the project from a constructivist perspective, they might have focused on the participants' experiences of the training. The research might have focused on how participants expressed themselves and the stories they produced, and how they might have had a say in how the research itself is constructed.

All three philosophical approaches would have involved observing the same training sessions, but the research questions asked and the findings of the research would have varied greatly. In the criticalist and constructivist approaches, the team might have considered how their own presence as non-Sudanese people participating in the journalism training programme affected the dynamics of the training itself. Indeed, this raises the question of how close to an insider experience a researcher who is structurally not able to become an insider can get.

The participant observation component of the project actually utilized a criticalist approach. Indeed, the media training was intended to provide Sudanese- and South Sudanese-Australians with journalism skills so that they themselves could influence the way they were being portrayed in the mainstream media.

GETTING IN

In order to conduct observational research you will generally need to get permission. Who you get this permission from will depend on the research site and what you are hoping to observe/try to understand, that is, your research questions. Gaining entry to a research site can be a common barrier to undertaking observational research, so you should do your homework beforehand in order to put forward a convincing case to the gatekeeper of your site.

Going back one step, what is your site? Observational research works best in relatively contained sites: a neighbourhood (Small, 2004); an organization (Spaaij, 2011); a village or town (Ellis, 2007); or perhaps a public place (Humphreys, 1972). It is difficult to do observational research on a city, for example, as it has many different facets and would be hard to integrate meaningfully. The site selected should be appropriate to the research questions. For example, exploring how cancer survivors interact online (Sharf, 1997) would necessitate an online site where that could be observed.

Once you have identified a site, you will need to identify the main gatekeepers. There may be no formal gatekeepers if it is a public place, like a public park or train station, or a website like 4chan where anyone can post completely anonymously to a variety of discussion boards (www.4chan.org). Most sites, though, will have gatekeepers who can enable or hinder access. The gatekeepers' view of the research will depend on the topic, who is commissioning the research, and what they expect or fear the outcomes might be.

The senior gatekeepers might enable entry to a site, but you would still need to convince the local people you would be interacting with to cooperate. For example, the principal of a school may agree to allow you to be a participant observer in a classroom, but if the classroom teacher does not agree, your study will not be possible. Likewise, the boss of a company may want you to evaluate one of its programmes. Because the boss has commissioned the evaluation, the employees may have to comply, but they may also feel threatened or vulnerable and perhaps be less than forthcoming with their cooperation. Similarly, in an online forum you may get permission from the forum owner/moderator/leader, but that does not necessarily mean that the forum members will be comfortable with you being there and happy about your presence. In these ways, gaining entry is a political process. We would suggest that the best way to gain permission is to have a solid rationale for the study and present this to the various gatekeepers, identifying any likely benefits to those at the site.

Nonparticipant observation in public places does not usually require gaining consent from gatekeepers. For example, if your site is a public park, it would be unnecessary to gain consent from the council or park service. However, if you were observing a park, and particularly if you were there alone for a long period of time taking notes, people using the park might question your presence because you are not exhibiting normal park behaviour. We would suggest that if that was to happen you should disclose your presence as a researcher.

Lofland and Lofland (1984: 7–10) suggest 'starting where you are'. This means researching what you are passionate about and have existing links to. This can facilitate entry as you may be an 'insider' and already have a trusting relationship with the gatekeepers. A disadvantage here is the potential lack of a critical eye regarding the taken-for-granted norms that you already operate within. A potential advantage, though, is a depth of understanding that might be difficult for an outsider to access. An integral element of both the constructivist and criticalist paradigms is reflexivity on the part of the researcher regarding the role they play in the dynamics in the field. Reflexivity can help to temper insider/outsider issues.

DISCLOSING THAT YOU ARE A RESEARCHER AND OTHER ETHICAL ISSUES

For participant observation research to be conducted ethically, in particular to be respectful to those who are being researched, a researcher must disclose that they are a researcher and give people the opportunity not to participate in the research if they so choose. In participant observational studies this can be an issue as an entire site can often be the object of investigation, and it can be difficult for particular individuals to be excluded from the study. It can also be challenging when the people at the research site are continually changing. How often should you re-disclose that you are a researcher? This can be especially fraught when undertaking participant observation in online sites, which may have people dipping in and out of participation regularly.

There are no straightforward rules about how frequently a participant observer should disclose their researcher status. We would advise erring on the side of caution and letting people in the research field know that they are part of a research project and getting their permission to participate. We would argue that this is respectful. If a person elects not to participate, then no data should be collected about them. But what about their interactions with others? There are no straightforward rules about this situation, and as a researcher you should carefully consider how to deal with that type of data in the context of their site and research questions. Excluding that person might change the research findings. It is important you consider other ways in which this can be mitigated.

Nonparticipant observers who are studying identifiable people also need to make their presence known and get permission to observe. For example, if a researcher is observing a group of children through a one-way mirror at a child care centre, they will need to get permission from the centre and the parents of the children as the latter would be too young to be able to consent for themselves. In the example discussed earlier about the AuSud Media Project, Farquharson and the research team got the consent of all of the participants in the project before conducting the observations. There is really very little difference in these examples between participant and nonparticipant observers in terms of gaining consent.

For purely observational studies at public places, the issue of consent is less fraught. This is because it is unlikely that the people being observed will be identifiable. If someone being observed is unidentifiable, observations of them are unlikely to cause them harm. As discussed in detail in Chapter 4, observational studies of online interactions are a grey area.

The debate about whether or not you need consent for these types of studies has not been resolved. The Association of Internet Researchers (AoIR) provides guidelines about how researchers may consider the issue (Markham and Buchanan, 2012), but there are no hard-and-fast rules. Rather than trying to be prescriptive, AoIR suggest that researchers consider the context of the Internet research, including the likelihood that the people being studied will be identifiable and if they are identified the likelihood of this causing harm. They also suggest that researchers consider the goals of the research, the types of data being used, and the 'ethical expectations' associated with that use (Markham and Buchanan, 2012: 9). Internet search engines will likely be able to identify direct quotes, and researchers should consider the consequences of this for the people they are quoting. As discussed in Chapter 4, your stance on this will depend on whether you view online discourse as text or conversation. It may also depend on the paradigm within which your research is operating.

Researchers in observational studies are often concerned about the impact of their presence on the research setting. This concern can be used to justify covert research (see Patton, 1990: 210–13, for a good discussion). However, the evidence to suggest that covert research is any more robust than research which is fully consented to is limited. There is much anecdotal evidence to suggest that when researchers are present at a research site over a period of time their presence becomes much less noticeable. Part of the reason for this is that it is difficult for people to change their behaviour consistently over a long period even when they know that researchers are present (Patton, 1990).

Ethics also needs to be considered in the analysis and reporting of participant observation data. The ethical values of research merit and integrity argue for accurately reporting the research findings, but this can go against the politics of the research site and the trusting relationships that a researcher may have developed with people on the research site. In reporting the findings of a participant observation study, researchers may have spent months working with and learning about people and their social relationships. What is their responsibility in accurately reporting their robust research findings when those findings might have negative outcomes for those at the research site? Post-positivist researchers would be likely to report the findings as an honest reflection of social reality. However, what if the study is coming from a criticalist perspective which aims to change social conditions in a positive way for the disadvantaged, but the findings are at odds with this goal? Are the researchers nevertheless obliged to report them? This is potentially in conflict with the idea that researchers should do no harm. Yet it may be that reporting the findings could shed light on a critical issue and lead to important positive changes in the future, even while currently making the participants look bad. Criticalist researchers might choose to report negative findings in this circumstance. Constructivist researchers might take another view, perhaps negotiating how the research is reported with the participants.

Ellis reflects on these issues with regard to an ethnographic study that she undertook where the findings were not well received by the people who were the subject of the study (Ellis, 2007). She argues for a relational ethics: '… relational ethics recognizes and values mutual respect, dignity, and connectedness between researcher and researched, and between researchers and the communities in which they live and work' (2007: 4). She suggests that researchers should re-check with research participants throughout the project that they still wish to be involved. She also strongly suggests that researchers encourage their research participants to read what the researchers write about them. Her research is compatible with a constructivist approach, while researchers from post-positivist and criticalist perspectives might disagree (although criticalists might support this approach on the grounds that it could be empowering for participants).

A relational ethics does not solve the problems involved with unflattering or actually potentially damaging research findings, but can provide some tools to consider in dealing with them. Our views of this problem will also be shaped by our epistemological positioning and the goal of the broader research project. If it was undertaken from a post-positivist perspective, we might be less concerned with the negative consequences for participants than if we were undertaking the research from a criticalist or constructivist perspective. In this way our approach to ethics can be shaped by our epistemological positioning.

A final ethical issue to consider is that of confidentiality. Confidentiality may be relevant even if the research has taken place in a completely public place and the researcher does not know who the participants are. For example, a person might wait at the same place in the same train station day after day. If a researcher were to report that they stood at the foot of the escalator rubbing their hands every morning, that person could be identifiable.

If confidentiality has been promised, it should be maintained. Internal confidentiality is particularly tricky as participants in participant observation studies are likely to be identifiable to each other. Ellis reported research findings from a project with the expectation that the participants would not read them (Ellis, 2007). She used pseudonyms that were easily identifiable to insiders, and those insiders were not happy with how they were portrayed. On reflection, she says she should have been clearer about the research with the participants and also should have paid closer attention to issues of internal confidentiality (see Chapter 4 for a further discussion).

COLLECTING THE DATA

Data from participant observation and observational studies are generally collected in the form of field notes, although sometimes video-recordings are used. The types of observations that are recorded by researchers vary widely. Things noted might include drawings of the layout of a room; descriptions of the setting; lists of the people present; the types of people present; the types of interactions that took place; what, where, when and how activities took place; how activities were organized and by whom; how the researcher felt about the goings-on; and whatever else might be relevant to the setting.

An observational project might develop a protocol to structure the observations. How structured the observational protocol/framework is would depend on the type of information being sought (i.e. the research questions) and who was doing the observing. In team projects there may be a more detailed observational protocol than where there is an individual researcher. This is because the project may want to make sure that all observers capture similar information, at least as a baseline. For example, Farquharson is part of a project that is observing how junior sports clubs manage diversity. That project, which is operating largely within the constructivist paradigm, will have different team members doing participant observation at different sports clubs. The team has developed an observation protocol that prompts each researcher to record particular types of information, but this also prompts the recording of any other observations that the researcher thinks might be relevant to the project.

Table 8.1 shows the amount of structure in an observational protocol according to research paradigm. Note that this table is identical to Table 6.1 in Chapter 6.

Table 8.1 The amount of structure in the observational protocol

RESEARCH PARADIGM	Positivist/post-positivist	Criticalist	Constructivist
Structured	✓		
Semi-structured		✓	✓

For the criticalist and the constructivist, the observational protocol can be very open-ended. The post-positivist will likely want particular types of observations.

In recording field notes it is necessary to remember that we don't notice everything that is going on at any given time. Our attention is selective. Having a clear research question and a well-developed observational protocol gives a focus to the data collection. For example, if we are productivity experts trying to work out how to improve efficiency in a workplace, we might notice that a worker has to walk down the hallway for five minutes every time they need to print something, and that they are spending an hour each day simply walking back and forth. Through our participant observation we may use the printer and also explore why that printer is so far away. Perhaps it is because people equally far in the other direction also use it frequently. Or perhaps there is no appropriate space closer. If we were to study the same workplace but with an eye to understanding how the workers collaborate rather than improving efficiency, we would notice very different things, such as who is talking to whom and about what. Further, the research paradigm underpinning the study would also influence both the goals of the study and the things recorded in the field notes.

There is no correct way to record field notes. As Clifford says, '… it is difficult to say something systematic about field notes, since one cannot even define them with precision' (1990: 53). Many observers will keep journals or notebooks to record their observations. It is usually advised that participant observers record their notes at least daily, but not when they are in the field. However, your comfort level about recording notes while in the field will probably depend on where you are observing and for what purpose. If you are doing an evaluation of a programme, you will probably be more comfortable openly taking notes than if you are conducting an exploratory study.

It is important to realize that field notes are interpretations of what has been observed. Even more, they are *'written* rhetorical constructions' (Clifford, 1990: 67, emphasis in original). A researcher very much shapes and frames the notes they collect and so these are not a neutral recording of events. Even if the events are video-recorded, which is not uncommon in nonparticipant observational studies, those recordings will still be interpreted and written up, with some things being noticed and others not. Moreover, the video itself will only capture what the camera is being pointed at, which necessarily excludes the surrounding contexts.

The issue raised at the start of this chapter, about researchers who are clearly not and cannot become insiders, is a vital one here. In the AuSud Media Project none of the researchers had a Sudanese or South Sudanese background, so none could share the embodied experience of being a Sudanese or South Sudanese Australian and all that that entailed. When one of the research team participated in the newsroom he was not a stakeholder in the project like the other participants were, because he did not have a Sudanese or South Sudanese background and did not write stories for those communities. So while he was involved in most aspects of the newsroom, his participation was as an outsider due to the structuring of the project which placed the Sudanese and South Sudanese participants as stakeholders and the non-Sudanese researchers as others. This type of participant observation is different from what Waller experienced while working as a ward clerk, as she was indistinguishable from the other ward clerks in the type of work she did (Waller et al., 2006).

So how long should a participant observer or an observer stay in the field? As with other aspects of observational research, this is both debated and dependent on the research question and the research paradigm underpinning the research. One answer is 'as long as is needed to get convincing answers to the research questions'. For in-depth studies a researcher may be in the field for one or more years. For a short evaluation of something specific, a much shorter period of time in the field might suffice.

CONCLUSION

As with other qualitative research techniques, how we go about observing people is very much shaped by the research paradigm we are operating within. This then shapes the questions we ask, the types of data we collect, how we analyze those data, and how we use these to support our conclusions. This chapter has discussed both participant and nonparticipant observation, but it has not provided clear rules about how observational research should be conducted, except perhaps that it is crucial that, as researchers, we pay attention to the issues of research ethics. This is because the approaches one might take to disclosing the research, to how much participation is needed, and to the other aspects of observational research, are very much debated and will differ by research paradigm. Being reflexive about where the research is situated should help provide some clarity about how to proceed.

Going further

Angrosino, M. (2007) *Doing Ethnographic and Observational Research*. London: Sage.

Includes an in-depth introduction to conducting observational research.

Denzin, N. and Lincoln, Y. (eds) (1998) *Collecting and Interpreting Qualitative Materials*. Thousand Oaks, CA: Sage.

Provides a comprehensive overview of qualitative research, including interviewing and observations.

Ellis, C. (2007) 'Telling secrets, revealing lives: relational ethics in research with intimate others', *Qualitative Inquiry*, 13: 3–29.

Here Ellis discusses the ethics around the Fisher Folk study. This was a famous case where the people she was studying read her research findings and many did not like what she had said. This article discusses the ethical aspects of participant observation.

Gold, R.L. (1958) 'Roles in sociological field observations', *Social Forces*, 36: 217–23.

The classic text for describing roles in observational research, this identifies the different roles of complete participant, complete observer, participant as observer, and observer as participant.

Patton, M.Q. (1990) *Qualitative Evaluation and Research Methods*. Newbury Park, CA: Sage.

An excellent discussion of qualitative research methods for evaluation, with an interesting examination of the pros and cons of observation in this context.

NINE

Observing things

CONTENTS

- Accretion measures — 122
  - Digital traces — 123
- Erosion measures — 124
- Advantages of studying physical traces — 125
- Disadvantages of studying physical traces — 125
- Analyzing physical traces — 127
- Conclusion — 127
- Going further — 128

In the previous chapter we explored observing people. In this chapter we shift the focus to observing things. By 'things' we mean the objects and other traces that people leave behind as they go about their lives. We can learn much about society by paying attention to how we use our environment, the items we make, and the traces we leave behind. Our approach to understanding physical traces will, like all other qualitative approaches, be shaped by the research paradigm underpinning our research. This chapter focuses on observing three-dimensional visual objects. (Textual and other two-dimensional visual objects are discussed in Chapter 10.) We use the term 'physical traces' rather than 'visual objects', although other researchers include physical traces as part of visual sociology (for example, Emmison et al., 2012). Another term that could be used is 'material culture', though this is not as commonly used in social science as it is in humanities.

Physical traces include things like gardens, statues, objects in our homes, graffiti, rubbish, traffic lights, paving, cemeteries, clothing, DNA, bottles and file folders – in other words, pretty much any object. They also include the non-textual digital traces we leave behind as we use the Internet, communicate using digital devices, and even as we walk around and are captured by surveillance videos. Physical traces are always located in a spatial context where their uses and presence are shaped, so when considering an object it must be studied in both its spatial and social contexts: 'Spatial settings, then, are of great importance in understanding objects and their relationships with humans' (Emmison et al., 2012: 107).

Physical traces can be useful as they provide evidence of what people do rather than what they say they do. Archaeologists use physical traces to try to understand the past. Forensic scientists use them to try to solve crimes. Physical traces can also be analyzed to help us understand the social world. The study of physical traces by social scientists is often to complement other qualitative techniques, but it can also be a key method in its own right.

The study of physical traces is a form of unobtrusive research. Unobtrusive research is research that does not require the active participation of others. It is also non-reactive – that is, the data exist independently of the research project. For example, an informal path through a public park can provide evidence of how that park is used. The path exists whether or not a researcher chooses to study it. Physical traces are usually considered using measures of two sorts: accretion and erosion (Webb, 2000). Accretion refers to things that accrue, while erosion refers to patterns of wear. In the park example, the park itself can be thought of as a measure of accretion, an intervention into the environment that takes what was originally there and shapes it for human use. The informal path is a measure of erosion, a way that the intended use of the space has been subverted by the park users. In the next sections we look at measures of accretion and erosion. This is followed by a discussion of the benefits and challenges associated with studying physical traces. We conclude with a discussion of how the research paradigm in which one is operating shapes the analysis of physical traces.

ACCRETION MEASURES

Measures of accretion look at the accumulation of deposits over a period of time (Webb, 2000). We can divide accretion measures into two categories: those that occur naturally and those that are controlled (Gray, 2009). Natural accretion includes things like fingerprints, litter, objects in the home, and other things that accumulate. Natural deposits occur during the course of everyday life and can provide insights into how people live. Controlled accretion of physical objects is less common than natural accretion. Controlled accretion refers to the researcher intervening in the accretion (Webb, 2000). Webb uses the example of checking the glass of museum displays for fingerprints and other evidence of touch on a daily basis as a way to measure how popular exhibits are. This is controlled because the researcher wipes the prints off each day. Social researchers are frequently interested in measures of accretion. Emmison et al. (2012: 110–11) argue that our objects can be signposts of social status and taste; can exhibit one's individuality; can indicate social activity in how they are used; and can have values encoded in them. We can analyze them for any of these.

Box 9.1

Analyzing graffiti

Graffiti is an accretion measure that social scientists have studied in a number of locales and ways. Otta (1992) studied graffiti written on restroom walls in Paolo, Brazil, finding that there were gender differences in both the amount and topics of the graffiti. Schreer and Strichartz (1997) also reported gender differences in the United States where they found men's restrooms were more likely to have scatological and insulting graffiti than women's, while women's restrooms were more likely to have political graffiti than men's. They found that sexual graffiti was equally likely to be present regardless of gender (Schreer and Strichartz, 1997). Both Otta and Schreer and Strichartz were examining graffiti as indicators of social values. McDonald (1999) took a different approach in his Australian study of graffiti. He was interested in identity and how graffiti indicated the identities and social hierarchies of its producers.

Digital traces

Digital data about us are being constantly and systematically collected and are a type of physical trace that accrues. This type of data has come to be termed 'big data'. Big data include textual and non-textual data such as the search terms we use on the Internet; who we are 'friends' with on social media; posts we make online; video collected of us as we walk along a road; what we click online; which websites we visit and for how long; purchases we make using a credit card; trips we make using a 'Smart' travel card or Google Maps enabled; and all manner of digital information that we routinely share as we live our lives. Although most closely associated with social computing and quantitative methods, big data can also be analyzed qualitatively. Most big data are being collected by private companies and are frequently used to tailor the type of information that pops up for us on our screens through processes called business analytics or data mining. These companies mainly use their big data to better target advertisements to put in front of us, but social researchers are increasingly seeking access to these so they can better understand the social world. The use of this type of accretion measure raises ethical issues, as we have likely not consciously consented to the use of this information for research purposes. How researchers will manage these ethical issues is still emerging. This is further discussed later in the chapter.

EROSION MEASURES

Measures of erosion look at patterns of wear (Webb, 2000), such as which books in a library are worn from use, or which paths through a park are most popular. Social scientists examine these patterns of wear and make conclusions about usage. Like accretion measures, erosion measures can also occur naturally or be controlled. Examples of natural erosion include analyzing potholes in roads to assess travel patterns or examining the wear on workers' shoes to assess the amount of work they are doing.

Forensic science regularly uses erosion measures at crime scenes (see Box 9.2) whereas other social scientists use these infrequently. A field where the study of erosion measures has provided useful insights is land management. One issue that has been raised in that field is whether policies that restrict campfires in national parks reduce park degradation. A study of national parks in the United States examined the impact of campfire management policies in parks with designated areas for campfires, no restrictions on campfires, and total campfire bans (Reid and Marion, 2005). The study looked at the number of campsites, fires and damaged trees (damaged due to the collection of firewood as well as other factors) in campsite areas. It found that there was evidence of campfires and damage to trees in all parks regardless of the campfire policy, suggesting that overly restrictive or permissive policies regarding campfires were not warranted. It also suggested that limiting axes, saws and other cutting implements would help maintain trees (Reid and Marion, 2005). This type of study of erosion measures is fairly common in land management, with many studies looking, for example, at the impact of mountain bike use and hiking on trails (see Pickering et al., 2010, for a meta-analysis of these studies) among other things.

Box 9.2

Forensic science

The fields of forensic science and investigative psychology commonly use accretion and erosion measures to reconstruct crimes. Both fields use police information, including statements from victims, criminals and witnesses, as well as computer files, video surveillance information, and other physical traces collected from crime scenes and other locations by the police (Canter and Alison, 2003). In this context, accretion measures include things like fingerprints, hair, blood, DNA, the position of bodies in a crime scene (Canter and Alison, 2003), and other things deposited as a result of crime. Erosion measures include the levels of trauma to bodies, decomposition, and – more benignly – items that have been stolen (Canter and Alison, 2003). Analysis of these items can provide insight into criminal behaviour, particularly when combined with other forms of data (Canter and Alison, 2003) including interviews.

ADVANTAGES OF STUDYING PHYSICAL TRACES

There are a number of advantages to using physical traces for social research. First, the study of physical traces is unobtrusive, the measures themselves are non-reactive, and permission may not be required for studies of this sort. The observation of objects can provide rich insights into social life.

Emmison et al. (2012: 150) identified a number of advantages to studying physical objects. They argued that objects were 'objective measures of social process' as they were indicators of actual behaviour. Because they were non-reactive they avoided things such as interviewer bias or bias in participant responses, which are important to post-positivists. They were also easy to categorize and count while still allowing for interpretive analyses.

Physical traces provide evidence of what people actually do rather than what they say they do. In this way such traces can be an important supplement to other types of data. For example, if you want to know what people actually eat at home, you might interview them and perhaps check their garbage. This garbage provides physical evidence that may or may not align with the information provided in interviews.

DISADVANTAGES OF STUDYING PHYSICAL TRACES

There are also a number of disadvantages associated with studying physical traces. Importantly, the type of information you get from studying physical traces, particularly accretion measures, is limited to what is present. Unless you are doing an analysis of rubbish, things that have not been saved cannot be studied. However, things that have not been saved might be important. Some things are so mundane that people might not think to accumulate them, but these may be central to how people live. For example, most of us would not save our personal items such as our undergarments or our intimate products. We must, then, take care in extrapolating from physical traces as the things that remain are almost always incomplete, providing only a partial picture of what has gone before. Think about the things you keep and the things you throw away. You probably only keep the special things, the things that have meaning for you or that you think will be useful. You probably throw away things that are mundane or perhaps that you consider to be disposable or even embarrassing. Therefore, if a researcher were to look at your belongings, they would get an incomplete picture of your everyday life.

The rates at which things accumulate and erode are not random. Some things erode more quickly than others. For example, vegetables rot at a different rate from processed foods, which is important if you are studying rubbish to find out what people eat. For example, if we were studying household rubbish in a culture where composting was common, we would not see any of the fresh produce consumed. We might assume, based on the rubbish, that the households studied did not eat fresh produce. This would be an erroneous assumption and highlights the limits of studies of physical traces. Also, things erode for many reasons, and your hypothesized reason may not be correct.

Some things accumulate, while others do not. Studies of accretion are limited to those things that can accumulate. Things that rot and/or disappear are difficult to study after a time. Similarly, measures of erosion are not randomly maintained. The absence of an erosion measure does not mean that there was nothing there. The walkway that might once have been somewhere may have been replaced by something else with a completely different use.

There are also some ethical issues associated with studying physical traces. For example, should you be able to sift through someone's garbage without their permission? What about their digital data? Does it make a difference if the sources of the physical traces are still alive? Some big data are so specific that it is possible to identify sources. For example, in 2006 AOL – a large Internet service provider in the United States – released the keyword search data of its 650,000 users for a three-month period. The goal of this release was to enable research. However, in its release of the search data AOL linked search terms to individual users (identified by a number), which made many users identifiable and caused embarrassment and harm. Although AOL quickly took down the data, these had already been distributed and are still available online.

In particular, the use of digital traces, both textual and non-textual, raises a number of vexing issues for social researchers. As with other physical traces, caution must be taken in extrapolating meaning or intent. For example, if a person is logged onto the home computer, the traces being tracked that will be attributed to them might actually have been left by their children, friends, partner, or even other relatives. So the information associated with that person would be a poor indicator of their actions. Most importantly, all the power is with the researcher in deciding what the data mean. Thus, this type of analysis is unlikely to be used by researchers operating in criticalist or constructivist paradigms. Even post-positivist researchers will recognize that we cannot intuit intent from traces without knowing the context for their production. A good example of this is the case of Justin Carter, an American teenager. In 2013 Carter stated on Facebook that he was going to 'shoot up a kindergarten', a statement he said was a joke made in the context of a computer game discussion and followed by the disclaimers 'LOL' and 'j/k', meaning 'laugh out loud' and 'just kidding' respectively. Carter was arrested and jailed as a result. This case highlights the importance of context. Digital traces taken out of context can be badly misinterpreted. A more benign example would be a person who ordered a lot of items online for other people who did not have their own credit cards, did not want to set up accounts, or for some reason did not want to buy online themselves. It might look like the person doing the ordering is wealthy and has particular tastes, but that may be incorrect.

More generally, because physical traces are non-reactive, the object of study was not developed specifically for research, so the researcher has to make do with what is there. For this reason, physical traces cannot be used to answer 'why?' questions.

Given the limitations of physical traces, it is necessary to carefully conceptualize those research projects that utilize them. They can work really well in conjunction with other research methods – studies that ask people about their physical objects can be very insightful. There should always be a critical element in the analysis of physical traces. By this we mean the researcher should always consider their context.

ANALYZING PHYSICAL TRACES

Studies of physical traces can be based on post-positivist, constructivist, or criticalist research paradigms. The analysis of physical traces from a post-positivist perspective can help identify what went on before. Their use by forensic scientists is a good example of this approach. Forensic scientists are trying to uncover what happened in a particular space and time. In this view, there is one factual version of events, not the multiple versions that might be uncovered by the criticalist and constructivist approaches. A crime was committed and the forensic scientists attempt to identify what happened and who the perpetrator was.

A criticalist study of physical traces would be examining physical traces from a particular ideological perspective. For example, a criticalist might study how the design of a street discourages women from walking at night. The goal of the research could be to highlight the importance of gender and gender norms around behaviour when designing built environments. A similar study might be done of statues. Statues are purposely present to put forward particular meanings. What might those meanings be and how might they be indicators of social hierarchies (see Emmison et al., 2012, for a discussion of how to study statues)?

Studies of physical traces have no participants present with whom to co-construct meanings, and are therefore difficult to undertake from a purely constructivist perspective. For a constructivist approach to work, physical traces would have to be combined with another type of qualitative method that involves participants. A good example of this approach was McDonald's (1999) study of graffiti. McDonald employed a mixed-method approach which analyzed both the graffiti and the graffiti writers' views of the graffiti, thus enabling a rich exploration of graffiti culture in Australia.

CONCLUSION

This chapter has provided an introduction to the study of physical traces, including non-textual digital traces. Physical traces can be divided into two categories: measures of accretion and measures of erosion. Within these we can think of natural measures and control measures (Webb, 2000).

The chapter has argued that physical traces can be a good way to find out what people actually do, and work well both in their own right but also in conjunction with other methods. As with other qualitative techniques, the research paradigm underpinning the research shapes the research question, the approach to analysis of the data, and the meaning made of it.

As passive modes of collecting data are increasingly present in our lives, increasing sources of data are becoming available to social researchers. These data provide exciting opportunities for researchers, but also raise questions about both the extent to which our everyday lives are under surveillance and our ability to consent to having our data used for research purposes which may not even be under consideration when the surveillance systems are being set up. As researchers, we need to be mindful of the potential ethical issues associated with these types of physical traces.

Going further

There is not a great deal of literature available on qualitative uses of physical traces. The recommendations below are a starting point for further research.

Emmison, M., Smith, P. and Mayall, M. (2012) *Researching the Visual*. London: Sage.

A very interesting and well-written discussion of analyzing a variety of visual data, including physical traces.

Hodder, I. (2012) 'The interpretation of documents and material culture', in J. Goodwin (ed.), *Sage Biographical Research*. London: Sage. pp. 171–87.

A comprehensive discussion of using material culture in social research.

Jenkins, T.M. (2014) 'Clothing norms as markers of status in a hospital setting: a Bourdieusian analysis', *Health (United Kingdom)*, 18 (5): 526–41.

This article describes the use of participant observation to enable the researcher to observe the clothing of hospital staff.

Schroeder, R. (2014) 'Big data: towards a more scientific social science and humanities?', in M. Graham and W.H. Dutton (eds), *Society & the Internet: How Networks of Information are Changing Our Lives*. Oxford: Oxford University Press.

This chapter introduces big data for humanities and social sciences and argues for its analysis.

Webb, E.J. (2000) *Unobtrusive Measures*. Thousand Oaks, CA: Sage.

A comprehensive introduction to the study of physical traces, including measures of accretion and erosion.

TEN
Observing texts

CONTENTS

- Thematic and discourse analysis: similarities and differences — 130
  - Thematic analysis — 130
  - Discourse analysis — 131
  - Critical discourse analysis — 132
- Locating and sampling texts — 133
  - Locating and sampling blogs — 134
- Doing a thematic analysis — 136
- Doing a discourse analysis — 137
- Conclusion — 138
- Going further — 139

'A woman has been repeatedly sexually assaulted after being kidnapped from Victoria and driven to New South Wales in the boot of a car'. ('Kidnapped, raped and locked in a cupboard: woman's 600km ordeal', *The Age*, 5 July 2011)

'A man has been charged after he kidnapped a woman and repeatedly sexually assaulted her'. (*Australian Institute of Family Studies*, 'Reporting on Sexual Assault' Media Backgrounder, www.aifs.gov.au/acssa/media/mbc.html)

Sexual assault is a violent and distressing crime that is often reported in the news media. Women are usually the victims of this crime and men are usually the perpetrators. Textual analyses of sexual assault media coverage consistently find that journalists have a tendency to use passive sentences (the first example) when reporting rape, despite the fact that the active voice (as in the second example) is usually encouraged in journalism training. The quotations above appeared in a set of ethical guidelines for journalists on best practice in reporting sexual assault (Australian Institute of Family Studies, 2014). The authors of those guidelines argued that using the passive voice in reporting sexual violence should be avoided because it had a range of political effects. It may distance the reader from the actions of the perpetrator, and focus undue attention on victims. Furthermore, researchers have also found that when crimes like rape are reported in the passive voice, people's attitudes are affected. They may become '… more negative towards rape victims, more accepting of rape myths and more accepting of physical violence towards women' (Henley et al., 1995: 80).

The above insights come from textual analysis of sexual assault reportage. They illuminate how language shapes the representation of social reality in powerful ways. Textual analysis is a method commonly used in making sense of newspaper articles and other language-based sources of information. It can also be used to scrutinize sources as diverse as blogs, social media sites, recipe books and medical textbooks. These are all sources that lend themselves to consideration of how various aspects of social life are represented, and the political or social effects of such representation. This chapter provides an overview of qualitative approaches to thematic and discourse analysis, methods which are commonly used in studying texts. Although visual materials such as photographs and films can also be analyzed as texts, the emphasis here is on written rather than visual texts. We provide case studies of how thematic and discourse analytic approaches to textual analysis can be used, and outline some sampling, data collection and analysis techniques.

THEMATIC AND DISCOURSE ANALYSIS: SIMILARITIES AND DIFFERENCES

Textual analysis is an umbrella term for a range of different approaches to the study of texts. Three popular qualitative approaches are thematic or qualitative content analysis, discourse analysis and critical discourse analysis (CDA). Broadly speaking, thematic analysis is consistent with some post-positivist and constructivist assumptions, depending on how it is used. Discourse analysis aligns with constructivism, and critical discourse analysis with criticalist approaches to qualitative research. All approaches are in common usage, and the method used will depend partly on the logic and values integral to your research question.

Thematic analysis

Thematic analysis focuses primarily on the content of texts, assuming there is a relationship between textual representations and the social reality beyond the text. An example of this approach is Mary Holmes's study of manners in online social media communications. Holmes (2011) was interested in developing norms about dilemmas of etiquette in online communications ('netiquette') and how these related to friendship norms more broadly. She conducted a thematic content analysis of websites giving advice about how to behave when using Facebook. Her assumption was that through analyzing websites devoted to netiquette we can learn something about how norms about the 'rules of engagement' for online friendships are similar to or different from those that guide the conduct of friendships offline. Holmes found that while etiquette websites offered competing advice when it came to appropriate behaviour regarding 'friending' and 'defriending', they all emphasized the importance of emotional self-awareness when peers, colleagues, bosses and family members may be included as Facebook friends. The blogs also revealed the perception that the emotional consequences of severing online ties through 'defriending' could be serious and needed to be done in a way that avoided overt rudeness or nastiness.

Discourse analysis

Discourse analytic approaches draw attention to the more formal or structural elements of language use in texts, and how these construct particular versions of social reality. Consider the difference, for instance, between the concepts of 'shyness' and 'social anxiety'. Although these concepts potentially describe similar behaviours, we could say they belong to different discourses or ways of constructing and categorizing the concept of a social inhibition. Social anxiety is an explicitly medicalized term. It puts social inhibitions into a category of psychological problem or abnormality that potentially has a treatment or cure that can be applied. Shyness, by contrast, belongs to a less value-laden discourse of personality traits, without the medicalized implication of abnormality.

There are numerous ways to conduct a discourse analysis. In broad terms, it varies from thematic analysis in the sense that greater attention is paid to the form of the text than the content, and to what is performed or accomplished by using language in a particular way. Discourse analysis also pays close attention to the assumptions underlying what is said or written and the worldview this is consistent with, as in the shyness/social anxiety example above. This aligns with the constructivist insight that language does not merely reflect and describe phenomena, but actively constructs them.

One area of social inquiry in which discourse analysis is popular is science and technology studies because it enables exploration of the assumptions that underpin the so-called value-free scientific method. Anthropologist Emily Martin (1991) conducted a very famous discourse analytic study of medical textbooks and concluded that these were not objective or value-free. She found that they portrayed male and female reproductive physiology in a way that drew heavily on sex stereotypes, and casted female reproductive processes in a more negative light. For instance, Martin found that menstruation was described in language emphasizing waste and shedding, although this language was rarely applied to the millions of sperm men produce and never 'use'.

The ovum was persistently portrayed as passive in that it was described as 'drifting' or 'being swept' along the fallopian tubes, in comparison to the active, frenetic language used to describe the behaviour of sperm. Martin contended that far from being accurate depictions of how sperm and ova actually behave, these descriptions could equally constitute social constructions of gamete behaviour based on gendered assumptions. Her research raised the prospect that these a priori constructions may influence how doctors and medical scientists view gamete behaviour and reproductive processes and what they see when they look at microscopic cells.

More recently, sociologists have used discourse analysis to illuminate how stem cell research agendas are represented as distinct from those research agendas that could pave the way for human reproductive cloning, even though both kinds of research may involve similar and controversial processes such as the manipulation and destruction of human and animal embryos. Petersen (2001) analyzes the term 'therapeutic' cloning in the genetic science research literature, to refer to stem cell research agendas that could in future lead to cures for many life-threatening and chronic diseases. The term 'therapeutic', used in this context, implies that the research is equivalent to therapy or treatment, when in reality the procedures are still highly experimental. He argues that the effect of language here is to downplay the potential risks associated with experimental medical procedures, and separate purported 'good' uses of science from the 'bad' agenda of reproductive cloning. One consequence of this is to detract attention from asking ethical or political questions about the 'good' science agendas, which may also be based on ethically questionable techniques.

Critical discourse analysis

Critical discourse analysis (CDA) is also an approach concerned with the manner in which language constructs particular versions of social reality, yet CDA goes further in its attention to the power dynamics of language and the social interests it serves. CDA, in contrast with other discourse analytic approaches, seeks to capture the relationship between language, power and ideology. Although there is a range of different approaches, in common is a focus on how power relations are exercised through textual representation (Machin and Mayr, 2012). Analysts working in this tradition usually openly declare their political allegiances, and see themselves as performing political activism or advocacy through their research endeavours. Critical discourse analysts typically scrutinize sources such as political speeches and documents, news media texts, or advertisements, with a view to exposing the ideological strategies underpinning language use in these texts. In Van Dijk's formulation, the goal of CDA is to 'understand, expose and ultimately resist social inequality' (2001: 352) as it is enacted through language use. Underpinned by a criticalist perspective, it is widely used by researchers interested in intervening in the political effects of media representations of race, ethnicity and migration, and is also popular among feminist researchers concerned with issues such as violence against women.

Mowat (2013) conducted a critical discourse analysis of media representations of the SlutWalk anti-sexual assault rally in order to find out how the media engaged with the feminist aims and politics of this form of social protest. In the global SlutWalk protests, women dress in 'slutty' or scanty attire as a form of activism. The SlutWalk social movement arose in response to a Canadian police officer's remark that women should avoid dressing like sluts in order to avoid rape. Mowat found that a discourse of personal responsibility that held victims individually accountable for the sexual violence inflicted on them underpinned much of the discussion of sexual assault generated by news coverage of the SlutWalk, along with a tendency to distance the movement from its feminist aims and objectives. Media coverage of the SlutWalk thus replicated many of the concerns that had led to the formation of the protest march in the first instance. Another feature of the coverage was to pit older feminists against younger feminists, and thus portray feminist politics as divisive and conflictual. Few articles provided information to contextualize the controversial dress of the marchers, and instead trivialized their 'raunchy' attire.

LOCATING AND SAMPLING TEXTS

Using textual sources can have a number of advantages and disadvantages for social researchers. Texts can often be sourced at the researcher's convenience, which can save large amounts of money or time. Unlike people, texts do not need to be recruited to research studies. They are never too busy to take part in an interview and they don't withdraw from a focus group due to illness. That said, finding the right kinds of texts for your study can be time-consuming and require perseverance, depending on the research questions guiding your study. Another drawback of this kind of source material is that it is not specifically tailored to your research questions. For instance, archival material such as letters and diaries may have systematic gaps that distort the historical record. This means researchers sometimes have to make do with what they find rather than use data that are ideal for the study.

Good source material for thematic or discourse analyses can be tracked down inexpensively. Old textbooks, newspapers, magazines, children's storybooks or recipe books can usually be located in free or low cost public or university library collections. Access to global news media, and other digital media sources, is now made easy through library-based 'one stop shop' online databases such as Factiva and Lexis-Nexis simply by searching on relevant key words. Blogs, or online web journals, can be found through the usual web-searching techniques, as well as via use of blog-specific Internet search engines such as Google Blog Search or Technorati. Postings to social media sites such as Facebook and Twitter also lend themselves to textual analysis, and browser plugins are freely available on the Internet which can help download various types of online data for analysis.

Box 10.1

Sampling for textual analysis

Sampling is a key consideration in studies based on textual analysis, and many of the considerations about rigour and generalizability discussed in Chapter 5 on sampling apply here. Textual analyses will generate at least four sampling questions:

1. Which sources will provide the material I need to answer my research questions?
2. How many of these will I need?
3. Within each source, which textual elements will be relevant to my study?
4. What timeframe or criteria is the basis for inclusion and what is the rationale for this?

How researchers make decisions about these questions will depend on the nature of the source, the demands of their research questions and feasibility, or the time, financial and human resources they have at their disposal.

For instance, Mowat (2013) was interested in how the mainstream Australian news media depicted contemporary feminist activism, and reasoned that the SlutWalk march was a good case study of such activism. This led to a decision to use newspaper articles discussing the SlutWalk as the data source. Through searching the Factiva database on the keyword 'Slutwalk' she gained access to 64 Australian newspaper articles that mentioned the march. Some of these were 'straight' news articles that were more objective in tone, and others were 'opinion pieces' in which the journalist or commentator who wrote the article was openly advocating a particular point of view. She decided to include both types of story in the analysis. Although it could be argued that opinion pieces lend themselves more to a discourse analysis because they could be expected to be more overtly ideological than 'straight' news reporting, Mowat reasoned that both kinds of articles were suitable. Previous research had established that 'straight' news reporting could be influenced by the political proclivities of the newspaper owners and editorial policy. The timeframe for selection of articles was not as critical for this study, given that it was feasible to analyze the entire population of Australian news media articles that the researchers found. The first SlutWalk march occurred in Australia in 2011 and there is only one march each year. As media coverage of the event was most intensive in the days immediately following the march, there was not a huge volume of material to select from. The only articles discarded were duplicates, or because the mention of the SlutWalk was too brief to be of analytic value.

Locating and sampling blogs

Blogs are becoming a popular online source for textual analysis because they are easily accessible and often conversational in tone, offering a source of everyday, naturalistic, 'commonsense' debate and dialogue. They are episodic, they may report on routine, often mundane events, and they can provide a way into the views, beliefs and experiences of their authors. They often take the form of regularly updated posts by a single author, which are then archived in reverse chronological order. Blogs generally have a feedback function that enables their followers to comment on posts, and these comments can also be a good source of data. There are many different genres of blogs in existence – for instance, those devoted to health, cookery, crafting and other 'lifestyle' issues, or news and current affairs-related themes. As Hookway (2008) notes, blogs originated as online personal diaries that provided a forum for individual bloggers to express their opinion and engage an audience. More recently, blogs have assumed some of the functions of the news media, and news media outlets will often use them as a way of encouraging public engagement. Many blogs also incorporate discussion forums, and posts to these forums are analogous to the 'letters to the editor' section of newspapers (Fozdar and Pedersen, 2013).

Sampling blogs can be relatively straightforward or difficult and time-consuming, depending on what you are looking for and the demands of your research question (see Hookway, 2008; Snee, 2010). Some research based on blog data uses a single blog as a case study, with online comments by blog audience members as the main data source. Conversely, some researchers require a larger sample of whole blogs in order to answer their research questions and only know which ones to use after painstaking and time-consuming work. Studies conducted by Fozdar and Pedersen (2013) and Hookway (2008) exemplify these two extremes, and the extent to which the blog sampling process very much depends on the demands of the research question.

Fozdar and Pedersen (2013) were interested in the extent to which blogs provide a forum for the expression and challenging of racist views, as opposed to a forum in which like-minded racists or anti-racists are simply affirmed in their views by people who agree with them. In order to explore this question they chose a single blog devoted to the discussion of asylum-seeker issues, on which the blog owner had posted newspaper articles about arrivals of asylum-seekers by boat. The blog owner allowed people to comment on postings. Due to the authors' interest in the debate generated by asylum-seeker arrivals, they chose to use a single case study to follow one debate in depth. The commentary on a single newspaper article posted to the blog they chose served as their main data source. It comprised 55 comments from members of the blog's audience, in response to this single blog post. From this group of comments, they were able to learn that there was a dialogue between those with pro-asylum-seeker and those with anti-asylum-seeker views. They also found evidence that a range of anti-racism strategies were being mobilized by the pro-asylum-seeker group.

Nicholas Hookway (2008) researched how Australians experienced morality in their everyday lives, particularly with regard to ideas about what it meant to live a 'good life' and how this related to the process of everyday moral decision making. To explore this topic online he required a sample of blogs written by Australian, single authors in a diary-like format. The blogs needed to contain posts that dealt with questions of morality and selfhood. Hookway described the painstaking and deliberative search process he embarked on in order to find his sample of blogs. Some blog-hosting sites do not have search engines, and most do not enable searching on common sociological descriptors such as age, gender and location. Hookway chose the blog content management service LiveJournal because it had a search engine, and appeared to host the kind of blogs he was looking for. He found he needed to trawl through the content and archives of each individual blog to discover whether it had suitable material, and this was a process that required many hours of work for each blog. To supplement this process and save time, Hookway eventually decided to post an advertisement on the LiveJournal Community page. This enabled him to find bloggers who identified their blogs as concerned with morality issues, rather than have to find the blogs himself.

As can be seen from these examples, sampling textual sources requires imagination, perseverance, and the exercise of judgement. Quantitative sampling techniques may be appropriate despite the fact that the main research approach is qualitative. Sampling decisions will depend on the amount of material available, and the demands of the research question.

DOING A THEMATIC ANALYSIS

Conducting a thematic or qualitative content analysis using texts such as newspaper articles or blogs is similar to the thematic analysis of interview or focus group data. We would emphasize that it is a conceptual process as much as a question of applying straightforward rules and techniques. The written source material needs to be coded, or read closely for meaning, and then categorized into thematically relevant 'chunks'. This may be done by pen or pencil on printed-out transcripts, or with the help of a computer-assisted qualitative data analysis program (CAQDAS) (see Chapter 12 for more details). Typically, texts are read and re-read several times to refine a coding scheme that works conceptually across all the data collected and progresses the analysis. When coding, researchers will typically begin with a large number of categories that are reduced as the coding process continues. Ultimately, a small number of themes will be generated which are then used to build an argument or a plausible answer to the research questions. Codes may reflect content that is manifest or latent in the text. A code based on manifest content is quite descriptive or literal and constitutes an 'at face value' reading of the data. Codes based on latent content are at a deeper level of interpretation and more closely related to the theoretical framing of the research question and/or move the researcher closer to answering the research question.

Recall Mary Holmes's interest in Facebook etiquette discussions as a case study of contemporary friendship norms. Holmes grouped the reporting of her data on etiquette under several main themes related to emotions and friendship. The discussion of these themes helped her build the following argument: online discussions of etiquette demonstrate that there is some uncertainty about the degree of emotional closeness appropriate to friendship these days, particularly when status differences exist between the people concerned, yet they largely reinstate the egalitarian principles applied to offline friendships.

Table 10.1 provides a visual representation and simplified version of how Holmes may have approached the coding and analysis of her data. Typically, analysis builds from an initial phase of coding the material into descriptive and latent codes, working towards a more concise set of themes. Codes tend to start out quite descriptive and then become more analytical as the analysis proceeds. For instance, it is possible to conceptualize the three segments of text provided in the first column of Table 10.1 as different kinds of pre-occupations with the norms of offline friendship and online Facebook communications. However, this conceptual linkage may not 'gel' until the researcher has read through many texts and become familiar with the data over time. It is quite common for coding to begin as quite descriptive on the first reading, as in the second column of Table 10.1, working towards a reduced number of themes that refine the analysis as more and more of the textual material is read and thought about in relation to the research question. The goal in this process of coding and theme generation is to find explanations that will shed light on the research questions (see Chapter 12 for more detail).

Table 10.1 From codes to themes

Text	Descriptive code	Possible sub-theme relating to hierarchies	Main theme relating to friendship norms
There should be fundamentally no difference between what you would do online and offline ... remember you are talking to real people with real feelings	Etiquette *vis-à-vis* online and offline behaviour	Online and offline behaviour rules	Manners online largely reinforce egalitarian principles of friendship offline and respect hierarchies that exist in the 'offline' world
I only accept people I know ... my students are split on this point with more and more leaning to taking no strangers	Friending behaviour	Divergences of opinion *vis-à-vis* hierarchy and online relationships	
I wouldn't dream of using **profanity in jest** on LinkedIn	Different platforms demand different behaviour	Work/professional relationships demand greater emotional distance	

Thematic analysis focuses on the content and meaning generated in the text, with the researcher grouping and reducing content and meaning in ways that will shed light on the research question.

DOING A DISCOURSE ANALYSIS

Discourse analysis, unlike thematic analysis, requires a focus on what and how things are said or written. As in thematic analysis, the methods used should be thought of as a conceptual toolkit rather than a way of stringently applying rigid techniques. As with good thematic analysis, discourse analysis begins with a close reading of the textual material. Becoming familiar with the data through reading and re-reading is key.

In a discourse analytic approach, the researcher is very attentive to issues such as sentence construction and the effect that this has on meaning as well as the kinds of imagery used in the text. Instead of using a process of interpreting meaning though coding, as described above, the researcher's attention will be more focused on words, phrases and grammatical features of the text, and how these interrelate to shed light on the research questions. Depending on the topic, the analysis proceeds guided by some or all of the following questions:

1. What view of the world or the situation is taken for granted in the text? How could this be different?
2. *Metaphors/imagery*: What are the recurring metaphors or imagery invoked in describing the phenomenon in question, and how do these contribute to representing the issue in a particular way?
3. *Tone*: Is the tone positive or negative, judgemental or neutral, and what are the consequences of this?
4. Are there recurrent words or phrases and what do these suggest about how the phenomenon is commonly understood? Are there other ways in which we could think about it?
5. What is being accomplished or enacted through the language use in the texts and how does this relate to power and resistance? For example, how are active and passive sentence constructions used and what is the effect of this?

Question 5 is particularly relevant to researchers working in the critical discourse analysis tradition who explicitly look for how power and resistance to dominant discourses are constructed and enacted through language use in texts.

CONCLUSION

We can learn a great deal about social processes, interactions and the power of representation through research methods that do not rely on researchers generating the raw material. Using traditional hard copy sources such as books, newspapers and magazines, as well as online sources such as blogs, textual analysis is often a feasible and low-cost alternative to research with human participants. At the same time, a major disadvantage of working with data that already exist is that these have not been specifically tailored for the research questions and systematic gaps may exist. Textual analysis includes thematic and discourse analytic approaches. Research questions that lend themselves to these methods tend to be concerned with explicating the assumptions and power dynamics of representation.

Going further

Australian Policy Online, http://apo.org.au (Australian Policy Online is a not-for-profit research database).

This comprehensive document archive is a great source of material suitable for textual analysis, particularly policy documents.

Gee, J.P. (2014) *An Introduction to Discourse Analysis: Theory and Method* (4th edition). London: Routledge.

This is a very accessible discussion of discourse analysis that provides a range of worked examples for the beginner.

Hookway, N. (2008) 'Entering the blogosphere: some strategies for using blogs in social research', *Qualitative Research*, 8 (1): 91-113.

This is one of the earliest comprehensive discussions of locating and sampling blogs to use in social research. It is still very useful in its attention to detail.

Snee, H. (2010) 'Using blog analysis', Realities Toolkit # 10, Morgan Centre, University of Manchester. Available at http://eprints.ncrm.ac.uk/1321/2/10-toolkit-blog-analysis.pdf (last accessed 19 September 2014).

This is a very practical guide to using blogs in social research. It discusses how to prepare and organize blogs for analysis.

Wodak, R. and Chilton, P. (eds) (2005) *A New Agenda in (Critical) Discourse Analysis*. Amsterdam: John Benjamins.

This interdisciplinary collection considers how critical discourse analysis is useful in various policy settings and contexts. This is more of a discussion of innovative projects or settings in which CDA can be applied than a 'how to' text.

DOING THE RESEARCH

THE RESEARCHER ASKS THE PARTICIPANTS TO PROVIDE THEIR OWN ACCOUNTS

ELEVEN
Narrative inquiry

CONTENTS

- Life history, personal narratives and autoethnography — 145
    - Life history — 145
    - Personal narrative — 145
    - Autoethnography — 146
- Using narrative research — 147
- Eliciting narratives — 148
    - Interview-based techniques — 148
    - Participant-controlled techniques — 149
- Analyzing life history and personal narratives — 150
    - Analyzing life history interviews — 150
    - Analyzing personal narratives — 152
- Evaluating narrative inquiry — 153
- Conclusion — 154
- Going further — 155

The most momentous act in the life of any lesbian or gay person is when they proclaim their gayness – to self, to other, to community. Whilst men and women have been coming out for over a hundred years, it is only since the 1970s that the stories have gone very public. (Plummer, 1995: 82)

> I'm worried that coming out positions non-White and transnational queerness as mere façade ... I mean, I haven't come out to my Asian family not because I'm afraid to but because we don't have a language for it. And yet, my partner and I are fully embraced. I've come out to my White side and they reject my queer-ness in total ... These stories can only be known when told and processed concurrently; never alone and never separate. (LeMaster, 2014: 51)

Many same-sex attracted adults and young people will have a 'coming out' story that they will tell at various times in their life to various audiences. It is a story about what it's like to come to the realization that you are gay, lesbian, bisexual or otherwise queer, claim an identity that sets you apart from the heterosexual majority, and tell others that you are same-sex attracted. Plummer (1995) analyzed coming out stories and found that despite differences in the detail of such stories from one individual to another, there were often strong similarities in the plot, genre and chronology of the stories told. In doing so, Plummer has drawn our attention to the cultural and social dimension of these stories. He calls the coming out story a 'late modernist tale' and 'a story of its time' that tells us not just about individual experience of same-sex desire and identity, but also about how homosexuality can be understood at this historical moment. LeMaster's (2014) autoethnographic variation on the genre utilizes a multi-vocal telling of the tale, and indicates that times are changing for the coming out story. In simultaneously narrating the story of his white family's open rejection of his homosexuality, alongside that of his Taiwanese family's unspoken acceptance, he attempts to give voice to the complexity of contemporary queer experience. He problematizes a unified, singular experience of sexual or racialized identity or coming out.

The coming out story is just one example of how people make sense of their lives through the stories they tell, hence the importance of narrative inquiry. Narrative inquiry is used in a range of interdisciplinary research settings, and can effectively be put to use where there is an opportunity to turn storytelling into a research strategy. Riessman (1993: 3) usefully defines narratives as '... talk organized around consequential events'. Through narrative we can explore issues of identity, loss, illness, suffering, healing, endurance and triumph over adversity, to name just a few of the big themes that loom large in the interdisciplinary research informed by this approach.

In this chapter, we examine narrative inquiry holistically with an emphasis on the design and execution demands of the approach. Obtaining stories in a form that lends itself to narrative inquiry is critical to successful research in this tradition. Although there are many different approaches, in common is an analytic focus on the structure as well as the content of the story told, and/or the importance of locating the individual story in a broader socio-cultural perspective. We discuss three popular approaches to narrative inquiry – life history, personal narratives and autoethnography – through recent and classic case studies drawn from interdisciplinary research settings. We also explain the ways in which researchers elicit stories suitable for narrative inquiry and some approaches to the analysis of narratives. In the final section of the chapter we consider ways in which narrative inquiry can be evaluated.

LIFE HISTORY, PERSONAL NARRATIVES AND AUTOETHNOGRAPHY

There is some debate about the differences between life history, personal narrative and autoethnography. For instance, some researchers, such as Squires (2008), regard life history as a form of personal narrative inquiry. We believe there is value in making some broad distinctions between these three approaches.

Life history

Life history research emphasizes the importance of understanding individual stories in context. There is an attempt to elicit a person's story in light of the social and historical contexts and experiences that have shaped the life lived and the story told about it (Dowsett, 1996; Stein, 1997; Plummer, 2001; Dempsey, 2006). Researchers working in this tradition will often draw on other sources of data, such as historical archives, to complement their analysis of individual stories. For instance, Arlene Stein's *Sex and Sensibility* (1997) documents lesbian identity among two generational cohorts of women – 'baby boomers' and 'Generation X' – who lived in the San Francisco Bay area of California. Stein, a sociologist, gathered what she calls 'self-stories' of the 'lives and loves' of lesbian-identified women. She assumed that the era in which the women were born would to some extent influence how they experienced their lesbian identities and made sense of their lives. In order to situate women's stories in an historical context, Stein interspersed her narration with material gleaned from articles in influential lesbian feminist publications of the time. Through analysis of the women's contextualized stories, Stein provided a vivid account of how feminism and the politics of the Women's Liberation Movement, and the subsequent 'decentring' of this movement, had been key influences on the development of lesbian identities.

Personal narrative

Personal narrative inquiry, by contrast, is more concerned with the story as a text with a structure and meaning. There is an emphasis on the formal elements of the story being told, and the cultural conventions on which the broader narrative, as opposed to the individual story, is based. Frank (2013) distinguishes between stories and narratives. Whereas stories are told by individuals, each individual story can only draw on a limited range of narrative tools which are culturally and historically specific. Researchers may be attentive to the plot, or the key 'moments' and occurrences in the story; the genre of the story (e.g. comedy, tragedy, thriller or adventure); and the chronology or timeline of the events.

For instance, in *The Wounded Storyteller* (2013), Frank proposed that all stories about illness were created with reference to three broader cultural narratives: chaos, restitution and quest. In restitution narratives, illness is seen as transitory. In terms of the narrative, 'It is a response to an interruption, but the narrative itself is above interruption' (Frank,

2013: 89). It is all about the body returning to its former image of itself, before illness. The illness has been managed, with the body likened to a car that had broken down and been repaired. Chaos narratives represent the opposite of restitution. They imagine life never getting better and the person speaks without self-reflection and without narration. In this sense they constituted, for Frank, anti-narratives. Quest narratives talk about what it's like to be in pain and share a person's hopes and fears, their sense (or lack of sense) about the meaning of suffering and the possibility of death. Frank (2010) argued that naming types of narrative was very useful for sick people as it could help them think about what kind of story they were telling as opposed to what kind of story they would have liked to tell about their illness. Stories told by the ill offer clues to prognoses and recoveries because they manifest qualities like despair, hope or a sense of personal power in the face of illness.

Psychologist Maggie Kirkman (2001) used a personal narrative approach in order to study infertility from the perspective of infertile women. Kirkman interviewed 31 Australian women who had had fertility problems, 12 of whom subsequently became mothers through use of either IVF or adoption or without medical intervention. From interviews Kirkman compiled chronological narratives that explained each woman's story of infertility. In analyzing these narratives she found that women likened their experiences of infertility to a quest, just as medieval quest narratives 'told of a knight undertaking an adventure to achieve a goal' and 'endured a time of trial to show himself worthy of achieving that goal' (Kirkman, 2001: 83). Kirkman's study explored various ways in which infertility can be likened to a quest, and found evidence that women often regarded the use of assisted reproductive technology as a necessary trial of courage and endurance, whether or not it ultimately resulted in the birth of a child. Her use of narrative inquiry was able to illuminate the meaning of children to infertile women, the difference between their narratives and those of radical feminist scholars who criticize reproductive technologies, and why women persist with fertility treatment, often against the odds of it being successful.

Autoethnography

Autoethnography, in contrast to life history and personal narrative, explicitly breaches the traditional division between researchers and the researched. Typically, the researcher studies their own biography as part of the research process, and is attentive to how emotions and personal experiences can illuminate the research questions. In autoethnography it is difficult to separate out the elicitation of the story from the analysis and writing process. In the words of Ellis et al. (2011: 2), it is an approach that 'acknowledges and accommodates subjectivity, emotionality and the researcher's influence on research, rather than hiding from these matters or assuming they don't exist'. In autoethnography, the storyteller is also an interpreter of the story.

For instance, in Jackie Liggins and colleagues' (2013) research into the healing capacities of an acute care mental health setting in New Zealand, the telling of Liggins' own story as a previous in-patient of an acute care mental health facility was critical to the study. Her experiences were narrated as part of the research process in order to reflect on her 'multiple roles as a compassionate observer, service-user and mental health professional' (2013: 105) and in order to develop unique insights into the acute care therapeutic landscape. Liggins' reflections on her own story were italicized in the text and represented as diary entries that explored what it was like for her to recover from a mental illness while institutionalized. These experiences were contrasted with her work experiences as a psychiatrist. The autobiographical reflections were interspersed with more 'objective' passages of text and analysis characteristic of conventional scientific writing. The stated goal of this approach is to encourage the reader to engage with the experience of mental illness and understand its complexity in a more meaningful way than is possible through a positivist approach to medical research.

It is important to keep in mind that these three approaches to narrative inquiry are not always mutually exclusive, and researchers can combine different elements in the one study. For instance, Kirkman's study of personal narratives is also a partial autoethnography. Kirkman had also experienced infertility and included herself as a participant in her study. Arlene Stein's life history method also incorporated elements of a personal narrative inquiry, in that the structure of her participants' coming out stories was an important focus, as well as the social and historical context of feminist activism.

USING NARRATIVE RESEARCH

Narrative research is generally agreed to be underpinned by constructivist assumptions, in that stories require an audience and their creation constitutes a social, interactive process (see Riessman, 1993; Plummer, 2001; Holstein and Gubrium, 2012). As Joyce (2013: 3) points out, these require 'a listener, a reader, a spectator (even where that audience might be the self, such as in the act of writing a diary)'. Stories constitute a co-creation by the researcher and the researched. They must be elicited and transformed into a format that makes them useable. The elements or components of storytelling can never be entirely creative: we all have limited repertoires of storytelling tools available as a consequence of our positioning in particular narrative cultures and social contexts. Frank (2010: 5) reminds us that stories always pose the question of what kind of truth is being told, but they are less successful at conclusively answering it: '… their work is to remind us that we have to live with complicated truths'.

Despite the above, and as Plummer (2001: 3) notes, life history as a biographical method has been criticized on the grounds of 'naïve realism', or the idea that stories provide a direct window onto research participants' experiences. It is true to say that post-positivist assumptions underpin some approaches to narrative inquiry, for example the biographic-narrative interpretive method, as outlined by Chamberlayne et al. (2002) in the UK. These researchers clearly state that they expect a story of an objective 'lived life' that can be corroborated under some circumstances (for example, by newspaper accounts or birth records), and a 'told story' that details meanings specific to the narrator. In this approach, post-positivist assumptions about the nature of the reality that can be found in stories co-exist with a more constructivist set of assumptions about storytelling (see also Dowsett, 1996; Plummer, 2001). It is important to keep in mind when using narrative approaches that stories can tell the researcher how participants see the world and what an experience was like from their point of view. Sometimes key events and experiences mentioned in the story have a documented basis in objective reality. However, stories cannot provide direct access to an indisputable 'truth' about reality or what happened. This is not the same as saying stories are lies or that storytellers' version of events can never be trusted.

ELICITING NARRATIVES

> Precisely because they are essential meaning-making structures, narratives must be preserved, not fractured by investigators, who must respect respondents' ways of constructing meaning and analyze how it is accomplished. (Riessman, 1993: 4)

Not all interview material is suitable for narrative inquiry. The interview data must take the form of a story, and it is difficult to create stories out of interview material that fits a conventional turn-taking question-and-answer approach. Short answers by a participant broken up by numerous interviewer questions do not lend themselves well to narrative analysis. At the research design stage of projects, it is necessary to think about how stories will be elicited. Stories suitable for narrative analysis can be generated entirely by the storyteller or they can be created through an interview process. Each approach rests on different assumptions about how, and the extent to which, the storytelling is an interactive process. We consider both approaches below.

Interview-based techniques

Personal narrative, life history and autoethnography interviews are typically longer than those used in other kinds of research, in order to capture sufficient richness and detail in the story. They are commonly at least one to several hours in length, with researchers interviewing the same participant multiple times. Squires (2008) gives a number of reasons why multiple interviews are often preferred by narrative inquiry researchers. They may be useful for a chronological follow-up, to check facts obtained in earlier interviews, to explore highly emotional issues in a sensitive way over time, to follow up on interesting phrases or omissions in earlier interviews that were insufficiently explored, or to give interviewees more control over the materials. Some interviewers may present the transcript of the initial interview to participants, and enable them to check or revise the story provided initially before moving on.

When life history or personal narrative inquiry is based on interviews, the interviewer acts as a guide who encourages the telling of the story (Kirkman, 1999; Plummer, 2001; Riessman, 2008). In this kind of interviewing, there is no strict interview schedule as such, although a very minimal series of prompts may be created. Researchers use open-ended questions that are worded in such a way that they will elicit a story in response. For example, Maggie Kirkman (1999) began each of her interviews with infertile women by asking 'Can you tell me the story of your infertility?' Riessman (2008) suggests ongoing gentle guidance to keep the storyteller on track and to encourage sufficient detail about important elements of the story, such as the timeline or chronology of events, and the relative significance of events in the story (e.g. What happened next? Can you remember a time when … ? Why do you think you remember that particular moment?). Photos may also be used as prompts to elicit storytelling, possibly those taken by the participants themselves.

Team-based autoethnographies can be based on interviews. For instance, Ellis et al. (1997) conducted an autoethnographic study of bulimia experiences. They called their process 'interactive interviewing' because it involved the three of them engaging in and recording emotional conversations about their personal experiences of bulimia and their opinions and feelings about cultural constructions of food consumption and women's bodies.

Participant-controlled techniques

Some researchers prefer not to use interviews to elicit life histories or personal narratives because they want to empower participants to generate stories on their own terms. For example, Yvonne Joyce's (2013) research on low-income single mothers returning to higher education aimed to find out 'How might disadvantaged single mothers embody or resist popular stories of single motherhood? What other narratives might inform their identities and help them make sense of their lives?' Joyce described her research method as 'self-recorded life narratives', and prefaced her discussion of method with the observation that single motherhood constituted a much-maligned identity, given single mothers were often viewed as undesirable and a social threat (that is, welfare cheats or a drain on taxpayers). Implicit in her research strategy was the desire to help participants find their own voice and speak their own stories about single motherhood into existence. For Joyce, this gave them as much control as possible in the research process, and might, in and of itself, constitute a transformative process. The method involved providing research participants with digital recorders for a two-week period so they could record themselves telling their life stories. Prior to the period of recording the stories, she provided some prompts to the participants to assist them to reflect on their experiences of higher education and single motherhood.

In autoethnography, it is also common for researchers as participants to tell their own story, either as sole researchers or part of a larger team. Ellis (2007) describes the process of conducting an autoethnographic study on the constraints to choice in abortion decision making, in which she and her partner Art Bochner, as co-researchers, wrote a script about their experience of an unwanted pregnancy. Two months after Ellis had had an abortion, she and Bochner separately wrote stories about their individual reactions to the experience. After these stories were written, the couple read each other's stories, discussed them, and then wrote a second version that was a negotiated co-construction of their joint experiences. Ellis (2007) comments that this process enabled them to explore emotional trauma without the fear of losing control over their stories to another researcher, or doing harm to vulnerable participants. She also wanted the story to help others going through a similar experience. To use Ellis's words, '… we wanted our work to reflect the human side of the lived experience of abortion – the meanings, feelings, contradictions and ambivalences embodied by the experience of choice' (2007: 22).

ANALYZING LIFE HISTORY AND PERSONAL NARRATIVES

Analysis of life history and personal narrative data can be more labour-intensive than other approaches to qualitative analysis. This is because people rarely tell their stories in a neat, linear fashion, and researchers may need to do considerable work in turning the stories collected into a form suitable for narrative analysis. One key difference between the analysis of narratives and other kinds of qualitative data is that it occurs within each story, as well as across a collection of stories. When narrative analysis is done using interview data, researchers will also need to produce written narratives from interview transcripts (see Chapter 12 for a longer discussion of transcription techniques and issues).

Analyzing life history interviews

One way to analyze life history interviews is to write thematized biographies or 'case histories' based on the interview transcripts. This enables interviews to be analyzed holistically and cross-sectionally. A holistic sense of each person's story in relation to the research topic can be created, as well as a means to compare individual stories to each other. Thematized case histories are created from close readings of the interview transcripts. Researchers can also incorporate other sources of data into these in order to situate the individual biography in a broader social and historical context.

Deb Dempsey (2006) conducted a life history-based study of family formation in an Australian queer community. She investigated how lesbian, gay and bisexual women and men cooperated and negotiated family formation using assisted reproductive technologies, and the meanings of family and relatedness that informed their decision making. She described her analysis process as follows:

> Several hard copies were made of each de-identified interview transcript. Transcripts were read closely for pre-determined and newly occurring themes, imagery, 'stand-out' words and phrases in an individual's biography. Extensive notes were scrawled in the wide margins. A comprehensive case history of each interview was then written, structured around a short biography of the participant, the themes that informed the initial interview schedule and emergent themes from the ongoing interviewing and analysis. The case histories were in the vicinity of 5,000 words in length. The early case histories were re-worked a number of times throughout the research process as themes that seemed important early on faded into insignificance with subsequent interviewing, reading, thinking and writing. (Dempsey, 2006: 97)

This is a complex, iterative process of analysis (see also Dowsett, 1996), which begins with the transcript, and then goes back and forth from this to the relevant literature as in most forms of qualitative analysis. Initial readings of the transcripts generate a list of themes, which are used to structure the case histories, keeping in mind the larger goal of answering the research questions. The thematized biography begins with a brief summary. Some of Dempsey's organizing themes for the case histories were as follows: meaning of fatherhood or motherhood; negotiations with partner about becoming parents; negotiating the reproductive relationship; meaning of bio-genetic paternity or maternity. Dempsey ended each case history with a section entitled 'significance of this story for the bigger picture' and 'interviews for comparison'. Through this process she could construct the bigger story that she wanted to tell in answer to the research questions.

Box 11.1

Sample partial case history from Dempsey (2006)

Summary

Keith Gower is a 36-year-old gay man who lives alone in an outer Melbourne apartment. He has little to do with his parents, brothers and sisters, all of whom rejected him for a time when he came out in his early twenties. Keith is now well-established in a career as a graphic designer.

It is Keith's intention to fully co-parent with Rowena, a single lesbian of similar age he has been friends with for many years. The two met through their involvement in queer community politics, have shared work networks and a close circle of mutual friends. Rowena and Keith have embarked on baby-making as a fifty/fifty shared commitment, an arrangement Keith feels is unusual for a lesbian and a gay man. Neither of them have a co-resident same-sex partner at the moment and, according to Keith, neither wants a future scenario where 'new sexual partners are more important than each other or the baby'.

Meaning of fatherhood

Fatherhood as a natural desire:

> I don't feel like I'm challenging the status quo or anything. It's just something I've always wanted to do ... It feels very natural. It's hard to describe it, it's like a burning need to fulfill this role as a father and no matter what anyone said to me, I was going to do it.

There was no sense in Keith's story that he saw gay fatherhood as an oxymoron or 'experiment' or as a political act. In the quote above he explains how he experiences his desire to become a father as 'natural' because he feels the desire very strongly.

(Continued)

(Continued)

Negotiating the reproductive relationship

> We put down in writing what we planned to do and what we understood the relationship would be and what we understand the responsibilities to be, the decision making process ... so we've got a base where we can go back to. We even went into the fact that if things should break down, what is the mediation process that we would go through to resolve conflict.

Keith and Rowena have a written agreement outlining the decisions they have made and the process they will follow regarding disputes about their child. Keith feels this is important, although his central emphasis is that the relationship is the contract, rather than the written contract *per se*.

Analyzing personal narratives

There is no standard set of procedures when it comes to doing narrative analysis, and the approach to analysis will to some extent be dependent on the research problem being addressed (Riessman, 1993; Squires, 2008). Much of what we describe in this section is consistent with what Squires (2008: 16) calls 'experience-centred' narratives, which assume four important characteristics:

- Narratives are sequential and meaningful.
- Narratives are definitively human.
- Narratives 're-present' experience, in the sense of reconstituting it.
- Narratives display transformation or change.

In contrast with life history methods, analysis of personal narratives generally emphasizes the form as well as the content of stories as a way to understand the phenomenon of interest. Frank (2013) argues that it is the researcher's task, through the process of analysis, to find or draw out the larger cultural narratives or structures of meaning on which the story is predicated. Some of the formal elements of narratives that can be analyzed include the employment or development of the story over time. For instance, does the story told indicate progress, regress or stability? What are the key 'moments' in the story that shed light on the research question? Riessman (1993) recommends beginning narrative analysis by looking at the overall structure of the text. For instance, how does the narrator organize the story? What do the speaker and the interviewer take for granted in their exchange? What would you expect to be there in the text that is omitted or glossed over? Another formal feature of stories that is of interest is the genre. For instance, is the story heroic, tragic, comic, romantic or satirical in tone, and what are the implications of this for answering the research questions? Does it combine one or more genres?

Narrative inquiry is generally underpinned by the constructivist belief that remembering is never merely an objective rendering of factual events about the past. Narrators tend to recall events in a sequence that has consequences for or sets the scene for events that happen later (see Riessman, 1993). This means that sequences of events in a story can be analyzed for what they assume about the connection of past events to the present and future. For example, in analyzing individual coming out stories, Plummer (1995) identifies common structural elements with regard to chronology, plot details and themes. Plummer also identifies that it is common for coming out stories to have a chronology that begins in early childhood and ends in early or late adulthood with a degree of resolution to the dilemma of sexual difference along the way, often through meeting like-minded others and discovering that one is not alone. Importantly, coming out stories often emphasize childhood gender nonconformity (i.e. feminine interests or appearance for boys, masculine or tomboy demeanour for girls) that in hindsight prefigure sexual identity. Through identifying the different narrative elements in his analysis, Plummer is able to make some observations about the relationship between individual stories and dominant Western cultural narratives about sexuality. One of these is the oft-made connection between gender nonconformity and sexual identities. We know from cross-cultural research into sexual identities and practices that this way of linking sexuality and gender presentation is by no means universal.

Kirkman (1999) gives a detailed account of her process in analyzing infertile women's narratives. As a first step, she read each woman's interview transcript and reconstructed it into a chronological telling of the infertility story. This reordering of the stories into chronological narratives made it easier to compare key plot events and sequences across each woman's narrative, in order to see a pattern of similarities and differences. As explained earlier, a notion of the quest was the main narrative device she detected in the women's stories. At the same time, Kirkman was concerned that this process might lead to some loss or distortion of meaning in the story told by the participants. To alleviate this, she sent each participant a copy of the reorganized narrative 'to check meaning and invite corrections'. Some women wanted to make minor revisions to her version of their story, while others were happy with the narrative she had constructed. When all the narratives were finalized, she sent each participant in the research a booklet that contained all of the revised participant narratives so that they each had access to other women's stories of infertility. The booklet included her own story of infertility, given that she was also a participant in the research.

EVALUATING NARRATIVE INQUIRY

The issue of validity, or the trustworthiness, of narrative inquiry is complex, as Riessman (2008) points out. She argues that two dimensions of validity are important in thinking about narrative research: that of the stories as told by the research participants, and the analysis or the story told by the researcher. Narrative truths cannot be objectively determined. By their very nature, they are partial. For Riessman, validity is always increased when researchers are explicit about their modes of inquiry and how they arrived at a particular analysis. She advises narrative researchers to keep a diary of the decisions and insights they arrive at along the way because this fosters reflexivity or a critical awareness about what was done, how it could have been done differently and the consequences of making certain decisions.

Riessman (2008) also remarks on 'correspondence', 'persuasiveness', 'coherence' and 'pragmatic use' as potentially important dimensions to assessing validity in narrative enquiry. 'Correspondence' refers to whether the narrative events match historical events, which may be important to some historical research. For instance, in the aforementioned life history study by Arlene Stein (1997), the researcher was interested in the history of the Women's Liberation Movement as a meaningful context for the development of lesbian identities, and was able to cross-check between her participants' life stories and archival sources. This criterion is less important for research informed by purely constructivist assumptions. 'Persuasiveness', for Riessman (2008), is enhanced when researchers present their data in ways that indicate they are genuine, and when the analysis presented is reasonable and convincing. This is strengthened, Riessman argues, when the researcher supports their claims with quoted evidence from their participants' narratives, and considers alternative explanations to the one they are putting forward. 'Coherence' is the degree to which a narrative 'hangs together' or makes sense in the context in which it is introduced. This does not mean the degree to which it reflects historical reality. It refers more to whether the narrators' assumptions about the world are articulated or commented upon plausibly in the way the story is told. 'Pragmatic use' relates to whether the researcher's analysis is accepted by the research community as illuminating or trustworthy. If a piece of narrative research is widely cited and becomes the basis for others' work in the future, this indicates it was a persuasive and plausible contribution to knowledge.

Laurel Richardson (2000: 15–16), writing about autoethnography, makes a more explicitly constructivist case for its artistic and emotional qualities as being key to understanding the contribution:

1. *Substantive contribution.* Does the piece contribute to our understanding of social life?
2. *Aesthetic merit.* Does this piece succeed as a piece of writing? Is it artistic in its form, sufficiently complex and interesting to read?
3. *Reflexivity.* Is there enough information about how the author came to write this text? Is it clear how the author's subjectivity has been both a producer and product of this text?
4. *Impact.* Does this affect me emotionally and/or intellectually? Does it generate new questions or move me to act?
5. *Capacity to express lived reality well.* Does the text provide a rich account of lived experience? Autoethnographic manuscripts might include dramatic recall and vivid turns of phrase so as to invite the reader to get emotionally close to the experiences of the author.

CONCLUSION

Narrative inquiry includes life history, personal narrative and autoethnography. It is a useful approach to qualitative research because it assists in making sense of the stories people tell about their lives. There are many research settings in which this can prove invaluable. For instance, in discerning whether a chronically ill person's story conforms to a quest, restitution or chaos narrative, as in Frank's famous (2013) typology in *The Wounded Storyteller*, the ill person can be helped to think about whether the kind of story they are telling is the story they need to tell in order to regain their well-being. We have emphasized throughout this chapter the constructivist nature of narrative inquiry and the importance of recognizing that this approach cannot give access to a singular 'truth' about social reality. This is not to say that 'anything goes' in narrative inquiry. As is the case with other approaches to qualitative analysis, its effectiveness is often a question of the trustworthiness of the research findings, and their capacity to illuminate the social phenomenon in a convincing way.

Going further

Chang, H., Hernandez, K. and Ngunjiri, F. (2012) *Collaborative Autoethnography.* Walnut Creek, CA: Left Coast.

A very practical guide to doing autoethnography in teams. It provides detailed advice on data collection, analysis and writing techniques.

Narrative Inquiry: The Forum for Theoretical, Empirical and Methodological Work on Narrative. Journal available at www.clarku.edu/faculty/mbamberg/narrativeINQ/HTMLPages/Editorial1.htm.

Qualitative research based on narrative methods in such a vast field it has its own interdisciplinary journal. This is a great resource to give you a sense of the richness and scope of narrative inquiry in a range of different research contexts.

Plummer, K. (1995) *Telling Sexual Stories: Power, Change and Social Worlds.* London: Routledge.

A highly readable account of a sociological approach to research based on storytelling. Plummer discusses various genres of sexual storytelling and places them in historical context.

Riessman, C. (2008) *Narrative Methods for the Human Science.* London: Sage.

A good introduction to a range of different approaches to narrative inquiry for the student or experienced researcher who has not worked with narrative methods before.

Stephens, C. (2011) 'Narrative analysis in health psychology research: personal, dialogical and social stories of health', *Health Psychology Review*, 5 (1): 62–78.

Narrative methods are used in many health disciplines and this is a good overview of the different approaches to narrative research in health psychology. The author discusses research topics in health psychology which could benefit from the use of narrative inquiry, and gives examples of using talk, texts, pictures and objects as narrative data.

TWELVE

Making sense: data management, analysis and reporting

CONTENTS

- Data management — 158
  - Setting up computer files — 158
- Keeping data secure and in good working order — 159
  - Transcribing data — 160
  - Ethics and transcription — 162
  - Preparing transcripts for analysis — 163
- Beginning data analysis — 163
- Initial exploration — 165
- Refining your analysis — 167
  - Memos — 168
- Using computer-assisted qualitative data analysis software (CAQDAS) — 168
  - Team-based qualitative data analysis — 172
- Analysis and writing — 172
- Writing theses, reports and articles based on qualitative research — 173
- Conclusion — 175
- Going further — 175

The qualitative analysis process is 'messy'. In many respects, it is an intellectual and creative process rather than a technical one. In this chapter, we consider some general principles and techniques of data management, analysis and writing. These complement our earlier more comprehensive discussions of narrative, discourse and thematic analysis. We consider how to store and manage data to ensure rigour, along with processes for the initial exploration and refining of an analysis. We discuss how computer-assisted qualitative analysis tools can help your analytic approach, along with issues associated with working in teams to analyze data. Finally, we give some brief tips for writing reports and journal articles based on qualitative data.

DATA MANAGEMENT

Qualitative research projects can generate an overwhelming amount of material. You are likely to have numerous computer files, print outs and field notes by the time your data collection is complete. One interview alone will need to be stored in at least three ways over the life of a project: as an audio file, an electronic text or word document, and a hard copy print-out. A printed interview transcript can easily run to thirty or more pages of text. Good data management and storage techniques preserve participant anonymity and confidentiality (where relevant) and for this reason are ethical requirements. They also help to ensure that you are systematic and thorough with data analysis. Deciding on a data management system early will save you time and make it easier to avoid chaos and potentially serious mistakes when analyzing or reporting results.

Setting up computer files

Every project requires a good password protected computer storage system that keeps project files in order and backed up to multiple locations. Unless your project is a thesis or dissertation, there will usually be more than one researcher who needs access to the project files, and even sole researchers will benefit from easy access to their files on different devices from a range of locations. Separate folders for data, administration (recruitment schedules, invoices, etc.), literature and Endnote libraries, research proposals and grant applications, ethics applications (including plain language statements and consent forms) and publications are a good idea, and you can set these up very early in the life of your project. Shared computer folders are usually available on file servers within organizations, but these may have limited storage capacity and be inaccessible for security reasons when off premises. If computer files are large (as is the case with videos, photographs and electronic recordings of interviews) or the research team is spread across different organizations, a web-based file sharing and storage program will save a lot of time. As long as the files inside are kept in logical order, it is much better than email at facilitating circulation of project materials and version control of documents.

Box 12.1

File sharing made easy

At the time of writing, *Dropbox* and *Basecamp* are two popular 'cloud' computing programs that are easy to use for research file sharing. Both allow you to access files from multiple locations, as long as you have an Internet connection, and will 'sync' files worked on by different people on multiple devices. *Dropbox* is a free, uncomplicated, folder-based program that allows you to earn extra storage space through signing up others to your shared folders. For modest monthly or yearly fees, you can buy additional amounts of storage if you need to use and share large computer files such as videos or photographs. *Basecamp* is a more sophisticated project management program that requires a small join-up fee. In addition to basic file sharing, it facilitates other useful project management functions, such as team calendars and meeting schedules, and enables you to easily keep track of multiple projects. Some researchers working with highly sensitive data are wary of these cloud computing programs due to concerns about privacy. If you are working with sensitive material and want the convenience of using these programs, it is possible to encrypt the data.

KEEPING DATA SECURE AND IN GOOD WORKING ORDER

Assigning code numbers to each item of data ('case') using a combination of letters and numbers will enable you to organize your data more efficiently. For instance, interview one in your study becomes IN01, and so on. With regard to electronic files, this code number should be placed in the header or footer of the electronic transcript and may appear on an interview coversheet. Setting up a table in a Word document or Excel spreadsheet that records each code number and basic descriptive information about your participants is a useful way to ensure you can find relevant data quickly

Table 12.1 Participant attributes – extract from sample file

Interview #	Gender	Relationship status	Age	Profession
1	F	Not in a relationship	38	PhD candidate
2	F	Married	62	HR administration
3	F	Married	40	Researcher
4	M	Divorced	25	unknown
5	M	Defacto	51	university administration
6	M	Married	36	TAFE teacher
7	F	Defacto	37	unknown
8	M	Married	62	Manager

(see Table 12.1). If you are using a computer program such as NVivo, you can enter this information as 'attributes' of the cases. Code numbers can also help you to file hard copy documents in order.

If you have print-outs of data, it is a good idea to keep these in a binder or other kind of secure and easily accessible file. Binders are easily labelled and stored, and contents can be flicked through, removed, and put back in order with ease.

When doing qualitative research based on people's interviews or stories, it is important to keep separate from the interview transcripts any information that can explicitly identify your participants. This is likely to be a requirement of gaining ethical clearance from most university-based human research ethics committees. Signed consent forms should be stored in a locked filing cabinet away from participants' data, as should any names and postal or email addresses obtained for the purpose of recruiting people to the study, or sending them information about the research results. It is good practice to ensure data in any form are not left lying around when not in use by the research team. It should always be put back in order and stored under lock and key in a filing cabinet or cupboard when not being used.

Transcribing data

Audio-recordings of interviews or focus groups are usually transcribed before qualitative analysis. Transcription can be done with the help of voice recognition software, a transcription machine, or a professional transcription agency. At the time of writing, voice recognition software was not sophisticated enough to accurately record a conversation played out loud from an audio-recorder. It does, however, enable you to listen to the interview through headphones and repeat it aloud as a means of converting the interview audio into digitized text. Although voice recognition programs are improving all the time, they still need to be trained to a single voice, and there can be accuracy problems. A more conventional transcription approach involves playing back the recording slowly through headphones (easy if you use a digital voice recorder) and typing the words as you hear them. Transcription kits (software and play-back machines) are costly but more efficient and less clumsy to use than a standard digital recorder, because the foot pedals enable you to pause, rewind and playback while typing.

If you are going to be doing your own transcription, or allocating it to a research assistant, it is important to be aware that it is a very time-consuming process. Professional transcription services usually charge for three hours of typing per hour of recording (more for focus and group interviews or low-quality audio-recordings) and the average non-professional typist will be at least twice as slow as this. Burke et al. (2010) estimate four to seven hours of typing per hour of interview for non-professional typists, depending on their skills, the complexity of the material and audio quality. Transcribing your own data soon after an interview helps with analysis, as it enables you to insert relevant non-verbal cues you can remember (for example, if the participant seemed embarrassed or nervous when they said something). It enables you to become familiar with the material and pick up nuances of meaning and tone that will never be present to the same degree in transcripts typed by someone who did not do the interview. That said, it is not always feasible for researchers to do their own transcription. When employing professional agencies or other individuals, transcripts must be checked for accuracy by playing back the original audio-recording and comparing it with the typed word-processing file. Due to the speed at which outsourced transcription is done, and given transcribers are usually paid for a set number of hours per hour of recording, there are often missed words and discrepancies between the transcript and the original audio-recording. These mistakes can affect meaning, which is why the checking process is so important.

If you are employing someone to transcribe your data, you must brief them clearly on how you want the transcription done. This will depend on your research questions and disciplinary biases. Unless you are a linguist doing conversation analysis, it is usually fine to transcribe for ease of reading. This means leaving out all the 'ums' and 'ahs' unless these are important to meaning, and punctuating for clear sentences. The transcripts should clearly distinguish between the researcher's questions and the participants' answers. Double-spacing and a wide right-hand margin will give you plenty of space to write on the transcripts. Devise a notation system so that the transcriber knows how to indicate missing words, disjointed sentences and meaningful pauses. An example we have found useful is provided in Box 12.2.

Box 12.2

One approach to transcript notation

Interviewer:	Introduces speaker's speech in indented quotations
David:	
–	Marks self-interruption or change of tack in sentence
[pause, footsteps]	Non-verbal cue
[indistinct]	Inaudible words
(oh, really?)	Interviewer's interjections when participant is speaking

---

A more detailed list of questions needing consideration before transcribing or outsourcing transcription is provided in Box 12.3.

> **Box 12.3**
>
> ## Questions you should ask yourself before doing or outsourcing transcription
>
> What information is needed at the beginning or on each page of the transcript (for example, interview number, date, location)?
>
> Will software be used to analyze the data later? If so, avoiding complex formatting is advisable.
>
> Do you plan on archiving your data? If so, check which file formats and preferences are suitable to save you having to make changes later.
>
> Do you want page numbers and where?
>
> Line numbers?
>
> How should the transcriber indicate a new speaker?
>
> How should the transcriber indicate when a speaker hesitates or makes a noise like 'um' or 'er'?
>
> How should laughter, jokes, or other non-verbal information, such as leaving and entering rooms, be indicated?
>
> How faithful to the actual words spoken should the transcriber be? For instance, many researchers will not want the transcriber to correct participants' grammar.
>
> How should the transcriber indicate words they couldn't understand? (A common way would be to note [unintelligible] and perhaps to include the exact point in the recording where this occurs [27:04] so the researcher can easily find it.)
>
> Would a glossary of unfamiliar words be helpful to the transcriber?
>
> (Source: Burke, 2011: 5)

Ethics and transcription

Ethical issues are also a consideration in that the transcription process needs to preserve confidentiality and ensure that the transcriber is not unduly exposed to distressing material without support.

Transcribers must be bound by confidentiality, in the sense that they are not to disclose any of the information they are privy to or leave copies of the materials they have transcribed in places where these could be read by others. Most reputable agencies will have a secure web-based file upload system that provides a safe and convenient way to send and receive files, but you also need to ensure that files will be managed confidentially by the actual person doing the transcription. You can ask your transcription person to sign a confidentiality agreement, or make sure you only source transcription services from reputable agencies that are used to working with confidential data. If in doubt, you should always ask whether the person or agency you are thinking of hiring has a sound understanding of confidentiality, and how they intend to store and dispose of copies of your audio files and data transcripts.

If your interview or written textual material is distressing or highly sensitive, it is important to consider how you will manage this both from the perspective of the transcriber and the participants. If you know that interview material is likely to be very upsetting to the average person, it is wise to discuss this with the transcription agency or transcriber first. There are times when sensitivities or the distressing nature of the material mean that the best decision may be to transcribe the material 'in house', or ensure that debriefing can be provided.

All the care you take with conducting your interviews and focus groups can be undone by poor quality transcription, so it is important that you can trust it has been done responsibly and accurately. If you are outsourcing transcription, it is often best to ask experienced colleagues for a recommended person or agency because quality and costs can vary greatly.

Preparing transcripts for analysis

Once you have transcripts, you will need to think about how you are going to de-identify them. It is very important to remove the main identifying information (for example, participants' names) from interview transcripts before you print these out or import them into a computer analysis program and begin work. Complete de-identification is usually a process rather than a one-off event because it is not always immediately apparent how much and what information will need to be changed in order to preserve a participant's privacy (see Chapter 4 for a recap of this point). At the very least you should allocate pseudonyms to your interviewees, and record each pseudonym on the front cover of the interview. It may also be appropriate to de-identify details such as their workplace and home suburb.

You should keep a separate 'anonymity log' containing the interview number, participants' real names and their pseudonyms, along with any other de-identification steps that you have taken. This is important because when there are a lot of interviews or multiple researchers, it can be easy to forget which interview transcripts have been de-identified and how. If this information is carefully logged in a separate file, there is a 'paper trail' that can be checked. It would be a severe breach of privacy, for instance, if a participant's real name or their child's real name were used when they had been promised anonymity in publications arising from the research. This is a possibility if the de-identification process is not managed well.

BEGINNING DATA ANALYSIS

In a *quantitative* research project, data collection and analysis are distinct phases of the research. The analysis will be inaccurate if you try to do it before all of the data are collected. In contrast, it is possible to begin analyzing *qualitative* data once you have your first interview, or newspaper article, or whatever it is that you are intending to analyze, and your project will be greatly enhanced by thinking of analysis as proceeding hand in hand with your data collection. If you transcribe all or some of your own data, this constitutes an early phase of data analysis in which you will begin to become really familiar with the material. If you are doing interviews, transcribe immediately after the first interview and read over your transcript carefully. Did some questions not work as well as they could have, or did you miss important opportunities to probe for more details? Did your participants frame the issue radically differently from the way you were expecting and could this have implications for your research focus? Picking up these problems early in your project, by analyzing as you go, is part of the 'logic in practice' of qualitative research.

Keeping a journal to record your thoughts and ideas as you progress through the fieldwork can also be a vital aid to analysis. After you turn off the tape recorder participants will often say very interesting things that you can note down in your journal and use to supplement your formally recorded interviews (as long as those participants do not specify that these comments were 'off the record'). The experience of doing an interview or reading through your other textual sources will often give rise to many ideas that will be lost to you later on unless you note them down at the time in a place where they can be easily retrieved. During the analysis process you can use your journal to sketch out maps or diagrams or lists that will help you work towards an answer to your research questions.

Depending on your chosen approach, qualitative analysis may involve you in thematic coding of your data, writing thematized life histories, composing chronologically sequential narratives, or conducting a discourse analysis. (These approaches have been discussed in some depth in earlier chapters of the book.) However, regardless of which approach you use, there are three 'golden rules' that should help:

1. *Use your research questions to guide the development of your analysis and keep things relevant but don't close down the possibilities too early.* Many common qualitative analysis techniques come from grounded theory (Strauss and Corbin, 1990), which specifies an initial phase of 'open coding' as a preliminary to a refined analysis that moves closer to answering the research questions. In this phase of the research, characterized by reading carefully to generate ideas and categories, you can note down anything that seems interesting about your data without censoring yourself too much. You will go through these notes and initial comments later, possibly discarding some that seem too detailed or collapsing others into smaller categories when it comes time to refine your analysis. If you are conducting a thematic analysis, these notes will help you generate an initial set of codes that you can build on and refine later on.

    At the same time, you don't have to pore over everything that is there in the data. For instance, when it comes to individual or group interviews the first few questions will often be about building a rapport with the participants, meaning there may be inconsequential small talk or 'white noise' to read through before you come to the valuable material. Sometimes small talk is an important way into the research themes but you can legitimately skip over idle chit chat, or even leave it out if you are the person doing the transcribing. It can be useful to write your research question(s) down where you can see them while you are exploring your data. Referring back to your research questions throughout the process of analysis will help you keep things focused.

2. *Immersing yourself in your data (reading and re-reading these, knowing them really well) is the path to good analysis.* Esterberg (2002: 157) calls this process 'getting intimate with your data'. You can't do good analysis unless you are very familiar with your material. Some researchers working with interview data like to play back the audio-recordings while they are driving or when they have down time at home as part of this familiarization process. Others like to spend at least part of each working day reading over their transcripts and making notes, before they get bogged down in other tasks. Transcribing the material yourself is also a great way to get intimate with your data. Whichever way you choose, knowing the material well makes it less likely that your analysis will be based on 'cherry picking' the things you have found out that fit with the literature or your pre-existing hunches. A good analysis will enable you to create arguments that answer your research question and that take into account nuances of meaning, as well as any similarities and differences across the material you have collected. When you are really familiar with your data and have been thinking about these for a long time, insights can come to you when you least expect them (for example, when washing the dishes or at 2am after a bad dream). Make sure you note down these random thoughts as they may prove important for your analysis. At the same time, as Bazeley (2013) warns, these 'Aha' moments do not substitute for working hard across your data set to refine and test your ideas. What this means is that you will need to test your hunches and impressions against the actual data.

3. *Go back and forth from your ideas to the literature.* Qualitative data analysis has been called an iterative process, in that there is constant to-ing and fro-ing from your data and the pre-existing social research and theories you have consulted to formulate your study. You are always making sense of your data in a context that includes making reference to the work that went before you. Just as you conceptualized your study and formulated your initial research questions by referring to the literature, you will need to return there in the process of making sense. This does not mean you are merely slotting your research findings into the categories or concepts that already exist in the literature. You will enter into a kind of dialogue between your data and relevant literature to come up with your own contribution.

INITIAL EXPLORATION

In the initial process of data exploration (sometimes called 'open coding'), the material is read intensively and everything that seems interesting is noted as descriptive comments or codes in the margins. Coding involves labelling a passage or excerpt of data according to what you understand it to be about. As Bazeley (2013) points out, this label or code serves both as a way to represent your data and as a means of accessing other data that are similarly labelled. In a thematic or discourse analysis, it is through the process of grouping data under similar codes, gradually refining those codes to a manageable and illuminating set, that you will move towards answering your research questions.

In life history and personal narrative methods that work with biographical data or stories rather than across an interview set, an initial phase of open coding will still help with getting to know the data.

Bazeley (2013) describes this initial exploration phase as comprised of 'read, reflect, play and explore strategies' that will help you get a feel for your data. She encourages researchers to be creative in how they do this. For instance, in addition to the usual techniques of scrawling notes on your transcripts or print-outs (see Figure 12.1),

```
IN46 4.4.12.                    page 5                          eye on prize =
                                                                baby naming
                                                                makes it more
                                                                real.

kept your (eye on the prize) I suppose as to why we were         yes
going through all this rubbish.

Facilitator:     Yeah so a name kind of signifies an actual baby that has been born?

Interviewee:     Yeah. So that's kind of how it was for us and as it     finding
                 was neither of the names came out of any of the         names
                 books - I mean obviously the names were in the          sources
                 books but we came upon them - well my partner
                 came upon them really quite separately. The name
                 books were just part of the process and it was
                 something - we both knew (it required a lot of thought.) We
                 were both probably a little - not anxious, but a bit    consequences of
                 nervous about picking a name that we later didn't       bad decision
                 like or was later shortened or bastardised in
                 some way that we didn't like.

                 I mean understanding there's only a certain amount      names at
                 of control you can have particularly once the kids      school
                 get to school in terms of how they represent their
                 names or how other kids shorten them or whatever,
                 but we wanted to - (we probably over-thought it in a    decision
                 lot of ways) but we wanted to make sure we didn't       making process
                 jump into anything too quickly. As it happened
                 because of the conception difficulties we didn't
                 jump into anything too quickly, it took ages.           good question!

Facilitator:     So what's at stake with choosing children's first names?

Interviewee:     Oh gosh, heaps. Heaps. I think it can be very           names identity
                 defining, rightly or wrongly, I think it's quite
                 defining particularly before you even meet
                 somebody, depending on your own background I
                 think you make a whole lot of assumptions around
                 other people's names. Those assumptions are in
                 many cases completely inappropriate, probably           consequences of
                 laden with all sorts of assumptions and judgements      bad decision
                 and all that sort of stuff, but I think that's the
                 reality of being human and I know I do it. It's in
judgement of others  the public sphere in terms of parents getting lampooned a bit for coming
naming decisions     up with creative spelling of names and changing ordinary names into -
                 changing a five letter name into an eight letter name that sounds the
                 same but looks very different and all that kind of stuff.

            requires a lot of thought because poverty get judged if they get it wrong?
```

Figure 12.1

creating mini diagrams or connecting lines to describe relationships, and noting down concepts or events that resonate with what you have already read about in the literature, you can try the following:

- Create a brief word picture to profile the person, event or situation that is described in your data source.
- Turn a transcript or part of a transcript into a poem, using the participants' words as much as possible.
- Identify a puzzle in your data to get you going with the analysis. Use your journal to write an imaginary dialogue with a colleague about this puzzle, having the colleague ask questions of you that will help you clarify the problem.

The goal of these techniques is to get you thinking and immersed in the material. If you are using thematic analysis, it is in this initial phase that your coding scheme will begin to take shape. At this stage, you will want your codes or categories to come from the data rather than rigidly applying a pre-organized schema. Although it can be a very confusing time when you are not sure what everything means yet, you will begin to develop important ideas at this stage. Don't get discouraged by your confusion! You may feel like you are wading through mud but this is a necessary stage and it will pass.

You may want to handwrite your notes on print-outs of transcript or electronically, using comment boxes in a word-processing program, or use the unstructured 'nodes' available to you in a specialist qualitative analysis program. Many researchers still prefer the so-called 'pen and pencil' method of printing out textual material and writing their initial comments and coding categories on the transcripts. Some people like to use highlighter pens or coloured sticky notes to mark distinctive features of the text. You can also easily highlight electronic text and add virtual sticky notes in word-processing programs.

REFINING YOUR ANALYSIS

After you have become familiar with your data through an initial phase of exploration, you will start to get a feel for the common categories that emerge across your data set, as well as what makes particular cases distinctive or unique. If you are doing a thematic or discourse analysis, developing codes that move you towards identifying a small set of themes or discourses in the data will be important. Remember, coding is a means to interpretation rather than an end in itself. As you progress with the analysis, you need to find ways to refine your coding scheme in a way that is moving you towards an argument (see Box 12.4). Remember that your argument is just the answer to your research questions, so it is vital to keep these in mind as you refine your analysis (see Mason, 2002, for a good discussion of constructing arguments in qualitative research).

> **Box 12.4**
>
> ### A strategy for reviewing and refining a coding scheme
>
> - Review your list of codes as a whole, simple list. How well does it reflect the concerns of your project? Show the list to someone who is not familiar with your project. Can they tell what your project is about from your list of codes? Underline those that seem particularly significant and query those that are unclear or may not be needed.
> - Where a code is too broad to be analytically useful, review its contents and refine.
> - Use a 'tree' structure to conceptually group your codes and revise it regularly.
> - Define each code in a codebook. In doing so you will be forced to clarify what data the code represents. Recode segments that are not relevant to a more appropriate category.
> - Merge codes that have a common or similar meaning.
> - Refining codes as specified above is much simpler when using computer-assisted qualitative data analysis software such as NVivo.
>
> (Source: adapted from Bazeley, 2013: 185)

Memos

Writing memos is a technique that many qualitative researchers will use in order to help them refine their analysis. Thinking through how to move from your codes to themes to answering your research questions means writing down your thoughts as you go. Esterberg (2002) describes memos as letters or notes that researchers write to themselves to help them understand their data. Analytic insights can emerge from giving shape to our thoughts through writing rather than just through the process of coding. Memos produced throughout the process of initial exploration and the refining of analysis may make their way into the thesis, journal article or report-writing process.

USING COMPUTER-ASSISTED QUALITATIVE DATA ANALYSIS SOFTWARE (CAQDAS)

Many qualitative researchers will use specialist computer software to assist with the analysis process, particularly when their research is based on thematic analysis and some forms of discourse analysis. There are a number of programs on the market of varying degrees of usability and sophistication (see Table 12.2 for some examples). At its most basic, CAQDAS assists researchers to manage and code large volumes of material. The search, retrieve and coding functions can be much more efficient than 'pen and paper' methods of printing out and coding transcripts, particularly for team-based projects conducted from multiple sites. Recent versions of programs enable researchers to store and analyze audio-visual as well as text files. These programs can also assist with theory

Table 12.2 Popular computer-assisted qualitative data analysis software packages and their websites

NVivo www.qsrinternational.com/products_nvivo.aspx
ATLAS.ti www.atlasti.com/index.html
HyperRESEARCH www.researchware.com/products/hyperresearch.html
MAXQDA www.maxqda.com/
Transana www.transana.org/

building from coded data, in that it is possible to build diagrams that display and hyperlink the relationships between codes or themes.

CAQDAS will not do your analysis for you. Just as a word-processing program will not teach you how to write good essays or reports, you will need to know how to do qualitative analysis before you attempt to use CAQDAS. These programs are tools that can assist in a range of different tasks: storing and manipulating data; breaking these down into manageable codes or segments and allowing you to compare these; searching and retrieving key words and terms; comparing and collapsing coded segments; and making diagrams and models that will help you make sense of your data.

A computer-assisted data analysis package can be used for an initial exploration of the data and to make refining a coding scheme less unwieldy. For instance, in the NVivo program codes are called 'nodes', and nodes can be created and assigned to chunks of text once these are imported into the program. Nodes can be 'free' or ungrouped, or 'tree' and hierarchical, meaning it is possible to create standalone codes, or those that are ordered or nested according to criteria. It is common to make liberal use of the free nodes in an initial phase of data exploration, and then, as the analysis progresses, articulate relationships between these codes through hierarchies and trees. Creating diagrams may also help you map the relationships between codes and refine or build theory from your analysis.

Box 12.5

Using NVivo to refine an analysis

Mowat (2013) used the NVivo program to initially explore her data, and then refine these to a set of key discourses she identified in media coverage of the SlutWalk protest marches. After an initial exploration phase, she drastically reduced her codes to six that seemed to represent the key discourses in the Australian media in their newspaper coverage of the SlutWalk. These were as follows: 'individual/personal responsibility', 'postfeminism', 'justice system', 'female sexual agency', 'feminisms at war', 'politics of appearance', and 'SlutWalk as hollow media spectacle'. Mowat later decided that many of the statements made by commentators that had been coded under 'justice system' were part of the larger discourse of holding

(Continued)

(Continued)

women individually or personally responsible for sexual assault, and was able to recode these in NVivo to reflect this. She further collapsed 'postfeminism', 'female sexual agency', 'politics of appearance' and 'SlutWalk as hollow media spectacle' into a new category 'buying into the patriarchy', which on reflection better encapsulated the discourse of 'selling out' or being co-opted that was common to the material captured within these earlier codes.

The screenshot in Figure 12.2 is from NVivo and shows the final structure of nodes for Waller's PhD thesis on home Internet use. By continually reordering the nodes, moving,

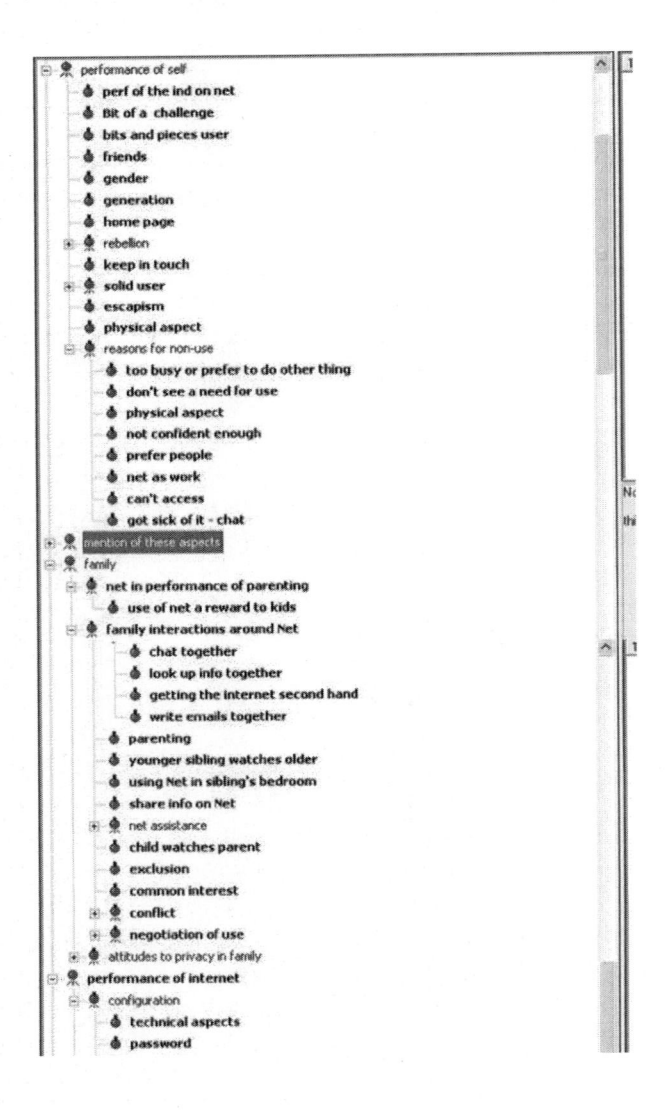

- performance of self
    - perf of the ind on net
    - Bit of a challenge
    - bits and pieces user
    - friends
    - gender
    - generation
    - home page
    - rebellion
    - keep in touch
    - solid user
    - escapism
    - physical aspect
    - reasons for non-use
        - too busy or prefer to do other thing
        - don't see a need for use
        - physical aspect
        - not confident enough
        - prefer people
        - net as work
        - can't access
        - got sick of it - chat
- mention of these aspects
- family
    - net in performance of parenting
        - use of net a reward to kids
    - family interactions around Net
        - chat together
        - look up info together
        - getting the internet second hand
        - write emails together
    - parenting
    - younger sibling watches older
    - using Net in sibling's bedroom
    - share info on Net
    - net assistance
    - child watches parent
    - exclusion
    - common interest
    - conflict
    - negotiation of use
    - attitudes to privacy in family
- performance of internet
    - configuration
        - technical aspects
        - password

Figure 12.2

splitting and combining them into groupings that made sense to her, she finally ended up with three main groupings: performance of self, performance of family, and performance of Internet. The main argument of her thesis became that the Internet, the family and the self are each performative, and her thesis provided an empirical examination of their intersecting performances.

CAQDAS has been criticized for a number of reasons, including expense and the tendency to decontextualize the data, or overemphasize comparisons across the data set rather than within a particular interview or other textual source. With regard to expense, many universities now buy multiple licences for popular packages, and make training available to staff and graduate students. The problem of decontextualization has improved with advances in the capacities of various programs. Recent versions of most CAQDAS programs do handle 'within text' and 'across text' searches easily, and allow you to view data in their original context as well as in segmented form.

Box 12.6

What CAQDAS can and cannot do

The software does ...

- structure work, enabling access to all parts of your project immediately;
- 'closeness to data' interactivity, allowing instant access to source data files (e.g. transcripts);
- explore data, using tools to search the text for one word or a phrase;
- code and retrieve functionality, creating codes and retrieving the coded sections of text;
- enable easy reorganization of coding, by the merging, splitting and moving of codes;
- project management and data organization, by managing the project and organizing the data;
- search and interrogate the database, by looking for relationships between the codes;
- writing tools, including memos, comments and annotations;
- output, by producing reports to view a hard copy or export to another package;
- helping with data visualization, by using some software that enables you to visualize the data in creative ways (for example, as word clouds).

The software does not ...

- do the analytical thinking for you, though it can do things that help you do that thinking;
- do the coding for you, as you will always need to decide what can be coded in what way (some software supports automatic coding of the results of text searches, but it is still important to check what has been automatically coded and to do additional manual coding);
- reduce bias, improve reliability or, on its own, improve the quality of your analysis (though it does have functions that can be used to help improve the quality of analysis);
- tell you how to analyze your data.

(Adapted from Lewins, A. and Silver, C. 2009)

Team-based qualitative data analysis

Much research these days is team based. This raises the question of how team members cooperate in doing qualitative data analysis, particularly in respect of the coding process. Discussions of team-based data coding often emphasize that it is important for researchers to develop shared understandings of what codes mean, and aim for consistency. As discussed in Chapter 2, the concept of intercoder reliability comes from positivist research traditions and refers to procedures that ensure researchers are working with the same definitions of coding categories and applying these in the same way. Practices used to ensure intercoder reliability include the careful definition of the meaning of codes to make them transparent to all members of the research team, and practice team-coding sessions where passages of data are coded, with the goal being to ensure the coding categories are being applied consistently. For researchers working with post-positivist assumptions, high intercoder reliability indicates that the analysis process is robust and the interpretation of data is reliable. High intercoder reliability will be met when the coding instructions are clear, coders are appropriately trained, trial runs of coding schemes are conducted, and coders are conscientious in their work.

From a constructivist and criticalist perspective, it is possible to question whether such standards of consistency can be met in a team-based qualitative analysis process. In this view, no amount of training in standardized procedures can dispel the effect of the 'researcher as instrument' who brings a unique set of social experiences and positionings to the research process. Within these research paradigms, it is more customary to think of team-based coding practices as socially constructed, based on discussions and negotiations between different members of the team. Sanders and Cuneo (2010: 327) call this 'social reliability', and see team-based analysis as '... a social process in which the personal backgrounds and theoretical and methodological preferences of team members interact in the social relationships of researchers with one another as they code the data'. In other words, as team members engage in the process of discussing the analysis, they will express agreement and disagreement, persuade each other, and at times pressure each other to accept their point of view.

ANALYSIS AND WRITING

Just as data collection and analysis are not discrete processes in qualitative research, it is also false to separate analysis from writing. In some forms of qualitative analysis, such as life history and personal narrative research, analysis is produced through the process of writing biographical histories or chronological narratives that can connect with the research question (see Chapter 11). Even with a thematic analysis that involves a more mechanical process of coding 'chunks' of data, and gradually refining this coding scheme, it is through the writing of results under refined themes that the final analysis and argument really start to come together. We would encourage you to leave yourself plenty of time for analysis and writing precisely because these are not mutually exclusive processes.

WRITING THESES, REPORTS AND ARTICLES BASED ON QUALITATIVE RESEARCH

Qualitative research results can be written in various ways. You may want to produce a report that is accessible to a community who have an interest in your research, a thesis for examiners, a report for government or industry, or an article for a peer-reviewed academic journal. Community reports or other accessible ways of disseminating the research findings are usually important from a criticalist perspective, in that they enable the people who were researched to learn about the findings and potentially benefit in some way. Relevance to your research question, or the sub-questions you have devised for your paper should always guide what you focus on in writing about your results. The audience for the research is also a consideration.

Organize your results section around thematic sub-headings which will usually be drawn from the coding categories you used in the analysis. You should try to write a reasonably flowing 'story' about what you found out in a manner that suits the method of analysis you used. In a qualitative research report, this usually involves making appropriate use of quotations from participants or texts. In telling this story, your job is to compare and contrast different responses, highlighting, where relevant, similarities and differences with previous findings in the literature. We would strongly discourage using percentages when reporting qualitative data. The word 'percentage' literally means 'of 100', and it is most unlikely that you will be reporting on more than 100 cases. Think carefully about whether or not it is appropriate to report on numbers at all. Exactly how many people said what is often irrelevant because you may be working with very small numbers, and using numbers can encourage the reader to focus on the numbers rather than the story you are telling. If you do want to refer to numbers, we suggest you do so in the following way: for example, 'Four of the seven participants who came from Australia said ...', 'All but one of the twelve women we interviewed explained ... '.

Different research approaches will demand different approaches to writing results (Box 12.7). For example, if you have done life history or narrative research, you will usually present fewer, longer stories in reporting your research. You may use certain stories in their entirety as illustrative examples. It is important to explain why you have chosen the stories you highlighted. Is it because they are typical, or atypical, or present the range of possibilities with regard to a given phenomenon? In autoethnographies or projects with an autoethnographic component, it is common for researchers to write elements of their own stories into the text, alongside those of their participants. Indeed, for researchers working in the constructivist tradition, presenting multiple perspectives and voices can be truer to the complexity of social experiences.

When reporting a thematic analysis, it is important to use quotations from your data to illustrate the themes you report. Discussing the themes you believe are illustrated in the quotations is critical because the meaning of quoted material is rarely self-evident. It is also both helpful to your audience and ethical to provide a substantial enough quote for the reader to assess the context. Some researchers will try to include the question that was asked, wherever possible, or to indicate whether what was said was prompted or unprompted, as this can affect meaning.

Box 12.7

A conventional approach to organizing a qualitative research report

Background: Introductory paragraph and setting the scene for why your research is important, topical or timely. (An anecdote or story of relevance to your research topic that explains its relevance can be a good launching point for a report, article or thesis.)

Literature review: See Chapter 3 for tips on writing literature reviews. If you have one you wrote for a research proposal, you may need to rework it to make it a more suitable frame for your results. The literature review should create an argument for why your research question is important and end with a statement of your research aims and questions.

Methodology: Includes a discussion of the methods, ethical issues, sampling, recruitment, reflections on the research process (including problems and how you dealt with them). Describe what you did under the following headings:

Methods (Did you conduct interviews? Focus groups? An analysis of texts? Give a broad description of your question topics and any piloting that was done beforehand.)

Ethical issues (What steps did you take to protect anonymity and confidentiality? How were the issues you anticipated different from what actually happened? How have you protected participants' anonymity in the reporting?)

Sampling (On what basis were people or texts selected? Strengths and limitations of your approach?)

Recruitment (How did you go about finding people to take part?)

Approach to analysis (For example, discourse/thematic or narrative analysis etc.)

Results: Analysis of findings, organized thematically. (In a qualitative study, there will usually be quotations from your source material.)

Discussion: The meaning and limitations of the results are discussed in light of the previous literature. For example, was the research question answered in the way you expected? What were the theories arising from your study? Were your results inconclusive? It is best to say so. What are the main implications of the findings?

In many qualitative research reports, the results and discussion are not separated out.

Conclusion: Summary of main findings and argument.

CONCLUSION

Analysis and writing are primarily about you and your conceptual skills: there are techniques and processes, but no formulae. No matter what your project or approach is, once you have finished with fieldwork or data collection you will need to become very familiar with your material, think hard about what it means, go back and forth between your data and relevant literature, decide on the best way to answer your research questions, and report this to relevant audiences. This constitutes the 'logic in practice' of qualitative analysis, and inevitably there will be dilemmas encountered along the way that will require you to use your judgement. Returning to the values and beliefs underpinning the research will assist you with this.

Computers can be very helpful organizational tools in assisting with the analysis process. They can help you manage large amounts of data and organize these into an easily retrievable coding scheme. At the same time, 'pen and pencil' methods still have their place and may be invaluable for smaller projects. Finally, how you write about your research will depend on the goals of your question, the audience you want to reach, the methods you used, and the kind of material you have: in other words, the paradigm most influential in your research. Be sensitive to the kind of data you have so as to let these shine through in your writing.

Going further

Bazeley, P. (2013) *Qualitative Data Analysis: Practical Strategies.* London: Sage.

A very detailed guide to CAQDAS, which contains many worked examples. It is particularly useful for those interested in fully exploring the capacities of CAQDAS.

Becker, H.S. (1998) *Tricks of the Trade: How to Think about Your Research While you are Doing It.* Chicago, IL: Chicago University Press.

A classic and highly readable account of the 'logic in practice' of qualitative research, along with writing tips.

Bird, C.M. (2005) 'How I stopped dreading and learned to love transcription', *Qualitative Inquiry,* 11 (2): 226-48.

An interesting discussion of the value for data analysis of doing your own transcription.

Clarke, A. (2005) *Situational Analysis: Grounded Theory after the Postmodern Turn.* Thousand Oaks, CA: Sage.

Situated analysis is a constructivist extension of grounded theory. It draws on the idea of situated knowledge and also explicitly includes discourse and non-human actors in the analysis.

(Continued)

(Continued)

Hesse-Biber, S. and Leavy, P. (2011) *The Practice of Qualitative Research* (2nd edition). London: Sage. Chapter 12.

This book provides very honest and practical examples of memo writing in the analysis process.

Mason, J. (2002) *Qualitative Researching* (2nd edition). London: Sage. Chapter 9.

Mason provides a very thoughtful account of the conceptual work involved in qualitative data analysis, particularly in the latter stages of the analysis process.

THIRTEEN

Combining approaches

CONTENTS

- Combining paradigms   178
- Combining qualitative methods   179
- Conclusion   180

We started this book by outlining the different sets of values and beliefs underlying research activities. We then explicitly linked the values and beliefs underlying a piece of qualitative research to the choice of research method, as well as the everyday decisions that a researcher has to make about the conduct of the research. This analytical framework is intended to help you in making your own critical assessment of the issues involved in using any qualitative research method and being able to justify your decisions when conducting qualitative research. It also assists you to judge the quality of other research. Now, analytic frameworks are intended to help you understand what is going on, but they are not necessarily a good description of real-world activities. We have made clear that the terms 'post-positivist', 'criticalist' and 'constructivist' are ideal types, and that in practice a researcher may conduct research that accords with more than one of these ideal types. In addition, a single research project will often include various pieces of research that will accord with more than one of these ideal types.

In this chapter, we conclude with some comments about these situations. First, we discuss combining different paradigms in the one piece of research, and then, using the example of ethnography, we discuss combining qualitative methods in a single piece of qualitative research.

COMBINING PARADIGMS

We described in Chapter 1 how quantitative research is underpinned by positivist values and beliefs, whereas qualitative research can be underpinned by post-positivist, criticalist or constructivist values and beliefs. In practice, many large research projects will involve both qualitative and quantitative components. For example, research on attitudes towards health promotion measures may include a quantitative survey measuring those attitudes as well as focus groups exploring them. These various components of a research project are inconsistent in terms of underlying values and beliefs. This does not, however, matter for the integrity of the research project. What it does mean is that pieces of research conducted according to the different paradigms are not commensurable, that is, they cannot be measured by the same standard. Each can only be measured by standards internal to the research paradigm. The following analogy with religious values and beliefs should make this clear.

There are people who hold religious values and beliefs, but also do not think that they have the monopoly on truth. They may recognize the truths contained in other religions, as illustrated in the following quote attributed to Muhammad Ali: 'Rivers, ponds, lakes and streams – they all have different names, but they all contain *water*. Just as religions do – they all contain truths.'

Similarly, we would recognize the contribution to knowledge of research within each of the paradigms. There is no need for research conducted within different paradigms to be commensurable, that is, to be measurable by the same standard. Rather, there is recognition of the truth, or contribution to knowledge, of research within each of the paradigms.

However, there is a catch. Some members of religions, for example some Christians, some Muslims, some Jews, would hold that they are upholders of the one true religion, and that other religions are not legitimate. Similarly, there are some positivists and post-positivists who would consider themselves to be the upholders of the one universal truth, and that research conducted within criticalist or constructivist paradigms is not legitimate. Such post-positivism is in ascendancy at this time (Denzin, 2010a, 2010b), sometimes going under the name 'scientifically-based research' or 'evidence-based research'.

In this book we have tried to demonstrate that values and beliefs underlie each research approach and that neither positivists, post-positivists, criticalists nor constructivists have a monopoly on justifiable research approaches. We have also argued that the quality of research depends on the data having been generated and interpreted in ways that are trustworthy, ethical and valid, and shown that ideas about trustworthiness and validity differ according to the underlying values and beliefs of the paradigm in which the research is conducted.

Following on from the issue of whether it is a problem when different pieces of research are underpinned by inconsistent values and beliefs, is the question of what to do when different methods of inquiry result in different stories about what is going on. As mentioned in Chapter 2, we should expect a variety of findings when using different methods of inquiry. Rather than being a problem, contradictions or conflicting data may indicate the need for further investigation of how contradictions are experienced and lived. Then again, as with the boxed example in Chapter 7, contradictions or conflicting data may simply reflect the messiness of the world in which we live and the variety of perspectives that exist.

COMBINING QUALITATIVE METHODS

Sometimes we may want to combine qualitative methods. It is possible to combine both methods and paradigms, as discussed above, but researchers who want to combine qualitative methods can also do so within the same paradigm. An example of this is ethnographic research or ethnography.

Ethnography refers to in-depth qualitative research usually about a particular location or context. At a minimum it combines participant observation and interviews and these can be supplemented by nonparticipant observation and document-based research. Ethnography usually includes a history of the topic and explains that topic in light of that history and the other evidence gathered through participant observation and interviews.

An example of ethnography was reported by Byron Good in *Medicine, Rationality and Experience: An Anthropological Perspective* (1994). In this study, Good used participant observation and interviews to understand the experience of attending medical school at Harvard and how it shaped medical understandings and practices. The study was situated in the broader context of the delivery of health care in the United States, the medical model and how it views illness and bodies, and the dominance of the scientific method in medical research and training. Good found that medical training fundamentally changed the ways that students viewed bodies. He further argued that medical training was embedded in cultural practices that were locally specific.

The benefit of combining different qualitative approaches is that they provide different lenses through which you can explore your topic. Interviews can tell you what people make of your topic. Participant observation can tell you how it feels for you to participate. Observation can indicate what people do, but not the meaning that they associate with their doings. Documents can tell you what is in the documents themselves, but usually not why they were made or who their audience was. For example, if you are interested in whether, how and why Muslim leaders try to shape their media portrayals and how successful their strategies are you could interview Muslim leaders and ask them. This could shed light on the strategies they employ (see Sohrabi Haghighat, 2013, for an example of this approach). It would probably be difficult to observe the Muslim leaders in action and to participate in their strategizing unless you were an insider. However, you might combine your interviews with media analyses to see whether the strategies they employ appeared to shape media portrayals of Muslims and Islam. This would then provide two sources of data that could be used to answer different aspects of your research question.

Newer and/or creative combinations and adaptations of qualitative methods enable exploration of the complexity and multifaceted nature of human interactions. For example, Jacqui Gabb (2008) argues convincingly that creative methods are needed to respect the different communication styles and capacities of children and adults, when researching families or intergenerational relationships. For instance, Gabb developed emotion maps as a way of enabling children and adults in families to communicate about intimate familial experiences in the family home. This is a research method that utilizes emoticon stickers that can be used by family members of all ages and literacy levels to communicate their feelings. According to Gabb, using emotion maps in conjunction with interviews with family members, along with other techniques that children enjoy, such as drawing, can encourage critical reflection and dialogue about sensitive and emotionally challenging topics.

As with research that combines pieces of research conducted according to different paradigms, the data collected by different qualitative methods are also not commensurable, even if these were collected within the same research paradigm. While these can be combined to provide a more holistic view of the research topic, and may even be analyzed using similar thematic categories, they should not be pooled as different approaches will measure different things.

Good's (1994) study appears to have been conducted within a constructivist paradigm. Indeed, he locates his research as firmly situated outside a positivist framework. However, we would argue that there is no reason why ethnography cannot be undertaken from a post-positivist perspective. In this book we have shown that while the paradigmatic approach taken shapes one's research question and one's research approach, many of the various techniques for qualitative research can be adopted from within any of the three research paradigms.

CONCLUSION

This book has been framed in terms of research paradigms, that is, values and beliefs about research. While we have outlined some of the more commonly used methods of qualitative research, we hope to have provided you with a conceptual apparatus to equip you to approach any method of qualitative inquiry. Whichever method you use, the principles outlined in this book can guide you. Using the analytical framework provided in the first two chapters, you can make your own critical assessment of the issues involved in using any qualitative research method not covered by this book. You will need to have a clear rationale for your research, and this means being clear about the values and beliefs underpinning that piece of research. Only then will you be able to articulate a research question that is framed appropriately for qualitative inquiry. Only then will you be able to make appropriate decisions about design issues, sampling, your relationship with your research participants, and your analysis, in order to produce research that is useful, ethical, trustworthy and valid. There is no 'magic recipe' that a beginning researcher can blindly follow. As a qualitative researcher you will need to engage your critical thinking skills at all stages of the research process.

May you live a good life and do good research!

References

American Sociological Association (1999) *Code of Ethics and Policies and Procedures of the ASA Committee on Professional Ethics*. Washington, DC: American Sociological Association.

Atkinson, P. and Hammersley, M. (1994) 'Ethnography and participant observation', in N. Denzin and Y. Lincoln (eds), *Handbook of Qualitative Research*. Thousand Oaks, CA: Sage. pp. 248–61.

Australian Bureau of Statistics (1998) *The Aboriginal and Torres Strait Islander Population of Australia – Census Counts, Concepts and Questions in the 20th Century,* Australia. cat. no. 1301.0. Canberra: ABS.

Australian Bureau of Statistics (2014) *Household Use of Information Technology,* Australia. cat. no. 8146.0. Canberra: ABS.

Australian Institute of Family Studies (2014) *Reporting on Sexual Assault Media Backgrounder, AIFS Australian Centre for the Study of Sexual Assault*. Available at www.aifs.gov.au/acssa/media/index.html (last accessed 29 September 2014).

Babbie, E.R. (2007) *The Basics of Social Research*. Belmont, CA: Thomson Wadsworth.

Bazeley, P. (2013) *Qualitative Data Analysis: Practical Strategies*. London: Sage.

Becker, H.S. (1988) *Tricks of the Trade: How to Think about Your Research while You're Doing It*. Chicago, IL: University of Chicago Press.

Berg, B.L. (2001) *Qualitative Methods for the Social Sciences*. Boston, MA: Allyn and Bacon.

Blaikie, N. (2007) *Approaches to Social Enquiry: Advancing Knowledge*. Cambridge: Polity.

Blee, K.M. (1998) 'White-knuckle research: emotional dynamics in fieldwork with racist activists', *Qualitative Sociology*, 21 (4): 381–99.

Bogdan, R. (1974) *Being Different: The Autobiography of Jane Fry*. New York: Wiley.

Bourdieu, P. et al. (eds) (1991) *The Craft of Sociology: Epistemological Preliminaries*. Berlin: Walter de Gruyter.

Bowker, N. and Tuffin, K. (2002) 'Disability discourses for online identities', *Disability and Society*, 17 (3): 327–44.

Bowman, D.D. (2007) 'Men's business: negotiating entrepreneurial business and family life', *Journal of Sociology*, 43 (4): 385–400.

Bowman, D.D. (2009) 'The deal: wives, entrepreneurial business and family life', *Journal of Family Studies*, 15 (2): 167–76.

Burke, H. (2011) 'Using an external agency or individual to transcribe your qualitative data', Realities Toolkit #15, Morgan Centre, University of Manchester. Available at www.socialsciences.manchester.ac.uk/morgancentre/methods-and-resources/toolkits/toolkit-15/ (last accessed 9 September 2014).

Burke, H., Jenkins, L. and Higham, V. (2010) 'Transcribing your own qualitative data', Toolkit #8, Morgan Centre, University of Manchester. Available at www.socialsciences.manchester.ac.uk/morgancentre/methods-and-resources/toolkits/toolkit-8/ (last accessed 9 September 2014).

Butler, J. (1990) *Gender Trouble: Feminism and the Subversion of Identity*. New York: Routledge.

Canter, D. and Alison, L.J., (2003) 'Converting evidence into data: the use of law enforcement archives as unobtrusive measurement', *The Qualitative Report*, 8 (2): 151–76.

Carrington, C. (1999) *No Place Like Home: Relationships and Family Life among Lesbians and Gay Men*. Chicago, IL: University of Chicago Press.

Chamberlayne, P., Rustin, M. and Wengraf, T. (eds) (2002) *Biography and Social Exclusion in Europe: Experiences and Life Journeys*. Bristol: Policy.

Clifford, J. (1990) 'Notes on fieldnotes', in R. Sanjek (ed.), *The Making of Anthropology*. New York: Cornell University Press.

Couch, D. and Liamputtong, P. (2013) 'Online dating and mating: the use of the internet to meet sexual partners', in C. Hine (ed.), *Virtual Research Methods*. London: Sage. pp. 283–304.

Creswell, J.W. (2014) Research *Design: Qualitative, Quantitative, and Mixed Methods Approaches*. Thousand Oaks, CA: Sage.

Crotty, M. (1998) *The Foundations of Social Research: Meaning and Perspective in the Research Process*. Thousand Oaks, CA: Sage.

Davis, M. et al. (2013) 'Reflecting on the experience of interviewing online: perspectives from the internet and HIV study in London', in C. Hine (ed.), *Virtual Research Methods*. London: Sage. pp. 195–204.

Decuir, J. and Dixson, A. (2004) '"So when it comes out, they aren't that surprised that it is there": using critical race theory as a tool of analysis of race and racism in education', *Educational Researcher*, 33: 26–31.

Deegan, A. (2012) 'Case: stranger in a strange land: the challenges and benefits of online interviews in the social networking space', in J. Salmons (ed.), *Cases in Online Interview Research*. Thousand Oaks, CA: Sage. pp. 69–90.

Dempsey, D. (2006) 'Beyond choice: family and kinship in the Australian lesbian and gay "baby boom". Unpublished PhD thesis, La Trobe University, Melbourne, Australia.

Denzin, N. (2010a) 'Moments, mixed methods, and paradigm dialogs', *Qualitative Inquiry*, 16(6): 419–27.

Denzin, N. (2010b) *Qualitative Inquiry under Fire: Toward a New Paradigm Dialogue*. Walnut Creek, CA: Left Coast.

Denzin, N. and Lincoln, Y.S. (eds) (2000) *Handbook of Qualitative Research*. Thousand Oaks, CA: Sage.

Denzin, N. and Lincoln, Y.S. (eds) (2011) *The SAGE Handbook of Qualitative Research*. Thousand Oaks, CA: Sage.

Deutsch, N. (2012) 'Case: implementing technology in blended learning courses', in J. Salmons (ed.), *Cases in Online Interview Research*. Thousand Oaks, CA: Sage. pp. 261–9.

Dowling, S. (2012) 'Case: online asynchronous and face-to-face interviewing: comparing methods for exploring women's experiences of breastfeeding long term', in J. Salmons (ed.), *Cases in Online Interview Research*. Thousand Oaks, CA: Sage. pp. 277–96.

Dowsett, G. (1996) *Practicing Desire: Homosexual Sex in the Era of AIDS*. Stanford, CA: Stanford University Press.

Ellis, C. (2007) 'Telling secrets, revealing lives: relational ethics in research with intimate others', *Qualitative Inquiry*, 13 (1): 3–29.

Ellis, C., Adams, T.E. and Bochner, A.P. (2011) 'Autoethnography: an overview', in *Historical Social Research/Historische Sozialforschung*. Available at www.qualitative-research.net/index.php/fqs/article/%0Bview/1589/3095 (last accessed 16 September 2014). pp. 273–90.

Ellis, C., Kiesinger, C. and Tillmann-Healy, L. (1997) 'Interactive interviewing: talking about emotional experience', in R. Hertz (ed.), *Reflexivity and Voice*. Thousand Oaks, CA: Sage. pp. 119–49.

Emmison, M. et al. (2012) *Researching the Visual*. London: Sage.

Esterberg, K.G. (2002) *Qualitative Methods in Social Research*. Boston, MA: McGraw-Hill.

Farquharson, K. (2005) 'A different kind of snowball: identifying key policy makers', *International Journal of Social Research Methodology*, 8 (4): 345–53.

Fielding, N. (2013) 'Virtual fieldwork using access grid', in C. Hine (ed.), *Virtual Research Methods*. London: Sage. pp. 375–93.

Fox, F.E. et al. (2013) 'Doing synchronous online focus groups with young people: methodological reflections', in C. Hone (ed.), *Virtual Research Methods*. London: Sage. pp. 319–32.

Fozdar, F. and Pedersen, A. (2013) 'Diablogging about asylum seekers: building a counter-hegemonic discourse', *Discourse & Communication*, 7 (4): 371–88.

Frank, A.W. (2010) 'In defense of narrative exceptionalism', *Sociology of Health & Illness*, 32 (4): 665–7.

Frank, A.W. (2013) *The Wounded Storyteller: Body, Illness and Ethics* (2nd edition). Chicago, IL: University of Chicago Press.

Gabb, J. (2008) *Researching Intimacy in Families*. Basingstoke: Palgrave Macmillian.

Glaser, B.G. and Strauss, A.L. (1967) *The Discovery of Grounded Theory: Strategies for Qualitative Research*. New York: Aldine de Gruyter.

Gold, R.L. (1958) 'Roles in sociological field observations', *Social Forces*, 36 (3): 217–23.

Good, B. (1994) *Medicine, Rationality and Experience: An Anthropological Perspective*. Cambridge: Cambridge University Press.

Gray, D. (2009) *Doing Research in the Real World*. Thousand Oaks, CA: Sage.

Guba, E.G. and Lincoln, Y. (1994) 'Competing paradigms in qualitative research', in N. Denzin and Y. Lincoln (ed.), *Handbook of Qualitative Research*. Thousand Oaks, CA: Sage. pp. 105–17.

Haraway, D.J. (1991) *Simians, Cyborgs and Women*. New York: Routledge.

Henley, N.M., Miller, M. and Beazley, J.A. (1995) 'Syntax, semantics, and sexual violence agency and the passive voice', *Journal of Language and Social Psychology*, 14 (1–2): 60–84.

Hesse-Biber, S. and Leavy, P. (2011) *The Practice of Qualitative Research*. Thousand Oaks, CA: Sage.

Hitzler, R. and Keller, D. (1989) 'Common-sense verstehen', *Journal of the International Sociological Association*, 37 (1): 95–113.

Holmes, M. (2011) 'Emotional reflexivity in contemporary friendships: understanding it using Elias and Facebook etiquette', *Sociological Research Online*, 16 (1): 11.

Holstein, J.F. and Gubrium, J.A. (2012) *Varieties of Narrative Analysis*. Thousand Oaks, CA: Sage.

Hookway, N. (2008) '"Entering the blogosphere": some strategies for using blogs in social research', *Qualitative Research*, 8 (1): 91–113.

Humphreys, L. (1972) 'Tearoom trade: impersonal sex in public places: issues, debates and controversies', in G. Ritzer, (ed.), *An Introduction to Sociology*. Boston, MA: Allyn and Bacon.

James, N. and Busher, H. (2013) 'Credibility, authenticity and voice: dilemmas in online interviewing', in C. Hine (ed.), *Virtual Research Methods*. London: Sage. pp. 229–44.

Jarrett, D. (2012) Fact sheet: 'The one tonne flight'. Available at: http://ecometrica.com/assets//one_tonne_flight.pdf (accessed 30 July 2015).

Joyce, Y. (2013) 'Single mother self-recorded life narratives: a method', Proceedings of The Australian Sociological Association (TASA) Conference, *Reflections, Intersections and Aspirations, 50 Years of Australian Sociology*, 25–28 November 2013, Monash University, Melbourne, Australia.

Karp, D. (1996) *Speaking of Sadness: Depression, Disconnection, and the Meaning of Illness*. New York: Oxford University Press.

Kazmer, M.M. and Xie, B. (2013) 'Qualitative interviewing in Internet studies: playing with the media, playing with the method', in C. Hine (ed.), *Virtual Research Methods*. London: Sage. pp. 175–94.

Kirk, J. and Miller, M. (1986) *Reliability and Validity in Qualitative Research*. Thousand Oaks, CA: Sage.

Kirkman, M. (1999) '"I didn't interview myself": the researcher as participant in narrative research', *Health Sociology Review*, 9 (1): 32–41.

Kirkman, M. (2001) 'Infertile women and radical feminism: conflicting narratives of assisted reproductive technology', in J. Daly, M. Guillemin and S. Hill (eds), *Technologies and Health: Critical Compromises*. Melbourne: Oxford University Press.

Ladson-Billings, G. and Tate, W. (1995) 'Toward a critical race theory of education', *Teachers College Record*, 97 (1): 47–68.

Laqueur, T. (1990) *Making Sex: Body and Gender from the Greeks to Freud*. Cambridge, MA: Harvard University Press.

Le, R. (2015) 'Risky business: understanding Vietnamese Australian women drug couriers'. Unpublished PhD thesis, Institute for Social Research, Swinburne University of Technology, Melbourne.

Lelkes, Y. et al. (2012) 'Complete anonymity compromises the accuracy of self-reports', *Journal of Experimental Social Psychology*, 48 (6): 1291–9.

LeMaster, B. (2014) 'Telling multiracial tales: an auto-ethnography of coming out/home', *Qualitative Inquiry*, 20 (1): 51–60.

Lewins, A. and Silver, C. (2009) 'Choosing a CAQDAS package', University of Huddersfield. Available at http://onlineqda.hud.ac.uk/Intro_CAQDAS/What_the_sw_can_do.php (last accessed 12 September 2014).

Liggins, J., Kearns, R.A. and Adams, P.J. (2013) 'Using autoethnography to reclaim the "place of healing" in mental health care', *Social Science & Medicine*, 91: 105–9.

Lincoln, Y. et al. (2011) 'Paradigmatic controversies, contradictions, and emerging confluences revisited', in N. Denzin and Y. Lincoln (eds), *The SAGE Handbook of Qualitative Research*. Thousand Oaks, CA: Sage. pp. 97–128.

Lofland, J. and Lofland, L.H. (1984) *Analyzing Social Settings: A Guide to Qualitative Observation and Analysis*. Belmont, CA: Wadsworth.

Luckmann, T. and Berger, P.L. (1971) *The Social Construction of Reality: A Treatise in the Sociology of Knowledge*. Harmondsworth: Penguin.

Machin, D. and Mayr, A. (2012) *How to do Critical Discourse Analysis: A Multimodal Introduction*. Thousand Oaks, CA: Sage.

Maffesoli, M. (1989) 'The sociology of everyday life', *Current Sociology*, 37(1): 1–16.

Malta, S. (2012) 'Using online methods to interview older adults about their romantic and sexual relationships', in M. Leontowisch (ed.), *Researching Later Life and Ageing: Expanding Qualitative Research Horizons*. London: Palgrave Macmillan. pp. 146–72.

Malta, S. (2013) 'Love, sex and intimacy in new late-life romantic relationships'. PhD thesis, Swinburne University of Technology, Melbourne.

Marjoribanks, T. et al. (2013) 'Resources of belonging: assessing the consequences of media interventions', in K. Howley (ed.), *Media Interventions*. New York: Peter Lang.

Markham, A. and Buchanan, E. (2012) *Ethical Decision-making and Internet Research: Recommendations for the AoIR Ethics Working Committee* (Version 2.0), Association of Internet Researchers. Available at: http://aoir.org/reports/ethics2.pdf (accessed 5 August 2015).

Martin, E. (1991) 'The egg and the sperm: how science has constructed a romance based on stereotypical male-female roles', *Journal of Women in Culture and Society*, 16 (3): 485–501.

Mason, J. (2002) *Qualitative Researching* (2nd edition). London: Sage.

McDonald, K. (1999) *Struggles for Subjectivity: Identity, Action and Youth Experience*. Cambridge: Cambridge University Press.

Merton, V. (1993) 'The exclusion of pregnant, pregnable, and once-pregnable people (a.k.a. women) from biomedical research', *American Journal of Law & Medicine*, 4: 369–451.

Milgram, S. (1963) 'Behavioural study of obedience', *Journal of Abnormal and Social Psychology*, 67: 371–8.

Milgram, S. (1974) *Obedience to Authority: An Experimental View*. London: Tavistock.

Morley, D. (1988) 'Domestic relations: the framework of family viewing in Great Britain', in J. Lull (ed.), *World Families Watch Television*. Thousand Oaks, CA: Sage. pp. 22–48.

Mowat, H. (2013) SlutWalk or Tart Parade? The de-politicisation of third-wave feminism and sexual violence prevention in Australian newspapers'. Unpublished Honours thesis, Hawthorn, Swinburne University of Technology.

Murphy, R.F. (1990) *The Body Silent*. New York: Norton.

National Commission for the Protection of Human Subjects of Biomedical and Behavioral Research (1979) *The Belmont Report: Ethical Principles and Guidelines for the Protection of Human Subjects of Research*. Washington, DC: Department of Health and Human Services.

National Health and Medical Research Council (2007) *National Statement on Ethical Conduct in Human Research*. Canberra: National Health and Medical Research Council.

Oakley, A. (1981) 'Interviewing women: a contradiction in terms', in H. Roberts (ed.), *Doing Feminist Research*. London: Routledge.

Otta, E. (1992) 'Graffiti in the 1990s: a study of inscriptions on restroom walls', *Journal of Social Psychology*, 133 (4): 589–90.

Patton, M.Q. (1990) *Qualitative Evaluation and Research Methods*. Newbury Park, CA: Sage.

Pekmezi, D.W. and Demark-Wahnefried, W. (2011) 'Updated evidence in support of diet and exercise interventions in cancer survivors', *Acta Oncologica*, 50 (2): 167–78.

Petersen, A. (2001) 'Biofantasies: genetics and medicine in the print news media', *Social Science & Medicine*, 52 (8): 1255–68.

Pickering, C.M. et al. (2010) 'Comparing hiking, mountain biking and horse riding impacts on vegetation and soils in Australia and the United States of America', *Journal of Environmental Management*, 91: 551–62.

Plummer, K. (1995) *Telling Sexual Stories: Power, Change and Social Worlds*. London: Routledge.

Plummer, K. (2001) *Documents of Life 2: An Invitation to Critical Humanism*. London: Sage.

Reid, S.E. and Marion, J.L. (2005) 'A comparison of campfire impacts and policies in seven protected areas', *Environmental Management*, 36 (1): 48–58.

Remenyi, D., Swan, N. and Van Den Assem, B. (2011) *Ethics, Protocols and Research Ethics Committees: Successfully Obtaining Approval for Your Academic Research*. Reading UK: Academic Publishing International.

Richardson, L. (2000) 'New writing practices in qualitative research', *Sociology of Sport Journal*, 17: 5–20.

Riessman, C.K. (ed.) (1993) *Narrative Analysis* (Vol. 30). Thousand Oaks, CA: Sage.

Riessman, C.K. (2008) *Narrative Methods for the Human Sciences*. Thousand Oaks, CA: Sage.

Robinson, O.C. (2014) 'Sampling in interview-based qualitative research: a theoretical and practical guide', *Qualitative Research in Psychology*, 11 (1): 25–41.

Salmons, J. (2012) *Cases in Online Interview Research*. Thousand Oaks, CA: Sage.

Sanders, C.B. and Cuneo, C.J. (2010) 'Social reliability in qualitative team research', *Sociology*, 44 (2): 325–43.

Schatzman, L. and Strauss, A. (1991) 'Social class and modes of communication', in P. Bourdieu, J.C. Chamboredon, J.C. Passeron and B. Krais, B. (eds), *The Craft of Sociology: Epistemological Preliminaries*. Berlin: Walter de Gruyter. pp. 169–78.

Schouten, J. W. and McAlexander, J.H. (1995) 'The cultures of consumption: an ethnography of the new bikers', *Journal of Consumer Research,* 22 (1): 43–61.

Schreer, G.E. and Strichartz, J.M. (1997) 'Private restroom graffiti: an analysis of controversial social issues on two college campuses', *Psychological Reports,* 81: 1067–84.

Seidman, I.E. (1991) *Interviewing as Qualitative Research: A Guide for Researchers in Education and Social Sciences.* New York: Teachers College Press.

Seymour, W. (2013) 'In the flesh or online? Exploring qualitative research methodologies', in C. Hine (ed.), *Virtual Research Methods.* London: Sage. pp. 261–82.

Sharf, B. (1997) 'Communicating breast cancer on-line: support and empowerment on the internet', *Women & Health,* 26 (1): 65–84.

Sharf, B. (1999) 'Beyond netiquette: the ethics of doing naturalistic discourse research on the internet', in S. Jones (ed.), *Doing Internet Research: Critical Issues and Methods for Examining the Net.* Thousand Oaks, CA: Sage.

Silverman, D. (2011) *Interpreting Qualitative Data.* London: Sage.

Skeggs, B. (1994) 'Situating the production of feminist ethnography', in M. Maynard and J. Purvis (eds), *Researching Women's Lives from a Feminist Perspective.* London: Taylor and Francis. pp. 72–92.

Slepian, M.L. et al. (2014) 'Thin-slice judgements in the clinical context', *Annual Review of Clinical Psychology,* 10 (March): 131–53.

Small, M.L. (2004) *Villa Victoria: The Transformation of Social Capital in a Boston Barrio.* Chicago, IL: University of Chicago Press.

Smart, C. (2009) 'Shifting horizons: reflections on qualitative methods', *Feminist Theory,* 10 (3): 295–308.

Snee, H. (2010) 'Using blog analysis', Realities Toolkit # 10, Morgan Centre, University of Manchester. Available at http://eprints.ncrm.ac.uk/1321/2/10-toolkit-blog-analysis.pdf (last accessed 19 September 2014).

Sohrabi Haghighat, M.H. (2013) 'Australian Muslim leaders, normalisation and social integration'. Unpublished PhD thesis, Swinburne University of Technology, Melbourne.

Spaaij, R. (2011) *Sport and Social Mobility: Crossing Boundaries.* London: Routledge.

Squires, C. (2008) 'Approaches to narrative research', National Centre for Research Methods, NCRM Review Papers, February. London: Economic and Social Research Council.

Stanley, L. and Wise, S. (1990) 'Method, methodology and epistemology in feminist research process. Feminist praxis: research, theory and epistemology', in L. Stanley (ed.), *Feminist Sociology.* London: Routledge. pp. 20–62.

Stein, A. (1997) *Sex and Sensibility: Stories of a Lesbian Generation.* Berkeley and Los Angeles, CA: University of California Press.

Stewart, K. and Williams, A. (2013) 'Researching online populations: the use of online focus groups for social research', in C. Hine (ed.), *Virtual Research Methods.* London: Sage. pp. 333–54.

Tates, K. et al. (2013) 'Online focus groups as a tool to collect data in hard-to-include populations: examples from paediatric oncology', in C. Hine (ed.), *Virtual Research Methods.* London: Sage. pp. 305–18.

Taylor, H.A. (2009) 'Inclusion of women, minorities and children in clinical trials: opinions of research ethics board administrators', *Journal of Empirical Research on Human Research Ethics,* 42 (2): 65–73.

Taylor, T.L. (2013) 'Life in virtual worlds: plural existence, multimodalities, and other online research challenges', in C. Hine (ed.), *Virtual Research Methods.* London: Sage. pp. 51–64.

Tolich, M. (2004) 'Internal confidentiality: when confidentiality assurances fail relational informants', *Qualitative Sociology,* 27 (1): 101–6.

Van Dijk, T.A. (2001) 'Critical discourse analysis', in D. Schiffrin, D. Tannen and H.E. Hamilton (eds), *The Handbook of Discourse Analysis*. London: Sage. pp. 352–71.
Venkatesh, S. (2008) *Gang Leader for a Day: A Rogue Sociologist Takes to the Streets*. New York: Penguin.
Waller, V. (2001) 'The consumption of the internet in household families'. Unpublished PhD thesis, Australian National University, Canberra.
Waller, V. (2007) 'The need for institutional integrity in responsive regulation: the case of the Australian Taxation Office "walk-in"', *Law and Policy*, 29 (1): 59–83.
Waller, V. (2012) '"This big hi-tech thing": gender and the internet at home in the 1990s', *Media International Australia, Incorporating Culture & Policy*, 143: 78–88.
Waller, V. et al. (2006) 'Development of a situated information systems analysis and design methodology: a health care setting', Alicante, Spain, European and Mediterranean Conference on Information Systems.
Webb, E.J. (2000) *Unobtrusive Measures*. Thousand Oaks, CA: Sage.
Weeks, J., (1995) *Invented Moralities: Sexual Values in an Age of Uncertainty*. New York: Columbia University Press.
Weeks, J., Heaphy, B. and Donovan, C. (2001) *Same Sex Intimacies: Families of Choice and Other Life Experiments*. London: Routledge.
Wilkinson, S. (1998) 'Focus groups in feminist research: power, interaction, and the co-construction of meaning', *Women's Studies International Forum*, 21 (1): 111–25.
World Bank (2010) *World Development Report 2010*. Washington, DC: World Bank.
Yin, R.K. (1994) *Case Study Research: Design and Methods*. Thousand Oaks, CA: Sage.
Zirakbash, F. (2014) '"I was just a housewife, a dentist and a servant": the lives of professional Iranian women in Australia'. Unpublished PhD thesis, Swinburne University of Technology, Melbourne.

Index

NB: page numbers in italic indicate figures or tables

Adams, A 72
Adato, M 105
aims of qualitative research 19–30, *29*, *29–30*
   judging quality of research (and) 22–8
      aim of validity 24
      reflexivity in constructivist research 27–8
      reliability and objectivity 22–4
      validity in how data are generated 24–6
      validity of interpretation of data 26–7
   research 20–21
      generating theory from the data 20–21
      useful and ethical 21–2
   selection and interpretation 20
Alison, L J 124
analysis and writing 172–3 *see also* writing theses, reports and articles
Anderson, A 72
Angrosino, M 120
approaching qualitative research 6–7
Association of Internet Researchers (AoIR) guidelines 115–16
Atkinson, P 65
Australia(n)
   Bureau of Statistics (2014) 87
   Institute of Family Studies (2014) ethical guidelines for journalists 130
   and the internet 87
   SlutWalk marches in 133, 134, 169–70 *see also* Mowat, H
AuSud Media Project 112, 115, 119

Babbie, E R 26
Bagnoli, A 91
Bazeley, P 165–6, 168, 175
Becker, H S 69, 175
Being Different: The Autobiography of Jane Fry 5–6, 16
beneficence (and) 50–53 *see also* research
   risks to the institution 52–3
   risks to research participants 51–2
   risks to the researcher 50

Berg, B L 76
Berger, P L 12
Bernard J 40
Bird, C M 175
Blaikie, N 8
Blee, K 50
Blumer, H 18
Bochner, A 149
Bogdan R 5–6, 16
Bourdieu, P 26
Bowker, N 84
Bowman, D 49, 51
Boydell, N 106
Brown, B 18
   and 'The power of vulnerability' 18
Buchanan, E 47, 57, 115–16
Burke, H 160, 162
Busher, H 85, 90
Butler, J 16

Canter, D 124
Carrington, C 111
Casey, M 106
Chamberlayne, P 147
Chang, H 155
Charmaz, K 30
Chilton, P 139
Clarke, A 175
Clifford, J 118–19
combining 177–80
   paradigms 178–9
   qualitative methods 179–80
computer-assisted qualitative data analysis software (CAQDAS) (and) 168–72, *169*, *170*
   team-based qualitative data analysis 172
   using NVivo to refine an analysis (Box 12.5) 169–71
   what CAQDAS can and cannot do (Box 12.6) 171
confidentiality 48–50
   internal, and risk to participants (Box 4.1) 49
   promises of 48–9

Corbin, J 164
Couch, D 84
Creswell, J W 80
Crotty, M 8
Cuneo, C J 172

data analysis (and) 163–5 *see also*
  computer-assisted qualitative data analysis software
  qualitative analysis: golden rules 164–5
  quantitative research 163–4
  team-based qualitative 172
data exploration 165–8
  initial (*aka* open coding) 165–6, *166*
  and refining your analysis 167–8
    by writing memos 168
    strategy for reviewing and refining a coding scheme (Box 12.4) 168
data management 157–63 *see also* data analysis *and* data exploration
  file sharing made easy: Dropbox and Basecamp (Box 12.1) 159
  keeping data secure/in good working order (and) 159–63, *159*
    approach to transcript notation (Box 12.2) 161
    ethics and transcription 162–3
    preparing transcripts for analysis 163
    questions to ask yourself (Box 12.3) 162
    transcribing data 160–63
  setting up computer files 158
Davis, M 84
Decuir, J 10
Deegan, A 87, 90
definition/s (of) 12, 100–112
  meaning of codes 172
  narratives (Riessman) 144
  validity 24
Demark-Wahnefried, W 11
Dempsey, D 102, 145, 150, 151–2
Denscombe, M 42
Denzin N. 8, 30, 72, 91, 120
Deutsch, N 86
digital methods –
  digital traces 123, 125
  observation 115–116
  interviews 82–90
  online focus groups 101–103
  ethics of, 48, 125–126
  thematic analysis 130–131, 133–36
Dixson, A 10
Dowling, S 85, 86, 89, 90
Dowsett, G 145, 148, 151
Durkheim E 12–13

Ellis, C 114, 116–17, 120, 146, 149–50
Emmison, M. 121, 122, 123, 125, 127, 128
Esterberg, K G 165, 168

ethics 46–54, 115–17 *see also* subject entries
  beneficence 50–53
  and confidentiality 117
  justice 53–4
  research merit, integrity and competence 53
  respect 46–50

Farquharson, K 55, 68, 112, 115
Fergie, G 106
Fielding, N 102
figures
  notes on transcripts/print-outs (12.1) 166
  screenshot: structure of nodes (12.2) *170 see also* Waller, V
Finch, J 39
Flyvbjerg, B 72
focus groups (and) 97–105 *see also* group interviews
  composition of 98–9
  designing moderator's guide for 100
  example from a moderator's guide (box 7.3) 100
  how many to conduct 99
  online 101–3
  recruitment for 99
  role of moderator 100–101
  strengths of 103–4
  typical 97–8
  uses for 104–5
foundations of qualitative research (and) 4–18
  approaching qualitative research 6–7
  how to find things out 15–18 *see also* research
  qualitative vs quantitative research as series of trade-offs 5–6
  qualitative social research *see subject entry*
  reality – can it be known? 9–12 *see also* reality
  relationship of the knower to the known 12–15 *see also subject entry*
  research paradigms – values and beliefs about research 7–9
Fox, F E 101, 102
Fozdar, F 135
Frank, A W 145–6, 152, 155

Gabb, J 43, 179–80
Gee, J P 139
Glaser, B G 64–5, 66, 72, 99
Gold, R L 110, 111, 120
Good, B 179, 180
Gray, D 122
grounded theory (Glaser and Strauss) 64–5, 69, 70, 164
group interviews 94–7
  example of interviewee with family present (Box 7.1) 95
  example of researcher interpretation when data are conflicting (Box 7.2) 96
  and group dynamic 95–7

Guba, E. G. 8, 10, 18
Gubrium, J A 147

Halkier, B 72
Hammersley, M 57, 65
Haraway, D J 15, 24
Henley, N M 130
Hernandez, K 155
Hesse-Biber, S 89, 97, 176
Hilton, S 106
Hitzler, R 14
Hodder, I 128
Holmes, M 131, 136
Holstein, J F 147
Hookway, N 135–6, 139
Humphreys, L 47, 52, 114

internet *see* digital methods
interviewing (and) 75–91
   anonymity and visual cues 86–7
   appropriate mode for research interviews 87–88
   designing the semi-structured interview 77–8
   effectively – the interview guide 78–82
     sample of semi-structured interview schedule (Box 6.1) 79
     sample of structured interview schedule: extract (Box 6.2) 80
   establishing rapport 88–90
     in asynchronous email interviews 90
     when interviewing in immersive digital environments 90
     through presentation and disclosure 89–90
     in real-time text interviews 90
   interviewing modes, practical considerations for *see subject entry*
   structured and semi-structured interviews 75–7, *77*
interviewing modes, practical considerations for 82–86, *82*
   synchronous interviews 83–6, 88
     asynchronous (email) 85–6
     audio only 83–4
     audio-visual 83
     immersive video environments 84
     text – synchronous 84–5

James, N 85, 90
Jarrett, D 17
Jenkins, T M 128
Joyce, Y 147, 149
justice 21, 46, 53–4, 56

Karp, D 22
Kazmer, M M 86, 88
Keller, D 14

Kirk, J 26
Kirkman, M 146, 147, 148, 149, 153
knower and the known *see* relationship of the knower to the known
Krueger, R 106

Lacqueur, T 11
Ladson Billings, G 10
Le, R 71
Leavy, P 89, 97, 176
Lelkes, Y 49
LeMaster, B 144
Lewins, A 171
Liamputtong, P 84
Liggins, J 146–7 *see also* research
Lincoln Y. 8, 10, 16, 18, 72, 120
Lofland, J 114
Lofland, L H 114
Luckmann, T 12
Lund, F 105
Lundgren, A S 91
Luther King, M. 10

McAlexander, J H 110
McDaid, L 106
McDonald, K 123, 127
Machin, D 132
McCormack, M 72
Maffesoli, M 17
making sense *see* analysis and writing; data analysis; data exploration; data management *and* writing theses, reports and articles
Making Sex: Body and Gender from the Greeks to Freud 11
Malta, S 69, 84, 85, 86, 87, 89, 90
Marion, J L 124
Marjoribanks, T 55, 112
Markham, A 47, 57, 115–16
Martin, E 131–2
Marx, K 10
   and analysis of class 10
Mason, J 24, 26, 31, 32, 35, 43, 167, 176
May, T 18
Mayall, M 128
Mayr, A 132
Medicine, Rationality and Experience: An Anthropological Perspective 179
Merton, V 54
Mhlongo, P 105
Milgram, S 51
Miller, M 26
Morley, D 95
Mowat, H 133, 134, 169–70
Murphy, R F 70
Murray, R 43

narrative enquiry (and) 143–55 *see also* stories
   analyzing life history interviews 150–52
      sample partial case history from Dempsey (2006) (Box 11.1) 151–2
   analyzing personal narratives 152–3
   autoethnography 146–7
      constructivist case for (Richardson) 154
   'coming out' stories 143–4
   eliciting narratives through
      interview-based techniques 148–9
      participant-controlled techniques 149–50
   evaluating narrative inquiry 153–4
   life history 145
   personal narrative 145–6
Newton, I 4
Ngunjiri, F 155
NVivo computer program 168, 169–70, *170*

Oakley, A 76, 91
observing people (and) 109–20
   collecting the data 117–19, *118*
   definitions of types of observation 110–12
   ethical issues and disclosure of researcher status 115–17
   gaining permission for the research 113–15
   paradigms and participant observation (Box 8.1) 112–13
   types of research question 112
observing texts (and) 129–39
   doing a discourse analysis 137–8
   doing a thematic analysis 136–7, *137*
   locating and sampling texts (and) 133–6
      blogs 134–6
      sampling for textual analysis (Box 10.1) 134
   sexual assault crime: ethical guidelines for journalists 129–30
   thematic and discourse analysis: similarities and differences *see subject entry*
observing things (and) 121–8
   accretion measures 122–3
      analyzing graffiti (Box 9.1) 123
      digital traces 123
   advantages of studying physical traces 125
   analyzing physical traces 127
   disadvantages of studying physical traces 125–6
   erosion measures 124
      forensic science (Box 9.2) 124
   physical traces 121–2
online methods *see* digital methods
Otta, E 123

Patton, M Q 30, 112, 116, 120
Pedersen, A 135
Pekmezi, D W 11
people *see* observing people
Petersen, A 132
Plummer, K 143, 144, 145, 147, 148, 153, 155

Pocknee, C 106
politics and ethics of qualitative research 45–57 *see also* ethics
politics in research (and) 54–6
   funding 55–6
   reporting research findings 56
   the researcher and the researched 54–5
   training and research participation (Box 4.2) 55
Pryce, J 18

qualitative vs quantitative research as series of trade-offs 5–6
qualitative research questions 34–5
qualitative social research 4
   and looking beyond taken-for-granted reality (Box 1.1) 4
quantitative research questions 35

reality 9–12
   constructivist view of 11–12
   criticalist view of 10–11
   positivist view of 9
   post-positivist view of 9–10
Reid, S E 124
relationship of the knower to the known 12–15
   constructivist – research as 'non-innocent conversation' 14–15
   criticalist – researcher as advocate 13–14
   positivist and post-positivist – the dispassionate researcher 12–13
   and Durkheim, E 12–13
Remenyi, D 51
the research *see* sampling
research (and) 15–17
   confidentiality 117
   constructivist 17, 18
   criticalist 16–17, 18
   ethics 115–17
   merit, integrity and competence 53
   in observational studies 116
   positivist and post-positivist 16, 18
   respect, beneficence, research merit and justice 46–50 **check** *see also* ethics
   risks to the institution, research participants and researchers 50–53
   unobtrusive 122
research (on)
   healing capacities of acute care mental health facilities (Liggins, 2013) 146–7
   how Australians experience morality in their everyday lives (Hookway, 2008) 135–6
researcher's questions 73–106 *see also* focus groups and group interviews *and* interviewing
respect 46–50 *see also* confidentiality; Humphreys, L *and* studies
   grey areas for 47–8
   online 47–8

Richardson, L 154
Riessman, C 144, 147, 148, 149, 152, 153–4, 155
Robinson, O C 67

Salmons, J 84, 89, 90
sampling (and) 61–72
 convenience 68
 generalizability 69
 hard-to-reach populations and research ethics 71
 peer-nominated reputational snowball (Box 5.1) 68
 a population 62
 process of 62
 purposive 67–8
 recruitment strategies 69
 sample size 70–71
 snowball 66–7
 theoretical 64, 66
 theory, starting with 63–4
 theory, starting without 64–6
Sanders, C B 172
Schatzman, L 28
Schouten, J W 110
Schreer, G E 123
Schroeder, R 128
Seidman, I E 70
Sex and Sensibility 145
Seymour, W 86
Sharf, B 47–8, 114
Shenton, A 30
Silver, C 171
Silverman, D 26, 27
Skeggs, B. 8
Slepian, M L 89
Small, M L 114
Smart, C 9
Smith, P 128
Snee, H 139
social media *see* digital methods
Sohrabi, H 67
Spaaij, R 114
Spencer, R 18
Squires, C 145, 148, 152
Stanley, L 63
Stein, A 145, 147, 154
Stephens, C 155
Stewart, K 102
story/ies 64–5, 69, 70, 144–55, 164, 173
 'coming out' 143–4
 of six blind men and the elephant 23–4, 28
Strauss, A L 28, 64–5, 66, 72, 99, 164
Strichartz, J M 123
studies (of/on)
 biker culture (Schouten and McAlexander, 1995) 110
 domestic labour in same-sex households (Carrington, 1999) 111

studies (of/on) *cont.*
 entrepreneurs and their spouses (Bowman, 2007, 2009) 49
 graffiti (McDonald, 1999) 127
 health and tobacco control policy elites in Australia (Farquharson, 2005) 68
 illicit drug-smuggling (Le, 2015) 71
 infertility in women (Kirkman, 2001) 146, 147
 men in tearooms (Humphreys, 1972) 47, 52
 obedience (Milgram, 1974) 51
 unannounced visits to car dealers (Waller, 2007) 111

tables
 amount of structure in the observational protocol *118*
 codes to themes *137*
 defining aspects of paradigms for everyday decision in qualitative research *29–30*
 modes of interviewing *82*
 participant attributes – extract from sample file *159*
 popular computer-assisted data analysis software packages and websites *169*
 typical amount of structure in an interview *77*
 underlying philosophical differences in research *29*
Tate, W 10
Tates, K 102, 103
Taylor, H A 54
Taylor, T L 87, 90
texts *see* observing texts
thematic and discourse analysis: similarities and differences 130–33
 critical discourse analysis 132–3
 discourse analysis 131–2
  carrying out a 137–8
  questions for 138
 source material for 133
 thematic analysis 130–31
  carrying out a 136–7, *137*
things *see* observing things
Tolich, M 49, 51, 57
from top to research design 31–43
 linking research questions to methods 40–41
 research proposal 41–2
  sample (Box 3.3) 41–2
 role of literature in developing research questions (and) 36–40
  sample literature review paragraph (Box 3.2) 39–40
  writing a literature review 39–40
 timely and feasible research 32–3
 topics and questions 33–6
  developing good qualitative research questions 33–6
  two research questions developed by students (Box 3.1) 34–5

Traianou, A 57
Tuffin, K 84
Turney, L 106

Van Dijk, T A 132
Venkatesh, S 50

Waller, V 14, 77, 83, 94–6, 100, 111, 119
    and thesis on home Internet use 170, *170*
Walsh, J 18
Warr, D J 106
Webb, E.J. 122, 124, 127, 128
Weeks, J 64
Wilkinson, S 101

Williams, A 102
Williams, M 18
Wise, S 63
Wodak, R 139
Women's Liberation Movement 145
The Wounded Storyteller 145, 155
writing theses, reports and articles 173–5
    conventional approach to (Box 12.7) 174

Xie, B 86, 88

Yin, R K 63–4, 69

Zirakbash, F 70

Printed in Great
Britain
by Amazon